OUTLINE OF ENGLISH GRAMMAR

IN FIVE PARTS

OUTLINE OF ENGLISH GRAMMAR

IN FIVE PARTS

BY

J. C. NESFIELD

GYAN

Published by

Gyan Publishing House
5, Ansari Road
Daryaganj, New Delhi-110002
Phone: 011-47034999, 9811692060
E-mail: books@gyanbooks.com

Distribution Network
gyanbooks.com
India, USA, Canada, UK, Australia

ISBN: 978-93-6280-391-7 (PB)
First Published, 1903

2nd Impression 2024

Printed at: Gyan Press, Delhi.

OUTLINE OF ENGLISH GRAMMAR
AUTHOR: J. C. NESFIELD

OUTLINE OF ENGLISH GRAMMAR

IN FIVE PARTS

I.—NOUNS, ADJECTIVES, PRONOUNS, ADVERBS, PREPOSITIONS, AND CONJUNCTIONS.
II.—VERBS AND THEIR INFLECTIONS.
III.—PARSING AND SYNTAX.
IV.—ANALYSIS AND CONVERSION OF SENTENCES: SEQUENCE OF TENSES.
V.—ANALYSIS AND DERIVATION OF WORDS: SOUNDS AND SPELLINGS.

BY

J. C. NESFIELD, M.A.

AUTHOR OF 'ENGLISH GRAMMAR PAST AND PRESENT,' 'HISTORICAL ENGLISH AND DERIVATION,' ETC.

London
MACMILLAN AND CO., LIMITED
NEW YORK: THE MACMILLAN COMPANY
1903

CONTENTS

PART I.—NOUNS, ADJECTIVES, PRONOUNS, ADVERBS, PREPOSITIONS, AND CONJUNCTIONS.

PART II.—VERBS AND THEIR INFLECTIONS.

PART III.—PARSING AND SYNTAX.

PART IV.—ANALYSIS AND CONVERSION OF SENTENCES: SEQUENCE OF TENSES.

PART V.—ANALYSIS AND DERIVATION OF WORDS: SOUNDS AND SPELLINGS.

PART I.—NOUNS, ADJECTIVES, PRONOUNS, ADVERBS, PREPOSITIONS, AND CONJUNCTIONS.

CHAPTER I.—HOW TO TELL THE PARTS OF SPEECH.

1. **How to tell the Parts of Speech.**—To find out the "Part of Speech" to which a word belongs, or in which it is used in any given example, ask yourself, "*What kind of work* does the word *do* in the sentence before me? What part does it play in helping to make the sentence?"

(1) If a word *gives a name* to some individual person or thing or to some kind of person or thing, the word is a **Noun**:—

James saw an *apple* fall to the *ground*.

Here "*James*" is the name of some person. "*Apple*" is the name of a kind of fruit. "*Ground*" is a name given to the earth we stand on. So *James, apple,* and *ground* are all nouns.

"Noun" and "name" mean the same thing. "Noun" is of Latin origin (*nomen*). "Name" is of Anglo-Saxon origin (*nama*).

(2) If a word *refers* to some person or thing *without giving a name* to the person or thing referred to, the word is a **Pronoun**. (If it gives a *name* to some person or thing, it is of course a Noun, not a Pronoun. Herein lies the essential difference between the one part of speech and the other.)

You and *he* came here a week before *me*.

Here "*you*" refers to the person spoken to without naming him; "*he*" refers to some person spoken of, whose name has been mentioned in a previous sentence; "*me*" refers to the person speaking without naming him. So all these words are pronouns.

The word "*pronoun*" means "for (Latin *pro*) a noun"; *i.e. a word used instead of a noun*, or as a substitute for a noun.

(3) If a word *adds* to the meaning of a noun so as to show

more clearly what person or thing the noun is meant to stand for, the word is an **Adjective** :—

This house. A *noble* character. A *white* brick.

The word "*this*" points out the house to which the writer or speaker alludes. The word "*noble*" shows what sort of character is meant. The word "*white*" describes one quality of the brick, namely, its colour. So all these words are adjectives. Each of them *qualifies* (*i.e.* adds something to the meaning of) the noun to which it is attached.

The word "*adjective*" (Latin *adjectivum*) implies addition: a word is added to a noun or pronoun in order to add to its meaning.

(4) If a word *says* something (*i.e.* makes some statement, or expresses some command, or asks some question) about a person or thing, the word is a **Verb** :—

The bird *has flown.* *Has* the bird *flown?* *Go* away.

In the first of these sentences "*has flown*" makes a statement about the bird. In the second it asks a question about it. "Has flown" is therefore a verb in either case. In the third sentence "*go*" expresses a command; therefore it is a verb.

The word "*verb*" is from Latin *verbum*, which means literally "word." It is called *the word* by way of distinction, because it is the most important kind of word in human speech.

(5) If a word expresses some *relation* between two persons or things (*i.e.* shows what the one *has to do* with the other), the word is a **Preposition** :—

A bird *in* the hand.

Here the word "*in*" shows what the hand has to do with the bird, or the bird with the hand. The bird might be *above* the hand, or *under* the hand, or *away from* the hand, or somewhere *near* the hand, or *in* the hand. The noun before which the preposition is placed is said to be its **Object**.

The word "*preposition*" means "placed before" (Latin *prae-* before, and *positus*, placed); *i.e.* placed before the noun or pronoun that is called its Object.

(6) If a word *joins* one sentence to another so as to make a larger sentence, or if it *joins* one part of speech to another of the same or a similar kind, the word is a **Conjunction** :—

(*a*) The thief was caught, *but* the money was lost.
(*b*) James *and* I went out for a walk.

In (*a*) the second sentence is joined to the first by the word *but*. In (*b*) the pronoun "*I*" is joined to the noun "*James*" by the conjunction *and*.

The word "*conjunction*" (from Latin *con* and *jung*-ere, *junction*-em) means the act of joining together or the thing that joins.

(7) If a word *adds* to the meaning of some verb, adjective, preposition, or conjunction, the word is an **Adverb** :—

(a) A snake moves *silently* in the grass.
(b) The day is *remarkably* cool.
(c) He swam *half* across the channel.
(d) He was despised, *merely* because he was poor.
(e) He walks *very* slowly.

In (a) the adverb "*silently*" qualifies (*i.e.* adds to the meaning of) the verb "moves." In (b) "*remarkably*" qualifies the adjective "cool." In (c) "*half*" qualifies the preposition "across." In (d) "*merely*" qualifies the conjunction "because." In (e) "*very*" qualifies the adverb "slowly."

"*Ad-verb*" means "added to a verb" (Lat. *ad verbum*). This is the main work of adverbs; but they are now used to qualify not only verbs, but adjectives, prepositions, conjunctions, and other adverbs,—in fact, any part of speech except a noun or pronoun.

2. The same word in different Parts of Speech.—Until we see a word in a sentence, we cannot say what kind of work it *does* in the sentence; and until we know this, we are often unable to say to what part of speech it belongs; for the same word may do one kind of work in one sentence, and another in another. The *form* that a word may have is often no guide at all; but the *work* that a word does is an unfailing guide. Take the following examples:—

(a) The *man* has come. *Man* the lifeboat.

Here the first "man" is a noun, because it gives a *name* to a kind of person. The second is a verb, because it *says* something to some one, *i.e.* it expresses an order.

(b) Bring me some *water*. Look at that *water* bird.

Here the first "water" is a noun, because it gives a *name* to a certain kind of thing. The second is an adjective, or rather a noun used as an adjective, because it *adds* to the meaning of the noun following by describing the bird.

(c) He hopes *for* pardon; *for* he knew no better.

Here the first "for" is a preposition, because it shows the *relation* between the act expressed by *pardon* and the feeling expressed by *hope*. The second is a conjunction, because it *joins* the sentence "he knew no better" to the sentence "he hopes for pardon."

(d) This is a *long* journey; we have *long* been travelling; and I *long* for rest.

Here the first "long" is an adjective, because it *qualifies* the noun "journey." The second is an adverb, because it *qualifies* the verb "have been travelling." The third is a verb, because it *says* something about the person denoted by "I."

Note.—It will be seen from § 4 that there are altogether eight different kinds of work that words can do, *i.e.* eight different parts of speech. Among these eight there are three, viz. Prepositions, Conjunctions, and Interjections, that have no **inflexion** or change of form. Adjectives have none except in the Plurals *these*, *those*, and in the degrees of comparison. Adverbs have no change of form except in the degrees of comparison. So the only parts of speech frequently subject to a change of form are Nouns, Pronouns, and Verbs.

3. The Parts of Speech defined.—From the account that has now been given, the parts of speech may be defined thus:—

(1) A **noun** is a word used for *naming* some person or thing.

(2) A **pronoun** is a word used *instead of* a noun.

(3) An **adjective** is a word used for *qualifying* a noun or pronoun.

(4) A **verb** is a word used for *saying* something about a person or thing (such as making a statement, asking a question, or giving an order).

(5) A **preposition** is a word used for showing in what *relation* one person or thing stands to another person or thing.

(6) A **conjunction** is a word used for *joining* one sentence to another sentence, or one word to another word of the same or similar part of speech.

(7) An **adverb** is a word used for *qualifying* any kind of word except a noun or pronoun.

4. Interjection.—To the seven parts of speech already named one more must be added to make the list complete, viz. the Interjection. So there are altogether eight parts of speech.

An interjection is unlike all the rest, because it *does* nothing in the sentence, *i.e.* it does not help to make the sentence as the other seven do. If it happens to occur in the middle of a sentence, it is not connected with any word either before or after. Sometimes it does not occur in any sentence, but stands quite alone.

Oh! ah! pooh! alas! fie!

These are merely exclamatory sounds intended to express some feeling of the mind. The word "*interjection*" (Latin *inter*, "amongst," and *jactus*, "thrown") means a word or sound "thrown into" a sentence, but forming no part of its construction, *i.e.* not contributing to the materials of which the sentence is built.

My son, *alas!* is dangerously ill.

If we cut out the word "*alas*," what remains makes quite as perfect a sentence as the original. Every other word *does* something to some other word or words. Thus *my* qualifies the noun *son;* the noun *son* is the subject of the verb *is; is* is the verb of the sentence, having *son* for its subject; *dangerously* is an adverb qualifying the adjective *ill; ill* goes with the verb *is*, and completes what the verb left unsaid. But the word *alas* goes with nothing, and can be cut out without altering the structure of the sentence.

CHAPTER II.—FORMS AND KINDS OF NOUNS.

SECTION 1.—NUMBER.

5. Singular and Plural.—When you speak of **one** thing at a time, the noun that you use is in the **Singular** number; as "a cow."

When you speak of **more than one** thing at a time, the noun that you use is in the **Plural** number; as "cows."

6. How Plurals are formed.—The main rules are—

(i.) Add *s* to the Singular. This is the general rule.

Singular.	*Plural.*	*Singular.*	*Plural.*
Cow	cows	Town	towns
Boy	boys	Star	stars
Bird	birds	Flea	fleas

(ii.) Add *es* to the Singular, if you find that you cannot pronounce the *s* without the help of *e*:—

Singular.	*Plural.*	*Singular.*	*Plural.*
Glass	glass-es	Brush	brush-es
Box	box-es	Branch	branch-es

Note.—Observe, then, that if the noun ends in *s*, *x*, *sh*, or *ch* in the Singular, you must add *es* to form the Plural.

(iii.) If the Singular ends in *y*, and the *y* is preceded by a consonant, change *y* into *ies*:—

Singular.	*Plural.*	*Singular.*	*Plural.*
Fly	flies	Army	armies
Cry	cries	Penny	pennies / pence
Duty	duties		

Note.—If the Singular ends in *ay*, *ey*, or *oy* (*i.e.* if the *y* is preceded by a vowel), simply add *s* and make no change in the *y*:—

Singular.	*Plural.*	*Singular.*	*Plural.*
Day	days	Ray	rays
Boy	boys	Monkey	monkeys

(iv.) If the Singular ends in *f* or *fe*, change the *f* or *fe* into *ves*:—

Singular.	*Plural.*	*Singular*	*Plural.*
Wife	wives	Loaf	loaves
Wolf	wolves	Thief	thieves

Note.—But there are about thirteen nouns ending in *f* or *fe*, which form the Plural by simply adding *s* to the Singular. The two nouns *scarf* and *wharf* sometimes form the Plural in *ves*:—

Singular.	*Plural.*	*Singular.*	*Plural.*
Chief	chiefs	Gulf	gulfs
Roof	roofs	Grief	griefs
Hoof	hoofs	Reef	reefs
Proof	proofs	Scarf	scarfs
Strife	strifes	Dwarf	dwarfs
Fife	fifes	Wharf	wharfs
Turf	turfs		

(v.) If the Singular ends in *o*, and the *o* is preceded by a consonant, add *es*, not *s*, to the Singular:—

Singular.	*Plural.*	*Singular.*	*Plural.*
Cargo	cargoes	Volcano	volcanoes
Hero	heroes	Potato	potatoes
Buffalo	buffaloes	Echo	echoes
Motto	mottoes	Negro	negroes

Note 1.—The following are exceptions:—*grotto, grottos; halo, halos; memento, mementos; proviso, provisos; tiro, tiros; piano, pianos; canto, cantos; solo, solos.*

Note 2.—If the *o* is preceded by a vowel, the Plural is formed by simply adding *s* to the singular, as:—*folio, folios; cameo, cameos.*

(vi.) If the noun is a compound, change the Singular of the *principal* word into a Plural:—

Singular.	*Plural.*	*Singular.*	*Plural.*
Court-martial	courts-martial	Maid-servant	maid-servants
Son-in-law	sons-in-law	Foot-man	foot-men
Step-son	step-sons	Hanger-on	hangers-on

Note.—Examples of double Plurals:—*man-servant, men-servants; lord-justice, lords-justices; Knight-Templar, Knights-Templars.*

7. **Exceptional Plurals** (see also Chapter XXXIII.):—

(i.) There are eight nouns, that form the Plural by changing the inside vowel of the Singular:—

Singular.	*Plural.*	*Singular.*	*Plural.*
Man	men	Goose	geese
Woman	women	Tooth	teeth
Foot	feet	Mouse	mice
Louse	lice	Dormouse	dormice

(ii.) There are four nouns, that make the Plural terminate in *en* or *ne*:—

Singular.	*Plural.*	*Singular.*	*Plural.*
Ox	oxen	Child	children
Cow	kine (or cows)	Brother	brethren (or brothers)

(iii.) There are a few nouns that have the same form for the Plural as for the Singular:—

Singular.	*Plural.*	*Singular.*	*Plural.*
Deer	deer	Trout	trout
Sheep	sheep	Cod	cod
Fish	fish	Brace	brace
Swine	swine	Dozen	dozen
Grouse	grouse	Score	score
Salmon	salmon	Stone	stone (weight)

Note 1.—Some nouns have no Singular:—

Annals	Gallows	Pincers	Victuals
Bellows	Statistics	Scissors	Tidings
Tongs	Suds	Shambles	News
Shears	Nuptials	Thanks	Means

In spite of the Plural form we say, "By *this* means," "*This* news is not true."

Note 2.—A noun like "earth," "sun," etc., can have no Plural, because there is only one earth and one sun.

Exercise 1.

In the following exercises—(1) *pick out all the nouns;* (2) *say whether each noun is Singular or Plural as it stands;* (3) *change every Plural into a Singular, and every Singular into a Plural:*—

1. There are many cities in England, many smaller towns, and an immense number of villages.
2. A cat and a dog are seldom good friends.
3. The earth goes round the sun in one day and one night.
4. When the cat is away, the mice play.
5. The branch of that tree has leaves of a bright green colour.
6. The cries of animals are many and various: a horse neighs; a dog barks; a cat mews; a swine or pig grunts; an elephant trumpets; an ass brays; an ox lows; a monkey chatters; a goose cackles; a boy laughs or weeps; a fish is silent.
7. If we stop in this wood, we shall be lost. So let us get back into the public road, before night comes on.
8. The wolf living in that forest killed many calves.
9. Some thieves broke into the house of my friend.
10. The stars are seen through the leaves and branches of that oak tree.
11. He went out fishing for salmon, and caught two dozen and more in his net, besides some trout to the number of two or three score.
12. Sheep cannot run as fast as deer; and so the sheep were caught first by the wolves.
13. The cat has caught two mice and one rat to-day.
14. Oxen are of more value than deer to a farmer.
15. The feet of men are larger than those of women; but the teeth are about the same in size.
16. The sun's light is brighter than the moon's; but the moon's rays are not so hot as those of the sun.

17. Joseph had eleven brethren, who sold him as a slave to some merchants on their way to Egypt.
18. A valley is usually hotter than the top of a hill.
19. He is a big man, and weighs fourteen stone.

SECTION 2.—GENDER.

8. **The Genders.**—A noun that denotes a male is of the **Masculine** gender; one that denotes a female is of the **Feminine** gender; one that denotes either sex is of the **Common** gender; one that denotes neither sex, that is, something without life, is of the **Neuter** gender.

So the genders of Nouns are four in number :—

1. *Masculine*—males.
2. *Feminine*—females.
3. *Common*—either sex.
4. *Neuter*—neither sex.

9. **Masculine and Feminine.**—These are distinguished in three different ways :—

1. *By a Change of Word.*

Masc.	*Fem.*	*Masc.*	*Fem.*	*Masc.*	*Fem.*
Bachelor	spinster, maid	Drake	duck	King	queen
Boar	sow	Drone	bee	Lord	lady
Boy	girl	Earl	countess	Man	woman
Brother	sister	Father	mother	Milter	spawner
Buck	doe	Friar, Monk	nun	Nephew	niece
Bull	cow	Gander	goose	Ram	ewe
Bullock, Steer	heifer	Gentleman	lady	Sir	madam
Cock	hen	Hart	roe	Sire	dam
Colt	filly	Horse	mare	Son	daughter
		Husband	wife	Stag	hind
				Uncle	aunt

2. *By a Change of Ending.*

Masc.	*Fem.*	*Masc.*	*Fem.*	*Masc.*	*Fem.*
Abbot	abbess	Host	hostess	Patron	patroness
Actor	actress	Hunter	huntress	Poet	poetess
Author	authoress	Lad	lass	Priest	priestess
Duke	duchess	Lion	lioness	Prince	princess
Emperor	empress	Marquis	marchioness	Prophet	prophetess
Giant	giantess	Master	mistress	Shepherd	shepherdess
God	goddess	Mayor	mayoress	Songster	songstress
Governor	governess	Murderer	murderess	Tiger	tigress
Heir	heiress	Negro	negress		

Peculiar Changes of Ending.

Masc.	*Fem.*	*Masc.*	*Fem.*	*Masc.*	*Fem.*
Fox	vixen	Hero	heroine	Sultan	sultana
Testator	testatrix	Widower	widow	Wizard	witch

3. *By placing a Word before or after.*

Masc.	*Fem.*	*Masc.*	*Fem.*
He-goat	she-goat	Bride-groom	bride
Land-lord	land-lady	Great-uncle	great-aunt
Man-servant	maid-servant	Pea-cock	pea-hen
Grand-father	grand-mother	Cock-sparrow	hen-sparrow

Examples of Nouns in the Common gender.

Parent	Cousin	Deer	Monarch	Pig	Calf
Relation	Bird	Baby	Person	Sheep	Foal
Friend	Fowl	Infant	Pupil	Elephant	Student
Enemy	Child	Servant	Orphan	Camel	Teacher

SECTION 3.—CASE.

10. Three Cases.—"Case" depends (1) upon the *change of ending* that a noun or pronoun incurs according to the purpose for which it is used in a sentence; (2) if there is no change of ending, upon the *grammatical relation* in which the noun or pronoun stands to some other word in the same sentence.

There are three Cases in English—(1) the Nominative, (2) the Possessive, (3) the Objective.

Pronoun.	*Noun.*
He, his, him.	Man, man's, man.

In pronouns each of the three Cases has a distinct form, as in Nom. *he*, Poss. *his*, Obj. *him*. But in nouns the only Case distinguished by a change of form is the Possessive, as *man's*. In such words the form of the Nominative is the same as that of the Objective, and hence the difference between Nom. and Obj. depends solely upon grammatical relation.

11. Possessive. — This is formed by adding *'s* (called *a-pos-tro-phe s*) to the Nominative of Singular nouns, and to the Nominative of those Plurals which do not end in *s*:—

Singular—man's. | *Plural*—men's.

If the Plural ends in *s*, as nearly all Plurals do, the Possessive is formed by simply adding the apostrophe :—

Singular.	*Plural.*	*Singular.*	*Plural.*
A cow's tail	cows' tails	A horse's foot	horses' feet
My niece's book	my nieces' books	A lady's cloak	ladies' cloaks
A thief's trick	thieves' tricks	A mistress's fan	mistresses' fans

12. Nominative.—A noun or pronoun is in the Nominative case, when it is used as Subject to a verb, or when it is used for purposes of address :—

(1) The *man* rides well. (2) Leave me, my *son*.

In (1) the verb "rides" expresses the action of riding. Who performs this action? The man. Therefore the noun "man" is in the Nominative case.

In (2) "son" is the person addressed. Therefore "son" is in the Nominative case.

13. Objective.—A noun or pronoun is in the Objective case, when it is the object to a verb or to a preposition:—

The man rode a fine *horse* . . . (*Verb.*)
The earth is moistened by *rain* . . (*Preposition.*)

Exercise 2.

Pick out every noun in the following sentences, and say—(a) what is its Gender, (b) what is its Case, and (c) what is its Number:—

1. A friend called at our house in the evening. 2. Did you see the elephant, that was led into Dover with one man walking by its side and another seated on its neck? 3. Between a cow and a dog, as between a cat and a dog, there seems to be a natural enmity; and between a cat and a cow there seems to be a natural friendship. 4. The Queen of England is monarch of a vast empire. 5. A herd of deer adds much to the beauty of a park. 6. How many sheep and how many goats are there in your flock? 7. There are certain animals, such as cats, jackals, foxes, owls, and tigers, that see things more clearly in the night than in the day: the brightness of the sun dazzles their eyes. 8. The heroine of that story was a poor lass, who was left an orphan at six years of age, but who conquered all difficulties and became a prosperous and happy woman. 9. The cattle are grazing on the side of the hill, and the cowherd is seated on the grass beside them. 10. The bridegroom will bring the bride to his house in a few days. 11. A peacock is one of the most beautiful of birds, and a lion is one of the stateliest of wild beasts. 12. A man, ignorant of the arts of reading, writing, and ciphering, is in point of knowledge more like a child than a man. 13. Cows are as fond of grass as bears are of honey. 14. Health is one of the greatest blessings that a man or woman can hope to enjoy in life. 15. The Czar of Russia, although he is lord of the eastern half of Europe and the northern half of Asia, besides being master of a huge army and a large fleet, cannot live in peace and safety with his own subjects, and cannot leave his palace without fear. 16. The love of money is the root of all evil; but by a proper use of money men can do much good.

Section 4.—The Kinds of Nouns.

14. Nouns are of five different kinds—(1) Proper, (2) Common, (3) Collective, (4) Material, (5) Abstract. (The fundamental division is into (*a*) **Concrete**, which includes (1), (2), (3), and (4), and (*b*) **Abstract**; see below, § 19.)

15. A **Proper** noun is a name given to *one particular* person or thing, and is not intended to denote more than one person or thing at a time; as *James* (person), *New Testament* (book), *York* (city), *France* (country).

Note.—The writing of a Proper noun, or of any other kind of noun when it is used as a Proper noun, should be commenced with a capital letter.

16. A **Common** noun denotes no one person or thing in particular, but is *common to all persons or things of the same kind*; as "man," "book," "country."

Here *man* does not point out any particular man, such as James, but can be used for *any and every* man. *Book* does not point out any particular book, such as the New Testament, but can be used for *any and every* book. *Country* does not point out any particular country, such as France, but can be used for *any and every* country in any part of the world.

17. A **Collective** noun denotes a *group*, *collection*, or *multitude*, considered as one complete whole.

For instance, there may be *many sheep* in a field, but only *one flock*. Here "sheep" is a Common noun, because it may stand for any and every sheep; but "flock" is a Collective noun, because it stands for *all the sheep at once* in that field, and not for any one sheep taken separately.

18. A noun of **Material** denotes the *matter* or *substance* of which certain things are made; as in the following examples:—

A cow eats *grass*. Seeds are grown in *soil*. *Salt* is necessary to life. Fish live in *water*. We cannot live without *air*. All things exist in *space*. *Fire* burns. That bar is made of *iron*. They had *fish* for dinner. We had *meat* with *bread* and *butter*. We shall dine on *wheat* to-day. *Milk* is the best of foods. Some men never eat *flesh*. We can write with *ink* or with *chalk*. A black-board is made of *wood*. *Air* is lighter than *water*.

Note.—Sometimes a Common noun has a Material noun that pairs with it; as *ox* (Common), *beef* (Material); *sheep* (Common), *mutton* (Material); *pig* (Common), *bacon* or *ham* or *pork* (Material); *deer* (Common), *venison* (Material); *tree* (Common), *timber* (Material), etc.

19. An **Abstract** noun denotes some *quality*, *state*, or *action* apart from any object or objects.

Quality.—Cleverness, height, humility, roguery, colour.
State.—Poverty, manhood, bondage, pleasure, youth.
Action.—Laughter, movement, flight, choice, revenge.

The four kinds named in §§ 15-18 all relate to *objects of sense*,—that is, to things which can be seen, touched, heard, smelt, or tasted, and all these kinds are called by the general name of **Concrete.** But an Abstract noun relates to things which cannot be seen or touched, etc., and which are thought of apart from any object or objects of sense.

For example—We know that stone is *hard.* We also know that iron is *hard.* We also know that a brick is *hard.* We can therefore speak of *hardness* apart from stone, or iron, or brick, or any other object having the same quality. "Abstract" means "drawn off" or "apart from" the object (Latin *abs*, off, and *tractus*, drawn).

How Abstract Nouns are formed.

20. Abstract nouns can be formed from Adjectives, or from Common nouns, or from Verbs, by adding some syllable or letter, which is called a suffix :—

(*a*) *Abstract Nouns formed from Adjectives.*

Adjective.	*Abstract Noun.*	*Adjective.*	*Abstract Noun.*	*Adjective.*	*Abstract Noun.*
Wise	wisdom	Prudent	prudence	Bitter	bitterness
Poor	poverty	Sweet	sweetness	Wide	width
High	height	Young	youth	Sole	solitude
Short	shortness	Proud	pride	Broad	breadth
Honest	honesty	Just	justice	Deep	depth
Dark	darkness	Great	greatness	True	truth
Long	length	Hot	heat	Cold	coldness
Brave	bravery	Sleepy	sleepiness	Humble	humility

(*b*) *Abstract Nouns formed from Common Nouns.*

Common Noun.	*Abstract Noun.*	*Common Noun.*	*Abstract Noun.*	*Common Noun.*	*Abstract Noun.*
Man	manhood	Agent	agency	Mother	motherhood
Child	childhood	Regent	regency	Rascal	rascality
Friend	friendship	King	kingship	Rogue	roguery
Boy	boyhood	Bond	bondage	Slave	slavery
Captain	captaincy	Hero	heroism	Infant	infancy
Priest	priesthood	Thief	theft	Owner	ownership

(*c*) *Abstract Nouns formed from Verbs.*

Verb.	*Abstract Noun.*	*Verb.*	*Abstract Noun.*	*Verb.*	*Abstract Noun.*
Serve	service	Relieve	relief	Seize	seizure
Live	life	Believe	belief	Laugh	laughter
Hate	hatred	Please	pleasure	Expect	expectation
Obey	obedience	Advise	advice	Protect	protection
Choose	choice	Defend	defence	Think	thought
Move	motion	Judge	judgment	Till	tillage
See	sight	Conceal	concealment	Steal	stealth

(*d*) *Abstract Nouns of the same form as Verbs.*

Verb.	*Abstract Noun.*	*Verb.*	*Abstract Noun.*	*Verb.*	*Abstract Noun.*
Fear	fear	Fall	fall	Laugh	laugh
Hope	hope	Stay	stay	Taste	taste
Desire	desire	Stop	stop	Ride	ride
Regret	regret	Walk	walk	Touch	touch
Order	order	Run	run	Love	love
Rise	rise	Step	step	Sleep	sleep

There are certain parts of a verb, which are equivalent to Abstract nouns, that is, have the same *force* or meaning as Abstract nouns, although they are not the same in *form*. These are—(1) the Verbal noun ending in *-ing*, as "working"; (2) the Infinitive form which is preceded by *to*, as "to work." There is no difference in meaning between an Abstract noun, a Verbal noun, and an Infinitive:—

Work is good for health . . . . (*Abstract Noun.*)
Working is good for health . . . . (*Verbal Noun.*)
To work is good for health . . . . (*Infinitive.*)

21. The class to which a Noun belongs depends on the sense in which the noun is used. The form does not always serve as a guide.

(*a*) Thus a Proper noun is sometimes used as a Common noun:—

A *Daniel* come to judgment.—SHAKSPEARE.

Here *Daniel* does not stand for the Jewish prophet, but for any man who resembles the Jewish prophet in wisdom and judgment.

Hence some Common nouns have been formed from Proper; as *epicure* (from Epicurus); *hansom* (from the inventor); *lumber* (from Lombard pawnbrokers); *mackintosh* (from the inventor); *currant* (from Corinth); *dunce* (from Duns Scotus); *calico* (from Calicut); *china* (from the country); *port* (from Oporto).

(*b*) An Abstract noun can be used as a Proper noun:—

The *Terror* set sail yesterday.
Whatever he did, *Fortune* smiled on him.

Here "*Terror*" stands for the name of a ship. "*Fortune*" is used as if it were the name of a person.

(*c*) An Abstract noun is sometimes used as a Common noun:—

{ He is a lover of *justice* . . . . . (*Abstract.*)
{ He is a *justice* of the peace . . . . (*Common.*)

In the first sentence *justice* means the quality of being just. In the second it stands for the man who is just, the judge.

{ She is a person of great *beauty* . . . (*Abstract.*)
{ She is the *beauty* of the place . . . (*Common.*)

In the first sentence *beauty* denotes the quality of being beautiful. In the second it denotes the person possessing the quality.

{ *Poetry* is one of the fine arts . . . . (*Abstract.*)
{ He wrote very good *poetry* . . . . . (*Common.*)

In the first sentence *poetry* denotes the art; in the second the poem or poems written by some one.

(*d*) The same word can be a Material noun in one sentence, and a Common noun in another:—

Fish live in water . . . . (*Common.*)
Fish is a good kind of food . . . . . (*Material.*)

In the first sentence the word *fish* denotes the animal; in the second its matter or substance.

Exercise 3.—*The kinds of Nouns.*

Point out the kind or use of each of the nouns occurring in the following sentences:—

1. A cow eats grass. 2. Seeds are sown in soil. 3. Give him the slate. 4. There is no slate to be got out of this quarry. 5. Is that chain of yours made of gold or brass? 6. Salt is necessary to life. 7. He is a man of great kindness. 8. He has done me many kindnesses. 9. We cannot live without air. 10. He is a man of very clear judgment. 11. The judgment that he gave on that case was too severe. 12. Milk is the best kind of food. 13. Some men never eat flesh. 14. A man, ignorant of the arts of reading, writing, and ciphering, is in point of knowledge more like a child than a man. 15. As soon as I heard that news, I was seized with wonder. 16. It is a wonder that he was not killed. 17. They had fish for dinner that day. 18. There are many fish in this river. 19. A black-board is made of wood. 20. We have a wood about half-a-mile from our house. 21. The Czar of Russia, although he is lord of the eastern half of Asia, besides being master of a huge army and a large fleet, cannot live in peace and safety with his own subjects.

CHAPTER III.—FORMS AND KINDS OF ADJECTIVES.

SECTION 1.—THE KINDS OF ADJECTIVES.

22. **Kinds of Adjectives.**—There are seven different kinds of adjectives:—

(1) **Proper**: formed from a proper name:—

A *Chinese* sailor = a sailor from China.
The *Turkish* empire = the empire of Turkey.
The *English* language = the language of England.

(2) **Descriptive**: showing of what *quality* or in what *state* a thing is. (These are sometimes called Qualitative.)

A *brave* boy. A *sick* lion. A *fertile* field. A *dark* night.

Note.—From such adjectives Abstract nouns are formed; as *bravery, sickness, fertility, darkness.*

(3) **Quantitative**: showing *how much* of a thing is meant:—

He had *much* (a high degree of) pain.
He ate *little* (a small quantity of) bread.
He walked the *whole* way back.
A *half* loaf is better than *no* bread.
He did not eat *any* (any quantity of) bread.

(4) **Numeral**: showing—(*a*) *how many* things are meant, or (*b*) *in what order* a thing stands:—

(*a*) Adjectives showing *how many* are called **Cardinals**:—

He had *seven* apples and *three* buns.

(*b*) Adjectives showing *in what order* are called **Ordinals**:—

He stood *seventh* in English and *third* in arithmetic.

Note.—Adjectives which refer to number, but specify no number in particular, are called **Indefinite** Numerals:—

All men are mortal. *Some* men are rich. *No* men are brutes. *Many* men are poor. *Few* men are rich. *Several* men have come. *Sundry* men have gone.

(5) **Demonstrative**: showing *which* or *what* thing is meant. The most common are *this, that* (with Singular nouns), *these, those* (with Plural nouns). Adjectives like *any, a certain, some, other, any other*, are called **Indefinite** Demonstratives.

This man came here to-day. *These* dogs are a nuisance.
That boat leaks: *those* persons will be drowned.
This is not the book I chose; I chose the *other* (book).
I did not choose *such* a book as that.
You must take *some* book or *other* (book).

Note.—There is a difficulty in classifying the adjective "some." (*a*) "I have *some* bread"; here *some* denotes quantity,—a certain quantity of bread. (*b*) "I have *some* loaves"; here *some* denotes number,—a certain number of loaves. (*c*) "You must take *some* book or other"; here *some* denotes neither quantity nor number, but is a vague kind of Demonstrative.

(6) **Interrogative**: asking *which* or *what* thing is meant:—

What book is that? *Which* book do you prefer?

(7) **Distributive**: showing that the things named are taken *separately* or *in separate lots*:—

The two men had *each* (man) a gun.
Every man was punctually in his place.
Take *either* side, whichever you like best.
Every four hours (that is, every period of four hours).

23. Articles.—It is convenient as well as customary to call *a* or *an* the Indefinite article, and *the* the Definite. But in point of fact these words are Demonstrative adjectives. *A* or *an* is merely a short form of *one*, and hence it is used only before nouns in the Singular number. *The* is merely a short form of *this*, *that*, *these*, or *those*, and hence it can be used before nouns in either number.

An is used before an open vowel or a silent consonant; as "an ox," "an hour," "an heir."

A is used before a consonant; as "a box," "a house." It is also used before a vowel in such examples as the following, in which the *sound* of the vowel (not the *spelling*) is preceded by the sound of *w* or *y* :—

A useful thing. *A* one-eyed man. *A* ewe-lamb.

24. How Adjectives are Formed.—Some adjectives are original or primary words, as *dry*, *hot*, *quick*, *wet*, *long*, *short*, etc. Others are formed by adding a letter or syllable (which is called a suffix) to some noun, and occasionally, though less frequently, to some other adjective, or less frequently still to some verb or adverb.

(*a*) *Adjectives formed from Nouns.*

Noun.	*Adjective.*	*Noun.*	*Adjective.*	*Noun.*	*Adjective.*
Stead	steadfast	Woman	womanish, womanly	Sale	saleable
Hope	hopeful, hopeless	Fop	foppish	China	Chinese
Grace	graceful	Might	mighty	Picture	picturesque
Fear	fearless	Worth	worthy	Statue	statuesque
Life	lifelike	Naught	naughty	Infant	infantile, infantine
Child	childish, childlike	Haste	hasty	Glory	glorious
Quarrel	quarrelsome	Part	partial	Labour	laborious
Toil	toilsome	Rome	Roman	Joy	joyous, joyful
Wretch	wretched	Hercules	Herculean	Pity	piteous, pitiful
Wood	wooden	Europe	European		
		Unit	unitarian		

(*b*) *Adjectives formed from other Adjectives.*

1st Adj.	*2nd Adj.*	*1st Adj.*	*2nd Adj.*	*1st Adj.*	*2nd Adj.*
Two	twofold	Full	fulsome	Pale	palish
Many	manifold	Whole	wholesome	Red	reddish
Four	fourteen, forty	Comic	comical	Middle	middling
Three	thirteen, thirty	Dramatic	dramatical	Sick	sickly
		Periodic	periodical	Poor	poorly
		Politic	political	Tacit	taciturn

(*c*) *Adjectives formed from Verbs.*

Verb.	*Adjective.*	*Verb.*	*Adjective.*	*Verb.*	*Adjective.*
Cease	ceaseless	Tire	tiresome	Snap	snappish
Resist	resistless	Talk	talkative	Move	movable

(d) Adjectives formed from Adverbs.

Adverb.	*Adjective.*	*Adverb.*	*Adjective.*	*Adverb.*	*Adjective.*
Up	upright	Fro	froward	In	inward
Down	downright	Fore	forward	Out	utmost

Exercise 4.

Pick out all the adjectives in the following sentences, and say to what class each of them belongs:—

1. Some persons were present, but I cannot say how many. 2. A live ass is better than a dead lion. 3. Twenty students are in the fourth class, and each has a book on English history. 4. A lazy boy gives much trouble to both his parents. 5. A little learning is a dangerous thing. 6. There is a forest of fine old oak-trees on either bank of the river. 7. Which pace do you like best in a horse, trotting or cantering? 8. The whole distance travelled on that day was thirty-two miles. 9. Roman history has been divided into several different periods; and the beginning of each period is marked by some great event. 10. The two great periods in the history of the Roman Empire are the pagan and the Christian. 11. London is the greatest city in the modern world, as Rome was in the ancient.

SECTION 2.—COMPARISON OF ADJECTIVES.

25. Adjectives have no change of form (such as nouns and pronouns have) to express Number, Gender, and Case.

The single exception is **this, that; these, those**. The two first are used with Singular nouns; as "this man," "that man." The two last are used with Plural ones; as "these men," "those men."

26. Degrees of Comparison.—But adjectives incur a change of form, according to the degree of comparison in which they are used.

There are **three degrees** of Comparison,—the Positive, the Comparative, and the Superlative.

The Positive denotes the simple quality; as "*fat* ox."

The Comparative denotes a higher degree of the quality; as "*fatter* ox." This is used, when *two* things are compared in respect of a certain quality.

The Superlative denotes the highest degree of the quality; as "the fattest ox." This is used, when one thing is compared with *all other* things of the same kind.

Note.—Of the seven kinds of adjectives named in § 22, the only one that admits of being freely used in different degrees of comparison is the Descriptive. Among Quantitative adjectives there are only two: *much, more, most;* and *little, less, least.* Among Numeral adjectives there are only two: *many, more, most; few, fewer, fewest.*

Among Descriptive adjectives there are some which from the nature of their meaning cannot have degrees of comparison.

(*a*) Shape, as *round*, *square*, *oblong*, *triangular*, *four-footed*.
(*b*) Material, as *golden*, *vegetable*, *leathern*, *wheaten*, etc.
(*c*) Time, as *weekly*, *annual*, *monthly*, *hourly*, etc.
(*d*) Place, as *Kentish*, *Canadian*, *insular*, *celestial*, etc.
(*e*) Natural objects, as *solar*, *lunar*, *sidereal*.
(*f*) Qualities in the highest degree, as *perfect*, *eternal*.
(*g*) Qualities in a moderate degree, as *reddish*, *palish*.

27. Regular Comparatives. There are two regular methods of forming the second and third degrees of Comparison :—

(1) By adding the adverbs *more* and *most*. This method can be used for adjectives of any number of syllables ; and it is the only method used for adjectives of more than two syllables :—

More beautiful (not beautifuller). Most beautiful (not beautifullest).
More famous (not famouser). Most famous (not famousest).

(2) By adding *er* and *est* to the Positive. This is called the Flexional method. Observe the following rules :—

(*a*) When the Positive ends in *two* consonants, or in a *single* consonant preceded by a *long* vowel, it incurs no change of spelling when *er* and *est* are added :—

Pos.	*Comp.*	*Super.*	*Pos.*	*Comp.*	*Super.*
Small	smaller	smallest	Great	greater	greatest
Thick	thicker	thickest	Brief	briefer	briefest
Bold	bolder	boldest	Deep	deeper	deepest

(*b*) When the Positive ends in a *single* consonant, and this consonant is preceded by a *short* vowel, the final consonant is doubled before *er* and *est* :—

Pos	*Comp.*	*Super.*	*Pos.*	*Comp.*	*Super.*
Thin	thinner	thinnest	Wet	wetter	wettest
Hot	hotter	hottest	Glad	gladder	gladdest

Note.—This rule applies to adjectives of *one* syllable. If the Positive is two syllables, the last consonant is usually not doubled ; as tender, tenderer, tenderest.

(*c*) When the Positive ends in *e*, *r* and *st* are added, not *er* and *est* :—

Pos.	*Comp.*	*Super.*	*Pos.*	*Comp.*	*Super.*
Brave	braver	bravest	Large	larger	largest
Free	freer	freest	Fine	finer	finest
True	truer	truest	White	whiter	whitest

(*d*) When the Positive ends in *y*, and the *y* is preceded by a consonant, the *y* is changed to *i* before *er* and *est*. But if the *y* is preceded by a vowel, it is not changed :—

Pos.	*Comp.*	*Super.*	*Pos.*	*Comp.*	*Super.*
Happy	happier	happiest	Grey	greyer	greyest
Dry	drier	driest	Gay	gayer	gayest

28. Irregular Comparatives.—In the words marked * the comparison is *defective* rather than irregular; that is, the Positive has no Comp. or Superl. of its own, but has borrowed them from an adjective that has no Positive of its own.

Pos.	*Comp.*	*Super.*	*Pos.*	*Comp.*	*Super.*
Good*	better	best	Old	older	oldest
Bad,* ill*	worse	worst		elder	eldest
Little*	less	least	Late	later	latest
Much*	more	most		latter	last
Many*	more	most	Fore	former	foremost, first
Hind	hinder	hindmost		further	furthest

Note.—"Fur-ther" is the comp. of *fore*, not of *forth*: cf. *far*, *far-ther*.

There are five words which are adverbs in the Positive degree, but adjectives in the Comparative and Superlative:—

Pos.	*Comp.*	*Super.*	*Pos.*	*Comp.*	*Super.*
Far	farther	farthest	Out	outer	utmost
In	inner	innermost, inmost		utter	uttermost
			(Be)neath	nether	nethermost
Up	upper	uppermost			

Exercise 5.

Write out the Comparatives and Superlatives of the following adjectives; and use, whenever you can, the forms er *and* est:—

Fierce, merry, short, loud, good, docile, permanent, handsome, sweet, able, little, bad, jealous, clever, much, pretty, large, late, rich, flat, few, red, soft, strange, idle, tall, kind, horrible, guilty.

CHAPTER IV.—FORMS AND KINDS OF PRONOUNS.

29. Kinds of Pronouns.—There are four different kinds of pronouns:[1]—

(1) **Personal**: *I, thou, you, he, she, it, they*, etc.
(2) **Demonstrative**: *one, this, that, such*, etc.
(3) **Relative** or **Conjunctive**: *who, which, that, as.*
(4) **Interrogative**: *who? which? what?*

[1] I exclude from the list of Pronouns such words as *any, each, every, some, either, neither.* These words are used **with** nouns, not **for** nouns; and therefore they are adjectives. As has been shown in § 22, these adjectives are either Demonstrative (*some, any*) or Distributive (*each, every, either, neither*). They **qualify** nouns expressed or understood, and are not **substitutes** for nouns. Therefore they are not Pro-nouns.

SECTION 1.—PERSONAL PRONOUNS.

30. The **Personal** pronouns are so called, because they stand for the three persons, viz.—

(*a*) The First, or the person *speaking;* as *I, we, myself.*

(*b*) The Second, or the person *spoken to;* as *thou, you, thyself.*

(*c*) The Third, or what is *spoken of;* as *he, she, it, himself,* etc.

The First Person, Masculine or Feminine.

Case.	Singular.	Plural.
Nominative . .	I	We
Possessive . .	My, mine	Our, ours
Objective . .	Me	Us

The Second Person, Masculine or Feminine.

Case.	Singular.	Plural.
Nominative . .	Thou	Ye or you
Possessive . .	Thy, thine	Your, yours
Objective . .	Thee	You

The Third Person, of all Genders.

Case.	Singular.			Plural.
	Masculine.	Feminine.	Neuter.	All Genders.
Nominative	He	She	It	They
Possessive .	His	Her, hers	Its	Their, theirs
Objective .	Him	Her	It	Them

31. The Possessive cases of most of these pronouns have, as you will have seen, two forms:—

	Singular.			Plural.		
First Form .	My	Thy	Her	Our	Your	Their
Second ,, .	Mine	Thine	Hers	Ours	Yours	Theirs

The first form is used, when it stands *before* the noun with which it is joined:—

My book, thy book, her book; our book, your book, their book.

The second form is used—(*a*) when it is separated from the noun by a verb coming between; (*b*) when a noun is not expressed after it; (*c*) when it is preceded by the preposition "of":—

(*a*) This book is *mine*. That house is *theirs*.
(*b*) My horse and *yours* (your horse) are both tired.
(*c*) That horse *of yours* is tired.

32. When the word "self" or "own" is added to any of the above pronouns, the pronoun is called **Re-flex-ive.**

I. *The First Person.*

Case.	Singular.	Plural.
Nom. or *Objec.*	Myself	Ourselves
Possessive	My own, mine own	Our own

II. *The Second Person.*

Case.	Singular.	Plural.
Nom. or *Objec.*	Thyself	Yourselves
Possessive	Thy own, thine own	Your own

III. *The Third Person.*

Case.	Singular.			Plural.
	Masculine.	Feminine.	Neuter.	All Genders.
Nom. or *Objec.*	Himself	Herself	Itself	Themselves
Possessive	His own	Her own	Its own	Their own

Exercise 6.

Put pronouns in the place of the nouns noted below:—

1. I told James that the snake seen by *James* in the garden would do *James* no harm, if *James* left *the snake* alone to go *the snake's* own way.

2. The girl went into the green field, and there *the girl* saw the sheep and lambs, as the *sheep and lambs* played about in *the field*.

3. A man brought round some wild beasts for a show. Among *the beasts* there was an elephant. *The man* threw cakes at the elephant, and *the elephant* caught *the cakes* in *the elephant's* trunk.

4. A dog was carrying an umbrella for *the dog's* master. Some boys tried to take away *the umbrella* from the dog. But *the dog* was too quick for *the boys*. *The dog* ran past *the boys* at full speed, and carried the umbrella safely out of *the boys'* reach.

5. When the camel is being loaded, *the camel* kneels down so that the load may be put on *the camel's* back. *The camel* loves men, if *men* treat *the camel* well.

6. The bees are flying towards the flowers. *The bees* suck *the flowers*, and fill *the bees'* bags with honey.

7. Wolves hunt in large packs, and when *wolves* are pressed by

hunger, *wolves* become very fierce, and will attack men and eat *men* up greedily.

8. A horse cannot defend *a horse* against wolves; but *a horse* can run from *wolves*, and *wolves* are not always able to catch *a horse.*

SECTION 2.—DEMONSTRATIVE PRONOUNS.

33. A **Demonstrative** pronoun points to some noun going before, and is used instead of it.

34. **This, that, these, those.**—These words are *adjectives*, when they are used **with** a noun (expressed or understood); but *pronouns*, when they are used **for** a noun :—

(1) Work and play are both necessary to health: *this* (namely play) gives us rest, and *that* (namely work) gives us energy.

Here *this* is a pronoun, because it is used instead of "play"; *that* is a pronoun, because it is used instead of "work."

(2) *This* house and *that* (house) are both to let.

Here *this* is not a pronoun, but an adjective, because it goes with the noun "house," and is not used instead of it. *That* is also an adjective, because it goes with the noun "house" understood after it.

35. **One, ones, none.**—When the antecedent noun is Singular, we use *one.* When it is Plural, we use *ones.* "None" is a shortened form of "not one," but it may stand either for a Singular or a Plural noun.

(1) I prefer a white horse to a black *one.*

Here *one* is a pronoun, because it is used instead of "horse."

(2) He came to my house *one* day.

Here *one* is an adjective, because it goes with the noun "day."

Note.—"They" and "one" are sometimes used without reference to any antecedent. They are then called **Indefinite** Demonstrative pronouns :—

They say that he is very clever.
One must take care of *one's* health.

Here *they* and *one* refer to no antecedent. They are Indefinite, and stand for no person or persons in particular.

Exercise 7.

Show whether each of the words printed in Italics in the following examples is a Demonstrative adjective or a Demonstrative pronoun. If it is a pronoun, show whether it is Definite or Indefinite :—

1. *This* horse is stronger than *that.* 2. Health is of more value than money; *this* cannot give such true happiness as *that.* 3. I prefer a house built of stone to *one* built of brick. 4. You will repent of this *one* day, when it is too late. 5. You have kept your

promise ; *this* was all that I asked for. 6. The faithfulness of a dog is greater than *that* of a cat. 7. *One* Mr. B. helped his friend in need ; *that* was a true friend. 8. Bring me *that* book, and leave *this* where it is. 9. The step you have taken is *one* of much risk. 10. A pale light, like *that* of the moon, begins to fringe the horizon.

SECTION 3.—RELATIVE OR CONJUNCTIVE PRONOUNS.

36. A **Relative** pronoun is so called, because it *relates* to some noun or Personal pronoun going before. Another name by which it is called is "**Conjunctive,**" because it joins two sentences. The noun or Personal pronoun to which the Conjunctive pronoun relates is called the **Antecedent.**

Case.	Singular and Plural.	Singular and Plural.
	Masc. and Fem.	Neuter.
Nominative . .	Who	Which
Possessive . .	Whose	Whose, or of which
Objective . .	Whom	Which

Exercise 8.

(*a*) *Point out the Antecedent to the Relative pronouns noted below, and say in what case each Relative is* :—

1. We love those persons *who* are kind to us.
2. The pen *whose* point was broken has been mended.
3. The ground *which* we dig will bear a fine crop.
4. That is the man *whom* we saw yesterday.
5. Is this a dagger *which* I see before me ?
6. We left the house in *which* we had long lived.
7. He lost the box of clothes *which* I brought.
8. The child *whose* parents are dead is an orphan.

(*b*) *Join each pair of sentences into a single sentence by putting a Relative pronoun in the place of the Personal pronoun* :—

1. This is the house ; Jack built *it*.
2. This book is a good one ; I read *it*.
3. This is the man ; I read *his* book.
4. The boy has come ; *he* lost his hat.
5. The girl has come ; you were looking for *her*.
6. These are the trees ; *their* leaves have fallen.
7. You built this house ; I have long lived in *it*.
8. These men have fled ; the ox was stolen by *them*.
9. Look at those boys ; we read in class with *them*.

(*c*) *Supply the Relative pronoun in the following sentences* :—

1. The box —— I bought was soon lost by him.
2. The man —— I met to-day was an old friend.
3. These are the only things —— I was looking for.
4. This is the book —— I won as a prize.

(*d*) *The Relative pronoun, provided it would be in the Objective case, is often omitted. Supply the omissions in the following*:—

1. Be so kind as to pick up the book I dropped.
2. The girl you teach is very clever.
3. Have you seen the boy I sent for?
4. This is the house we lived in.
5. These are the wolves I shot to-day.

37. That, as, but.—"*That*" and "*as*" can be used for "who," "whom," or "which," but not for "whose." "*As*" was originally a conjunction, but is now used as a Relative pronoun after *such* and sometimes after *same*.

The man *that* we were looking for has come.
This is the *same* book *as* yours.
He is not *such* a clever student *as* you are.

But.—This conjunction is sometimes used as if it were a Relative pronoun signifying *who* . . . *not* or *which* . . . *not*.

There is no one *but* agrees to it=
There is no one *who* does *not* agree to it.

"*But*," however, is not really a Pronoun, but a Conjunction: "There is no one, *but he* agrees to it"; It never rains *but it* pours." In the sentence "There is no one but agrees to it," the pronoun "he" has been omitted, and must therefore be understood.

Section 4.—Interrogative Pronouns.

38. The name **In-ter-rog-a-tive** is given to those pronouns that are used for asking questions:—

Who spoke?	(*Nominative to the verb.*)
Of *whom* did he speak?	(*Objective after preposition.*)
What did he say?	(*Objective after verb.*)
Who are you?	(*Complement to the verb.*)
Whose book is that?	(*Possessive case.*)
Which of them won the prize?	(*Nominative to the verb.*)

CHAPTER V.—FORMS AND KINDS OF ADVERBS.

Section 1.—The Kinds of Adverbs.

39. Three kinds of Adverbs.—The three kinds of adverbs are—

I. Simple. II. Interrogative. III. Relative or Conjunctive.

40. Simple Adverbs.—These are distinguished from one another according to their meaning:—

(*a*) **Quality** or **Manner.**—He acted *thus.* He did his work *slowly,* but *surely.* He behaved *foolishly.* We must *needs* try again.

(*b*) **Quantity** or **Degree.**—He is *almost,* but not *quite,* the cleverest boy in the class. He is *very* clever, but *rather too* indolent.

Note.—The word "*the,*" when it is placed before an adjective or adverb of the Comparative degree, is not the Definite article, but an *adverb of Quantity.* "*The* sooner, *the* better."

(*c*) **Number.**—He *seldom* failed, and *always* did his best. Try *again.* He has tried *twice* already.

(*d*) **Time.**—He did this *before,* and you have done it *since.* He will *soon* be here. He has *already* come. Some time *ago.*

(*e*) **Place.**—We must rest *here,* and not *there.* *South-ward, home-ward, on-ward. In-side, out-side.*

Note.—The adverb *there* is used with Intransitive verbs, when the verb is placed *before* its Nominative instead of *after* it; as "*There* stood a man at the gate." In such connections *there* is merely introductory, and has no signification of place.

(*f*) **Affirming** or **Denying.**—He will *probably* return to-day. We shall *certainly* succeed. He did *not* come.

41. The **Interrogative** adverbs are those used for asking questions:—

(*a*) **Quality** or **Manner.**—How (in what manner) did he do this? How (in what state of health) is he to-day?

(*b*) **Quantity** or **Degree.**—How far (to what extent) is this report true?

(*c*) **Number.**—How often did he come? How many persons came?

(*d*) **Time.**—When did he come? How long will he remain here? How soon will he go?

(*e*) **Place.**—Where did he go? How far (to what distance) did he go? Whence has he come.

(*f*) **Cause.**—Why (for what reason or cause) did he say this? Wherefore does she weep?

42. Relative or **Conjunctive adverbs.**—The Interrogative adverbs, when they are not used for asking a question, but *relate* to some antecedent, are called **Relative** adverbs. They are also called **Conjunctive,** because they join sentences:—

This is the place *where* (=in which) we dwell.

Sometimes the Antecedent is not expressed:—

This is *where* we dwell.

Here the adverb *where* does two things—(1) it modifies the verb of its own sentence "we dwell," as if it were a Simple adverb; (2) it joins its own sentence to the previous sentence "this is," as if it were a conjunction.

SECTION 2.—COMPARISON OF ADVERBS.

43. Adverbs, like adjectives, take no change of form, except when they are used in different degrees of Comparison.

(*a*) If the adverb is of one syllable, we add *er* and *est* to the Positive :—

Fast	faster	fastest	Long	longer	longest
Hard	harder	hardest	Loud	louder	loudest
Near	nearer	nearest	Late	later	latest or last

Note.—The adjective "near" has two adverbial forms, *near* and *nearly*, but their meanings are not the same : "He stood *near* : he *nearly* fell." The adjective "early" has the same form *early* for its adverb.

(*b*) In some adverbs the Comparative forms are irregular :—

Well	better	best	Much	more	most
Badly	worse	worst	Little	less	least
Far	farther	farthest	Fore	further	furthest

(*c*) Adverbs ending in *-ly* form the Comparative and Superlative by adding *more* and *most* :—

Wisely	more wisely	most wisely
Beautifully	more beautifully	most beautifully

The only adverbs that freely admit of degrees of Comparison are Simple adverbs of Quality. These might be called **Descriptive** adverbs. They answer to the Descriptive adjectives mentioned in § 26, *Note*, the only kind of adjective that freely admits of Comparative and Superlative forms.

SECTION 3.—THE FORMS OF ADVERBS.

44. Some Adverbs have the same form as the corresponding adjectives. In this case the one must be distinguished from the other by the *work that it does* (§ 1) in the sentence. Both are qualifying words ; but an adjective qualifies a noun or pronoun, while an adverb qualifies any part of speech except a noun or pronoun ; see § 1 (3) and (7).

Adverb.	*Adjective.*
He was *much* pleased.	There is *much* sickness here.
He stayed *long*.	He went on a *long* journey.
He spoke *loud*.	There is a sound of *loud* voices.
He came *early*.	He woke up at an *early* hour.
He hit him *hard*.	This is a *hard* piece of wood.
He came *quick*.	They rode along at a *quick* pace.
Stand *near* while I speak.	He is my *near* relation.
He was *a little* tired.	There is *a little* hope now.
He came *only* once.	This is my *only* son.
He has slept *enough*.	He has eaten *enough* bread.

45. Adverbs in "ly"—Most Adverbs are formed from adjectives by adding *ly*.

Adjective.	*Adverb.*
Wise	wisely (*Adverb of Quality or Manner*)
Whole	wholly (*Adverb of Quantity*)
First	firstly (*Adverb of Number or Order*)
Former	formerly (*Adverb of Time*)
Distant	distantly (*Adverb of Place*)
Certain	certainly (*Adverb of Affirming*)

But this form of the Adverb occurs most frequently in Simple adverbs of *Quality* or *Manner;* and there is generally an Abstract noun which can be placed between the Adjective and the Adverb:—

Adjective.	*Abstract Noun.*	*Adverb.*
Wise	wisdom	wisely
Poor	poverty	poorly
High	height	highly
Short	shortness	shortly

46. Adverbs formed from Pronouns.—

		Adverbs.				
		Rest.	Motion to.	Motion from.	Time.	Manner.
Dem.	This	there	thither	thence	then	thus
	He	here	hither	hence	...	...
Rel.	**Who**	where	whither	whence	when	how
Inter.	**Who?**	where?	whither?	whence?	when?	how?

Many of the above adverbs can be compounded with prepositions:—

From "there" we get *therein, thereto, thereat, therefore, therefrom, therewith, thereout, thereon, thereby, thereof.*

From "here" we get *herein, hereto, heretofore, hereat, herewith, hereon* or *hereupon, hereof, hereby, hereafter.*

From "where" we get *wherein, whereto, wherefore, whereon, whereof.*

From "hither" we get *hitherto* (=up to this point of place or time).

From "thence" we get *thenceforth, thenceforward.*

From "hence" we get *henceforth, henceforward.*

47. Adverbs ending in "s."—These have been formed from the Possessive cases of nouns:—

Needs (=of need, necessarily). *Once* (=of one, or of one time). *Twice* (=of two times). *Sometimes* (=of some time). *Always* (=of all way). *Sideways* (=of a side-way). *Length-ways* (=of a length-way). *Else* (=of other, from an old form, "elles," of another).

48. Adverbial Phrases.—There is a large class of words in

English which are made up of two or more words, and may be called Adverbial phrases :—

(1) A preposition followed by a noun :—*At random* (aimlessly); *of course* (necessarily); *at length* (finally); *in fact* (actually); *to boot* (moreover); *of a truth* (truly).

(2) A preposition amalgamated with a noun :—*Indeed* (actually); *betimes* (punctually); *besides* (in addition); *between* (in the middle); *to-day* (on this day); *to-morrow* (on the next day); *asleep* (in a state of sleep); *abed* (in bed); *away* (on the way).

Note.—The "*be*" is an old form of the preposition "by." The "*a*" is a contracted form of the preposition "on."

(3) A preposition followed by an adjective. Some noun is understood after the adjective :—*In general, in particular, in short, at large, in vain, on high, of old, after all, at first, at last, at least, at all, at most, at best, in future, at present.*

(4) A preposition amalgamated with an adjective. Here, as before, some noun is understood after the adjective :—*Below, beyond, behind, abroad, anew, awry, across, along, aloud,* etc.

(5) A noun qualified by an adjective ;—*Meantime, meanwhile, midway, yesterday,* etc.

(6) Miscellaneous phrases :—*By all means, by no means, by the by* (something said in passing), *by the way* (the same meaning as *by the by*), *once on a time, inside out, upside down, to be sure* (certainly), *head foremost* (with the head in front), *head downwards, topsy-turvy, head over heels* (the head being thrown over the heels).

49. Adverbs sometimes go together *in pairs*, the one being connected with the other by the conjunction "and" :—

> He is walking *up and down, to and fro.*
> He is walking *here and there, hither and thither.*
> The mice run *in and out, backwards and forwards.*
> He comes here *now and then* (occasionally).
> He works *off and on* (irregularly).
> You will see him *by and by* (in a short time).

CHAPTER VI.—PREPOSITIONS.

50. Preposition and Adverb.—A Preposition must not be confounded with an Adverb, though the two words are often identical in form. The only way to distinguish them is to look to the *work that each of them does.* Whenever an Adverb is used, only *one* factor in the sentence is affected by it, viz. the word or phrase which it qualifies; as "He walked *about.*" Here the word "about" qualifies the verb "walked" and nothing more. Whenever a Preposition is used, *two* factors at least are affected by it, viz. (1) the word that is its object, and (2) the word that is connected with its object by the Preposition. "He walked *about* the field." Here "about" connects its object "the field" with the verb "walked." The Preposition shows what the field *has to do with* the act of walking, or in what relation the one stands to the other, § 1 (5).

Examples.

Adverb.	*Preposition.*
The man ran *past*.	He came at half-*past* seven.
The *above*-named book.	The sky is *above* the earth.
He swam *across*.	The house stands *across* that field.
I saw him once *before*.	He stood *before* the door.
Go *along* quickly.	Let us walk *along* the bank.
You must go *behind*.	A man stood *behind* the door.
He sat *below*.	He stood *below* me in the class.
There is nothing *beyond*.	They went *beyond* the mark.
The horse was going *by*.	*By* whom was this done?
Sit *down* here.	The boat floats *down* the stream.
He sat *inside*.	The book is *inside* the box.
The men stood *around*.	They walked *around* the fields.
He is standing *near*.	Your house is *near* mine.
He died two years *since*.	*Since* that year I have been ill.
Stand *up* as straight as you can.	Walk *up* the hill.
He lived *on* for two years.	A book is *on* the slate.
He came a few days *after*.	He came *after* a few days.
Bees fly *in* and out.	Fish swim *in* water.
There were four men *besides*,	and ten more *besides* these.
The house was clean *within*.	I slept *within* the house.
The house was clean *without*.	Men die *without* sleep.

51. A Preposition, according to the definition given in § 3 (5), shows in what relation one thing stands to another thing. Some examples of such relations are given below :—

1. *Place, Situation, Circumstance.*

In.—Stand *in* the water. He is *in* a bad temper.

Into.—Go *into* the water. Water can be changed *into* steam.

Through.—Go *through* the door. He passed *through* many dangers.

Past or **beyond.**—*Beyond* the boundary. This is *past* endurance.

On or **upon.**—Sit *on* the box. *On* this condition I will trust you.

At.—He is not *at* home. He was much *at* fault.

By.—Sit *by* me. I will abide *by* my promise.

With.—I will go *with* you. All *with* one exception failed.

Over or **above.**—Air is *above* the earth. He spends *above* his income.

Below or **under.**—Snakes live *under* ground. The matter is *under* inquiry.

Behind.—The dog is *behind* you. There is a smile *behind* his frown.

Before.—Stand *before* the door. Duty *before* pleasure.

To.—He has gone *to* England. This is much *to* your credit.

For.—He starts *for* home. He worked hard *for* a prize.
From.—He starts *from* home. We are now free *from* danger.
Of.—He shot wide *of* the mark. He was robbed *of* his purse.
About.—Walk *about* the streets. He went *about* his business.
Near.—Come *near* the spot. His success is *near* my heart.
Along.—The boats were tied *along* the shore.
Among or **amid.** ·Let us walk *amid* the trees. They quarrelled *among* themselves. (This is used for *more than two* things.)
Between.—*Between* the two banks of the river. He still halts *between* two opinions. (This is used for *two* things only.)
Up, down.—The monkey ran *up* and *down* the tree.
Across.—He sailed *across* the sea. Sit *across* the saddle.
Around or **round.**—Describe a circle *round* a given centre.
Beside.—He sat *beside* me. He is *beside* himself with anger.
Besides.—He has two sons in India *besides* one in England.
Against.—It is not easy to swim *against* the stream.
Without.—He stands *without* (outside) the gate. Men cannot live *without* food.
Within.—He is *within* the house. This is not *within* my power.

2. *Time.*

In.—He finished the work *in* ten days. He arrived *in* time.
Into.—He slept late *into* the day.
Through.—He has been a lazy man *through* or *throughout* his whole life.
Past or **beyond.**—He is now *past* or *beyond* the age of forty.
On.—I will expect you *on* Monday next.
At.—Bats fly out *at* night; but retire *at* daybreak.
By.—The sun shines *by* day; the moon *by* night.
With.—*With* the return of the hot winds the grass fades.
Above or **over.**—He was absent *above* or *over* two weeks.
Under.—You will not finish that work *under* two months.
Behind, after.—He arrived *behind* time. He returned *after* many days.
Before.—He commenced work *before* seven o'clock A.M.
To.—*To*-day, *to*-night, *to*-morrow. The train is not up *to* time.
For.—He was made a prisoner *for* life.
From.—They commence work daily *from* ten o'clock.
About.—It is now *about* three o'clock P.M.
Between.—He arrived *between* four and five o'clock P.M.
During.—I will remain here *during* your pleasure.
Pending.—Nothing more can be done *pending* his arrival.
Till or **until.**—They worked all day *till* sunset.
Within.—This was finished *within* the time fixed.

Note.—When one Preposition does not express fully the relation that is intended, two Prepositions can be used with the same object:—

He stood *over against* the bank. The seed sprouted *from under* the ground. One man stood out *from among* the rest. The mouse crept *in between* the planks.

52. **Forms of Object.**—The object to a Preposition is usually

a noun or a pronoun. Sometimes, however, an adverb is made the object, sometimes a phrase, and sometimes a sentence :—

This news has come from *afar*. (*Adverb.*)
I bought this for *under-half-its-value*. (*Phrase.*)
This depends on *what-he-promises-to-do*. (*Sentence.*)

53. Omission of Object.—This never occurs except when the object, if it were expressed, would be the Relative pronoun, *whom, which, that.*

The man you were looking for has come.

Here the object to "for" is *whom* or *that* understood.

54. Prepositions in the form of Participles.—Such words, originally Participles, can now be parsed as prepositions :—

Pending fresh orders. *During* the summer. *Notwithstanding* his anger. All *except* one (all, one being excepted). The hour *past* sunset. *Considering* his age, he did well. *Owing* to this. Inform me *concerning*, *touching*, or *regarding* this matter.

55. Phrase-prepositions.—Sometimes a Preposition takes the form of a *phrase*, and not of a *single word*. But a phrase-preposition almost always ends in a Simple preposition.

By means of; because of; in front of; in opposition to; in spite of; on account of; with reference to; with regard to; for the sake of; on behalf of; instead of; in lieu of; in the place of; in prospect of; with a view to; in the event of.

Note.—In the following examples, the phrase has no Simple preposition at the end of it :—

On this side (of) the river. *On board* (of) the ship.

55*a*. Disguised prepositions, as in the following examples :—

Fourpence *a* (on) day. I go *a* (on) fishing. One *o'* (of) clock.

CHAPTER VII.—CONJUNCTIONS.

56. A **Conjunction** is a word used for *joining*. It joins :—

(1) One word to another word.
(2) One sentence to another sentence.

One Word joined to another Word.

57. When two words are joined together by a Conjunction, they are usually of *the same* or of *a similar* part of speech.

Thus, a noun is joined to a noun or pronoun; a verb to a verb; an adjective to an adjective or participle; an adverb to an adverb or to a phrase which does the work of an adverb; a preposition to a preposition.

The cat slowly *and* silently approaches. James *and* I went away at four o'clock. The horse is lame *as well as* thin. She sat down *and* wept. The bird flew into *and* through a cloud. He returned happy *and* smiling.

He is poor, *but* honest. They are sad, *but* or *but yet* hopeful. Take this book *or* that. Do not walk up, *but* down the hill.

Point out all the parts of speech which are joined together by the Conjunctions in the above sentences.

58. **Correlative** Conjunctions are those which go in pairs.

He is *both* wise *and* good. Take *either* the one book *or* the other.
He is *neither* wise *nor* good. The goat was *not only* killed, *but also* eaten.

One Sentence joined to another Sentence.

59. Among those Conjunctions which join one sentence to another sentence, the most common are given in the following examples:—

First Sentence.	*Conjunction.*	*Second Sentence.*
My father says,	*that*	this book is mine.
I trust his word,	*because*	he speaks the truth.
The boy will come,	*if*	he is allowed to do so.
I wish to know,	**whether*	I am excused or not.
She walked slowly,	*lest*	she should fall down.
He will do this,	*unless*	he is stopped by you.
The boy returned,	*although*	the day was still wet.
You may go out,	*as* or *since*	the rain has now ceased.
He left his bed,	**when*	the sun was seen to rise.
We could not tell,	**whence*	the noise of voices arose.
No one could find out,	**where*	the cow was lying hid.
The mice will play,	*while*	the cat is away.
Can you tell me,	**whither*	he intends to go.
You must wait here,	*until*	your father comes back.
They could not tell,	**why*	they were so heavily fined.
The girl is quick,	*and*	she reads very well.
She went to bed,	*for*	she was feeling quite tired.
He was so badly hurt,	*that*	he died soon after.
I will trust you,	*provided*	you sign your name.
We must believe it,	*since*	you say so.
Pay that debt,	*or*	you will not be trusted.
I wish to know,	**how*	the sick man is to-day.
He will die some day,	*however*	rich he may be.
He closed his house,	*after*	his friends had gone.
He cleaned his house well,	*before*	his friends came.
The girl is clever,	*but*	the boy is a dunce.
He left the house,	*as soon as*	the rain stopped.
He could not pass,	*though*	he tried often.
Your horse is swifter	*than*	mine (is).

Note.—The conjunctions marked with an asterisk, namely, *whether*, *when*, *whence*, *where*, *whither*, *why*, and *how*, are Conjunctive or Relative adverbs (see § 42), *i.e.* partly adverbs and partly conjunctions. Such a word does the work of *two* parts of speech. So far as it *qualifies* the verb of its own sentence by stating the time, place, manner, etc., of the event, it is an **Adverb**. So far as it joins one sentence to another, it is a **Conjunction**.

60. Conjunction and Adverb.—Care must be taken not to confound a Conjunction with an Adverb, or with a Preposition, or with any other part of speech. There is no fear of any confusion, if the student will ask himself, *What work does the word do in the sentence before him?* If it joins one word or sentence to another word or sentence, it is a Conjunction. If it shows in what relation one thing stands to another thing, it is a Preposition. If it qualifies some word, it is an Adverb.

Conjunction.	*Preposition, Adverb, etc.*
We will go *after* you have dined.	We will go *after* dinner (*Prep.*).
	He came a few days *after* (*Adv.*).
He went *before* he had dined.	He went away *before* dinner (*Prep.*).
	I have never seen him *before* (*Adv.*).
He is shrewd, *but* unlearned.	All *but* four escaped (*Prep.*).
	There is *but* one present (*Adv.*).
He is *either* a fool or a knave.	He is ruined in *either* case (*Adj.*).
He fled ; *else* he would have been caught.	We could do nothing *else* (*Adv.*).
I cannot beg ; *for* I am ashamed.	He has been ill *for* a long time (*Prep.*).
Neither you nor I can do that.	I agree with *neither* side (*Adj.*).
Do what you *like ; only* keep quiet.	I heard of this *only* yesterday (*Adv.*).
	The *only* dog I had was stolen (*Adj.*).
We must trust it, *since* you say so.	I have not been *since* Sunday last (*Prep.*).
	I took this four weeks *since* (*Adv.*).
The time is up ; *so* we must go.	Do not walk *so* fast (*Adv.*).
I heard *that* you had come.	The book *that* you gave me is here (*Relative Pron.*).
	The light of the sun is brighter than *that* of the moon (*Demon.* (*Pron.*).
	I am no admirer of *that* book (*Demon. Adj.*).
I like this more *than* (I like) that.	No drink other *than* water suited him (*Prep.*).
Wait *till* I return.	Wait here *till* sunset (*Prep.*).
As the sun is up, let us start.	He is not such a man *as* you (*Rel. Pron.*).

PART II.—VERBS AND THEIR INFLECTIONS.

CHAPTER VIII.—THE KINDS OF VERBS.

61. Three kinds of Verbs.—There are three kinds of verbs,—the Transitive, the Intransitive, and the Auxiliary.

I. **Transitive.**—A Transitive verb denotes an action that is directed towards some object:—

The man *killed* a snake.

Note.—The word "Transitive" means "passing over." Verbs of Class I. are called Transitive, because the action expressed by such a verb as "killed" does not stop with the doer, but *passes* from the doer to the object denoted by "snake."

II. **Intransitive.**—An Intransitive verb denotes an action that stops with the doer, and concerns no person or thing except the doer:—

Men *sleep* to preserve life.

Sleep what? That is nonsense. No word or words can be placed as object after such a verb as *sleep*. The verb *sleep* is therefore Intransitive.

Note.—An Intransitive verb, that is made Transitive by having a preposition added to it and can be used as such in the Passive voice, is called **a Prepositional verb**:—

We *act-on* this rule. This rule is *acted-on* by us.

III. **Auxiliary.**—An Auxiliary verb is one that *helps* other verbs, Transitive or Intransitive, to form some of their parts. It happens that very few of our tenses are formed by inflection, that is, by a change of inside vowel or by a change of ending. So for forming most tenses verbs require help, and this help is given them by the special class of verbs, which are for this reason called Auxiliary (Latin *auxiliaris*, helpful).

(1) I *have* slept well. (2) He *will* sleep well.

Here the Auxiliary *have* goes with the verb "slept." The two verbs thus joined make a compound tense, which could not have been expressed by any form of the verb "sleep" alone.

Similarly, the Auxiliary *will* goes with the verb "sleep." The two verbs thus joined make a compound tense, which could not have been expressed by any form of the verb "sleep" alone.

62. Transitive Verbs used Intransitively.—There are two ways in which Transitive verbs can become Intransitive :—

(*a*) When the verb is used in such a general sense that no object or objects are thought of in connection with it :—

Men *eat* to preserve life (Intr.).	He never *eats* meat (Trans.).
He *writes* well (Intr.).	He *writes* a good letter (Trans.).

A new-born child *sees*, but a kitten is born blind. I *see* a ship.

(*b*) When the Reflexive pronoun is omitted :—

He *drew* (himself) near me.	He *made* (himself) merry.

The following are common examples of Transitive verbs which have acquired an Intransitive force by omitting the Reflexive pronoun :—

Transitive Verb.	*Intransitive Counterpart.*
Get you (=yourself) gone.	*Get* out of my way.
Give him a penny.	The shoe *gives* after it is worn.
He *obtained* a place.	This doctrine *obtained* (held its ground) for a long time.
The fire *burnt* up the house.	He *burnt* with rage.
Do not *stop* me.	Let us *stop* here a little.
They *open* the doors at nine.	School *opens* at ten o'clock.
A man *breaks* stones with a hammer.	The day *breaks* at six.
The ox *drew* this cart.	He *drew* near to me.
Move away this stone.	*Move* on a little faster.
He *broke up* the meeting.	School *broke up* at three.
The mouse *steals* food.	The mouse *steals* into its hole.
They *bathed* the child.	Let us *bathe* here.
He *rolls* a ball down the hill.	The ball *rolls* down the hill.
He *burst* the door open.	The storm has *burst*.
Bad men *hide* their faults.	Bats *hide* during the day.
He *turned* me out of the room.	He *turned* to me and spoke.
They *drop* the boat into the water.	Rain *drops* from the sky.
They *keep* the boat on the left bank.	The boat *keeps* on the left bank.
He *sets* the school in order.	The sun *sets* at six P.M.
He *feeds* the horse on grain.	Many men *feed* on rice.

There are a few verbs, in which the difference between Transitive and Intransitive is shown by a difference in the inside vowel. Here the Transitive verb has a **causal** sense: thus "to *fell*" means "to *cause to fall*."

Intransitive.	*Transitive.*
The tree *falls.*	He *fells* the tree with an axe.
The sun will *rise* at six.	I cannot *raise* this box.
The cow *lies* on the grass.	The man *lays* down his coat.
We must not *sit* here.	He *set* the books in order.
He will *fare* well.	He will *ferry* me across.
The enemy *quails.*	He *quells* the enemy.
The fish *bite* well to-day.	I took care to *bait* them well.
His chains *clink* on him.	Help me to *clench* this nail.

63. Verbs that require a Complement.—"Complement" means that which *fills up* or *makes complete.* A verb that requires a complement may be either Transitive or Intransitive.

(*a*) Those Transitive verbs that not only take an Object, but require the help of some other word or words to supply what has still to be said about the *Object,* are called **Factitive.**

Subject.	*Verb.*	*Object.*	*Complement.*	
They	made	him	king . .	(*Noun compl.*)
The judge	set	the prisoner	free . .	(*Adjective compl.*)
They	found	him	out . .	(*Adverb compl.*)

(*b*) Those Intransitive verbs that require a Complement to supply what the verb left unsaid about the *Subject* are called **Copulative.** They *couple* the Complement with the Subject.

Subject.	*Verb.*	*Complement.*	
That beggar	turned out	a thief . . .	(*Noun compl.*)
His progress	has been	satisfactory . .	(*Adjective compl.*)
The results	are	out	(*Adverb compl.*)

Note.—**Complete and Incomplete Predication.**—A verb that makes a complete sense so that nothing more need be added to it is called a verb of Complete Predication; as, Hogs *grunt.* All such verbs are Intransitive.

Verbs of Incomplete Predication are of three different kinds—(1) A Transitive verb that requires an object only; (2) a Transitive verb that requires both an object and a complement, *i.e.* a Factitive verb; (3) an Intransitive verb that requires a complement, *i.e.* a Copulative verb.

CHAPTER IX.—THE PARTS OF A FINITE VERB.

64. Finite and not Finite.—The various different forms that a verb can take are subdivided under two main headings: I. The Finite; II. The non-Finite. The present chapter deals with the Finite only.

Any part of a verb can be called Finite, which is connected with some Subject :—

(1) The tree *fell* (Finite). (2) The *falling* tree (non-Finite).

In (1) the verb *fell* is preceded by its Subject "tree"; the verb *fell* is therefore Finite. In (2) the word *falling*, though it is a part of the verb "fall," is not preceded, and cannot be preceded, by any Subject: it is, in fact, a kind of adjective that qualifies or goes with the noun "tree." This part of the verb, therefore, is non-Finite.

Note.—The word Finite means "limited," that is, limited or bound to its Subject.

65. The Finite moods.—"Mood" means the *manner* or *mode* of the action expressed by the verb. There are three Finite moods :—

I. Indicative. II. Imperative. III. Subjunctive.

I. In the **Indicative** mood we assert or indicate some action as a *fact*, and sometimes as a condition :—

He *comes* (fact). If he *comes* (condition).

II. In the **Imperative** we *command* or *advise* some action :—

Come. *Go.* *Sweep* the room.

In these three examples the Subject "thou" or "you," though not mentioned, is implied.

III. In the **Subjunctive** mood we express some action, not as a fact, but as a *doubt* or as a *desire* or as a *purpose* :—

If he *come* (older form) }
If he *should come* } . . . (*Doubt.*)
May he *come!* . . . . . (*Desire or wish.*)
He eats that he *may live* . . . (*Purpose.*)

66. Number and Person.—The number and person of a Finite verb depend upon the *number* and *person* of its Subject :—

Number.
- If the Subject is Singular, the verb must be Singular; as, Rain *is* falling.
- If the Subject is Plural, the verb must be Plural; as, Rain-drops *are* falling.

Person.
- If the Subject is in the First person, the verb must be in the First person; as, I see. We come.
- If the Subject is in the Second person, the verb must be in the Second person; as, Thou seest. You see.
- If the Subject is in the Third person, the verb must be in the Third person; as, He sees. They see.

67. Tense.—Tense is the form assumed by a verb for showing —(*a*) the *time* in which an event occurs; (*b*) the *degree of completeness* ascribed to an event at the time of its occurrence.

(*a*) Now as regards the question of *time* the verb may tell you—

(1) That an action *is done* in **Present** time; as, He *comes*.
(2) That it *was done* in **Past** time; as, He *came*.
(3) That it *will be done* in **Future** time; as, He *will come*.

(*b*) As regards the question of *completeness*, there are four degrees, which give rise to four different forms of Present, Past, and Future time:—

I. **Indefinite**; which denotes Present, Past, and Future time in its simplest form, the degree of completeness being left indefinite; as, *I see, I saw, I shall see.*

II. **Continuous**; which denotes that the event (in Present, Past, or Future time) is still *continuing*, or not yet complete; as, *I am seeing, I was seeing, I shall be seeing.* (This is sometimes called the Imperfect form of tense.)

III. **Perfect**; which denotes that the event (in Present, Past, or Future time) is in a completed or *perfect* state; as, *I have seen, I had seen, I shall have seen.*

IV. **Perfect Continuous**; which combines the force of the two preceding forms; as, *I have been seeing, I had been seeing, I shall have been seeing.*

68. Voice is that form of a verb which shows whether what is named by the Subject *does* something or *has* something *done* to it.

In the **Active** voice the person or thing denoted by the Subject is said *to do* something to some other person or thing:—

Tom *threw* a ball.

In the **Passive** voice the person or thing denoted by the Subject is said to *suffer* something from some other person or thing:—

A ball *was thrown* by Tom.

Note 1.—It will be seen from these examples that when the verb of a sentence is changed from Active to Passive, the object to the Active verb becomes the subject to the Passive one.

Note 2.—An **Intransitive** verb has no Passive voice, unless it takes a Cognate object (§ 95) in the Active. Even then the Passive can be used only in the third person:—"I ran a race"; "a race was run by me."

69. Conjugation of the Finite moods.—The conjugation of a verb, that is, the different forms that it can take in the Finite moods, is shown in the following tables. It will be observed that the only tenses formed by inflection, that is, without the help of Auxiliary verbs, are the Present and Past Indefinite, and these only in the Active voice.

A. Active Voice of Do.

I.—*Indicative Mood.*

Tense.		Singular. 1st Person.	Singular. 2nd Person.	Singular. 3rd Person.	Plural. 1st, 2nd, 3rd Persons.
Present	*Indefinite*	do	doest or dost[1]	does	do
	Continuous	am doing	art doing	is doing	are doing
	Perfect	have done	hast done	has done	have done
	Perf. Cont.	have been doing	hast been doing	has been doing	have been doing
Past	*Indefinite*	did	didst	did	did
	Continuous	was doing	wast doing	was doing	were doing
	Perfect	had done	hadst done	had done	had done
	Perf. Cont.	had been doing	hadst been doing	had been doing	had been doing
Future	*Indefinite*	shall do	wilt do	will do	1. shall / 2, 3. will } do
	Continuous	shall be doing	wilt be doing	will be doing	1. shall / 2, 3. will } be doing
	Perfect	shall have done	wilt have done	will have done	1. shall / 2, 3. will } have done
	Perf. Cont.	shall have been doing	wilt have been doing	will have been doing	1. shall / 2, 3. will } have been doing

[1] *Dost* is used only when the verb is Auxiliary; as "Thou *dost* arise."

II.—*Subjunctive Mood.*

Tense		Singular. 1st Person.	2nd Person.	3rd Person.	Plural. 1st, 2nd, 3rd Persons.
Present	*Indefinite*	do	do	do	do
	Continuous	be doing	be doing	be doing	be doing
	Perfect	have done	have done	have done	have done
	Perf. Cont.	have been doing	have been doing	have been doing	have been doing
Past	*Indefinite*		(*Same as Indicative*)		
	Continuous	were doing	wert doing	were doing	were doing
	Perfect		(*Same as Indicative*)		
	Perf. Cont.		(*Same as Indicative*)		
Future	*Indefinite*	should do	wouldst do	would do	1. should, 2, 3. would } do
	Continuous	should be doing	wouldst be doing	would be doing	1. should, 2, 3. would } be doing
	Perfect	should have done	wouldst have done	would have done	1. should, 2, 3. would } have done
	Perf. Cont.	should have been doing	wouldst have been doing	would have been doing	1. should, 2, 3. would } have been doing

III.—*Imperative Mood.*

Present Singular 2. do (thou). *Plural* 2. do (ye or you).

Note.—The Indefinite Present Subjunctive can also be expressed by *may*, as *may do;* and the Indefinite Past by *might*, as *might do*. *Should* is used for *would* in the 2nd and 3rd persons to express a condition.

B. Passive Voice of **See.**

This, if we omit the Past Participle "seen," gives a complete conjugation of the Finite forms of the verb "*to be.*"

I.—*Indicative Mood.*

Tense.		Singular. 1st Person.	2nd Person.	3rd Person.	Plural. 1st, 2nd, 3rd Persons.
Present	*Indefinite*	am seen	art seen	is seen	are seen
	Continuous	am being seen	art being seen	is being seen	are being seen
	Perfect	have been seen	hast been seen	has been seen	have been seen
	Perf. Cont.		(*None*)		
Past	*Indefinite*	was seen	wast seen	was seen	were seen
	Continuous	was being seen	wast being seen	was being seen	were being seen
	Perfect	had been seen	hadst been seen	had been seen	had been seen
	Perf. Cont.		(*None*)		
Future	*Indefinite*	shall be seen	wilt be seen	will be seen	1. shall / 2, 3. will } be seen
	Continuous		(*None*)		
	Perfect	shall have been seen	wilt have been seen	will have been seen	1. shall / 2, 3. will } have been seen
	Perf. Cont.		(*None*)		

II.—*Subjunctive Mood.*

Tense.		Singular. 1st Person.	Singular. 2nd Person.	Singular. 3rd Person.	Plural. 1st, 2nd, 3rd Persons.
Present	*Indefinite*	be seen	be seen	be seen	be seen
	Continuous		(*None*)		
	Perfect	have been seen	have been seen	have been seen	have been seen
	Perf. Cont.		(*None*)		
Past	*Indefinite*	were seen	wert seen	were seen	were seen
	Continuous	were being seen	wert being seen	were being seen	were being seen
	Perfect		(*Same as Indicative*)		
	Perf. Cont.		(*None*)		
Future	*Indefinite*	should be seen	wouldst be seen	would be seen	1. should, 2, 3. would } be seen
	Continuous		(*None*)		
	Perfect	should have been seen	wouldst have been seen	would have been seen	1. should, 2, 3. would } have been seen
	Perf. Cont.		(*None*)		

III.—*Imperative Mood.*

Present Singular 2. be (thou) seen. *Plural* 2. be (ye or you) seen

Note.—The Indefinite Present Subjunctive can also be expressed by *may*, as *may be seen*; and the Indefinite Past by *might*, as *might be seen*. *Should* is used for *would* in 2nd and 3rd persons to express a condition.

Exercise 9.

Point out the Voice, Mood, Tense, Number, and Person of every Finite verb noted below:—

1. *Come* and *tell* me what you *have heard*. 2. If you *should be* at home when I *call* at your house, I *shall be* glad. 3. He *came* to my house at four o'clock in the afternoon. 4. You *will be killed*, if that stone *falls* upon your head. 5. Why *were* these books *brought* to me? 6. My father *will* not *return* for some time. 7. If he *should return* to-morrow, I *should be* much *surprised*. 8. *Will* you *come* soon to see me? 9. He *told* them to call for him at four o'clock. 10. *Put* away the books, and *shut* the door of the room. 11. The cow *is* a quiet and useful animal. 12. Oxen *draw* the plough. 13. I *see* four men coming. 14. They *see* the sun rising. 15. We *see* the hills in the distance. 16. Thou *art* the wisest man in the room. 17. The horse *carries* its rider. 18. That the horse *is* lame *is seen* by all of us. 19. How to do this *was* not *understood*.

Exercise 10.

(*a*) *Change the following sentences from the Active to the Passive:—*

1. A cat chased a mouse, and a dog chased the cat. 2. He brought six apples for me. 3. The lower animals do not need tools. 4. But they possess limbs as useful to them as tools. 5. Man alone knows how to make tools. 6. God has given no such mind to other animals. 7. We must find out the reasons of things. 8. This king conquered that. 9. Who made you and all the world?

(*b*) *Change the following sentences from Passive to Active:—*

1. The shops are closed by all the dealers. 2. This book was brought here by my servant. 3. The roof of the house was blown off by the wind. 4. The ripening wheat was destroyed by a storm of hail. 5. The soil of the earth is made fertile by rain. 6. That fine tree was split by lightning. 7. The walls of the house were cracked by an earthquake in several places. 8. The men were ordered by the king's messengers to go away. 9. Four men must be sent by us to the market. 10. How to spell, read, and write is known by man alone. 11. His death was bewailed by all of us.

CHAPTER X.—PARTS OF A VERB THAT ARE NOT FINITE.

70. Non-Finite parts of a verb.—Any part of a verb which is not connected, and from the nature of its meaning cannot be connected, with a *Subject*, comes under the heading of non-Finite (§ 64). Such a verb may be called a Verb Infinite.

The non-Finite parts of a verb are three in number:—(1) the **In-fin-i-tive** mood; as, "I wish *to retire*"; (2) a **Par-ti-cip-le**; as, "A *retired* officer"; (3) a **Gerund**; as, "I think of *retiring.*" Not one of the three forms here noted can have a noun or pronoun placed before it as Subject, and hence not one of them is a Finite part of the verb "retire."

71. Infinitive.—The Infinitive mood is that part of the verb which names the action without reference to any doer. It may denote either Present or Past time:—

	Tense.	*Active.*	*Passive.*
Present	*Indefinite* .	To send	To be sent.
	Continuous .	To be sending	(*Wanting.*)
Past	*Perfect* . .	To have sent	To have been sent.
	Perf. Contin.	To have been sending	(*Wanting.*)

The Infinitive is usually preceded by "*to,*" but not always. "*To*" is not used after the verbs *hear, see, feel, make, let, bid, watch, behold, know;* nor after the Auxiliary verbs *shall, will, may, do;* nor after the verbs *must, can;* nor after the negative forms *need not, dare not*:—

I hear thee *speak* of the better land.
You need not *send* these books to me.
I do *hope* you will *return* soon.
Let me *see* what you have done.

Note.—Observe the last example "let me *see.*" Here *let* is the second person Imperative—the only person which can be expressed by a verb in the Imperative mood. To express the first or third person, we use the verb "let" in such forms as "let *me* see," "let *him* see." In all such examples "see" is in the Infinitive mood.

72. Participle.—A Participle (when it is not part of a tense) is a Verbal adjective, that adds to the meaning of some noun or pronoun as ordinary adjectives do. It may denote either Present or Past time:—

		Active voice.	*Passive voice.*
Present or Continuous .	.	Loving	Being loved.
Past	*Indefinite* . . .	(*Wanting*)	Loved.
	Perfect . . .	Having loved	Having been loved.

Note.—The form *loving* stands for both Present and Continuous time. These are not the same in meaning:—

(*a*) *Hearing* this he was much surprised . . (*Present.*)
(*b*) He went away *sorrowing* . . . . . (*Contin.*)

In (*a*) the action is completed. In (*b*) it is continuous.

We have no form of Participle to express *Future* time. This is expressed by the Infinitive; as, "The world *to come.*" To express a very near future, we add the words *about* or *going* to the Infinitive:—

The house is *about to fall.*
The house is *going to fall.*

Or we may express a very near Future by the following phrase:—
The house is *on the point of falling.*

73. A Participle is in one respect a verb, in another an adjective :—

(*a*) It is a verb, because (if the verb is Transitive) it can be followed (like a Finite tense) by an object :—

Having eaten *his dinner*, he returned to work.

(*b*) It is an adjective or like an adjective, because—(1) it can have degrees of Comparison ; and (2) it goes with some noun or pronoun, as ordinary adjectives do :—

(1) Faded (*Positive*) ; more faded (*Comp.*) ; most faded (*Superl.*).
(2) *Having eaten* his dinner, *he* returned to work.

In (2) the participle *having eaten* goes with the pronoun *he*.

Exercise 11.

Pick out every Infinitive and every Participle in the following sentences, and say what time it denotes :—

1. I saw him take aim with his bow. 2. Being tired of work the men went home. 3. I feel the cold air strike against my face. 4. The returned soldier was received gladly by his parents. 5. Grazing in the fresh grass, the lambs soon became strong. 6. To stay awake at night is bad for health. 7. A vicious and kicking horse gives much trouble to its master. 8. He dared not say this in open day. 9. Pleased at seeing me return, he made me come and sit by his side. 10. I have often known him laugh for nothing. 11. The boy that you see there painting a picture is my brother. 12. My wife, expecting me to return shortly, did not leave the house. 13. A man-eating tiger must be shot at once, if you can do it. 14. I was told that I might go away, and so I went. 15. He hears his daughter singing a new song. 16. The days of youth are passed, never to return to us again.

74. Gerund.—A Gerund is a kind of noun which names the action or state denoted by the verb. It has four forms,—two for the Active voice, and two for the Passive :—

	Active.	*Passive.*
Present or Continuous	Loving	Being loved.
Past	Having loved	Having been loved.

The *forms*, then, are identical with those of the Participle ; but their *use* is entirely different. A Gerund is a kind of *noun* ; a Participle is a kind of *adjective*.

Exercise 12.

In the following sentences, say whether the words noted below are Gerunds or Participles :—

1. The oats will grow well in the *coming* rains. 2. We heard of his *coming* back to-day. 3. Did you hear of his *having won* a prize? 4. The boy, *having won* a prize, was much praised. 5. She was fond of *being admired*. 6. *Being admired* by all, she was much pleased.

7. The cow, *having been killed* by a tiger yesterday, could not be found. 8. The boy was ashamed of *having been beaten* in class by his sister. 9. I am tired of *doing* this work. 10. *Doing* this work every day, you will soon improve. 11. *Spelling* is more difficult than *writing*. 12. He was in the habit of *boasting* of his cleverness. 13. A *boasting* man is much despised. 14. He was pleased at *having found* his son. 15. *Having found* his son, he returned home at once. 16. Foxes do not enjoy *being hunted*, but men enjoy *hunting* them. 17. The fox *being hunted* fled into its hole.

75. A Gerund is in one respect a verb, in another a noun :—

(*a*) It is a noun, because it has all the uses of a noun ; for it can be the subject, object, or complement to a verb, or the object to a preposition .—

Spelling is more difficult than writing . . . (*Subject to verb.*)
He teaches *spelling* with much success . . . (*Object to verb.*)
The hardest thing to learn in English is *spelling* . (*Compl. to verb.*)
He is very clever at *spelling* . . . . . (*Obj. to Prep.*)

(*b*) It is a verb, because it can express Present or Past time, and can be in the Active or Passive voice (for examples see § 74). Moreover, if the verb is Transitive, it requires an Object in the same way that the Finite forms of the verb do :—

He made two mistakes in spelling *that word*.

Here "word" is the Object to the verb "spelling."

But if we place *of* after "spelling," and *the* before it, then "spelling" is a pure noun, and not a verb at all. To distinguish this from a Gerund we call it a **Verbal Noun**, *i.e.* a noun formed from a verb.

He made two mistakes in *the* spelling *of* that word.

Here "spelling" is a pure noun, and "that word" is not the object of "spelling," but of the preposition "of."

CHAPTER XI.—STRONG AND WEAK VERBS.

76. Verbs are distinguished into **Strong** and **Weak** according to the manner in which they form the Past tense and the Past participle. (Sometimes, but with less propriety, Strong verbs are called Irregular, and Weak verbs Regular.)

I. *How to tell a Weak verb from a Strong* :—

(*a*) All verbs, whose Past tense ends in a *-d* or *-t*, which is not in the Present tense, are Weak :—

Live, live-*d*. Fan, fann-*ed*. Carry, carri-*ed*. Plunge, plunge-*d*. Sleep, slep-*t*. Burn, burn-*t*. Shoe, sho-*d*. Flee, fle-*d*. Pay, pai-*d*. Bend, ben-*t*. Build, buil-*t*. Send, sen-*t*. Gird, gir-*t* or gird-*ed*. Think, though-*t*. Work, wrough-*t*. Sell, sol-*d*. Owe, ough-*t* or owe-*d*.

(*b*) All verbs, whose Past tense is formed by shortening (not changing) the vowel of the Present tense, are Weak :—

Bleed, bled. Shoot, shot. Lead, led. Light, lit or light-*ed*.

(*c*) All verbs, whose Past tense is the same as the Present, are Weak :—

Cut, cut. Hurt, hurt. Put, put. Rid, rid. Spread, spread.

II. *How to tell a Strong verb from a Weak* :—

(*a*) All verbs, which form the Past tense by *changing* (not merely shortening) the inside vowel, and do *not* add on a final -*d* or -*t*, are Strong :—

Fight, fought : (but "buy, bough-*t*" is Weak, because, after changing the inside vowel, it adds a final -*t*). Hold, held. Stand, stood. Sit, sat. Find, found. Drive, drove.

(*b*) All verbs, which form the Past participle in -*en* or -*n*, are either wholly or partly Strong :—

Wholly.—Draw, drew, draw-*n*. Shake, shook, shake-*n*. Slay, slew, slai-*n*.

Partly.—Saw, saw-*ed*, saw-*n*. Cleave, clef-*t*, clov-*en*. Lade, lade-*d*, lade-*n*.

Observe that the verbs in the last line are Weak in the Past tense and Strong in the Past participle. These are classed as "Mixed."

77. Lists of Strong Verbs.—Though we have many Strong verbs still left, yet the Strong conjugation is practically obsolete, because (1) no *new* verbs have ever been so conjugated, (2) many verbs that were once Strong have become Weak.

Group I. (50 *verbs*).—Final -*n* or -*en* retained in Past Participle.

Present Tense.	*Past Tense.*	*Past Part.*
Arise	arose	arisen
Bear (produce)	bore	born
Bear (carry)	bore	borne
Beget	begot, begat	begotten, begot
Bid	bade, bid	bidden, bid
Bind	bound	*bounden, bound
Bite	bit	bitten, bit
Blow	blew	blown
Break	broke	broken
Chide	chid	chidden, chid
Choose	chose	chosen
Draw	drew	drawn
Drink	drank	*drunken, drunk
Drive	drove, drave	driven
Eat	ate	eaten
Fall	fell	fallen
Fly	flew	flown
Forbear	forbore	forborne
Forget	forgot	forgotten
Forsake	forsook	forsaken
Freeze	froze	frozen
Get	got	*gotten, got
Give	gave	given
Go, wend	went	gone
Grow	grew	grown
Hide	hid	*hidden hid

Present Tense.	*Past Tense.*	*Past Part.*	*Present Tense.*	*Past Tense.*	*Past Part.*
Know	knew	known	Steal	stole	stolen
Lie	lay	lain	Stride	strode	stridden
Ride	rode	ridden	Strike	struck	*stricken, struck
Rise	rose	risen	Strive	strove	striven
See	saw	seen	Swear	swore	sworn
Shake	shook	shaken	Take	took	taken
Shrink	shrank	*shrunken, shrunk	Tear	tore	torn
Sink	sank	*sunken, sunk	Throw	threw	thrown
Slay	slew	slain	Tread	trod	trodden, trod
Slide	slid	slidden, slid	Wear	wore	worn
Smite	smote	smitten, smit	Weave	wove	woven
Speak	spoke	spoken	Write	wrote	written

Note.—The seven participles marked * are now chiefly used as adjectives, and not as parts of a tense :—

Adjective.	*Part of some Tense.*
Our *bounden* duty.	He was *bound* by his promise.
A *drunken* man.	He had *drunk* much wine.
A *sunken* ship.	The ship had *sunk* under the water.
A *stricken* deer.	The deer was *struck* with an arrow.
The *shrunken* stream.	The stream has *shrunk* in its bed.
Ill-*gotten* wealth.	He *got* his wealth by ill means.
A *hidden* meaning.	The meaning is *hid* or hidden.

Group II. (32 *verbs*).—Final *-n* or *-en* lost in Past Participle.

Present Tense.	*Past Tense.*	*Past Part.*	*Present Tense.*	*Past Tense.*	*Past Part.*
Abide	abode	abode	Sing	sang	sung
Awake	awoke	awoke[1]	Sit	sat	sat
Become	became	become	Sling	slung	slung
Begin	began	begun	Slink	slunk	slunk
Behold	beheld	beheld, beholden[2]	Spin	spun	spun
Cling	clung	clung	Spring	sprang	sprung
Come	came	come	Stand	stood	stood
Dig	dug	dug	Stick	stuck	stuck
Fight	fought	fought	Sting	stung	stung
Find	found	found	Stink	stank	stunk
Fling	flung	flung	String	strung	strung
Grind	ground	ground	Swim	swam	swum
Hold	held	held	Swing	swung	swung
Ring	rang	rung	Win	won	won
Run	ran	run	Wind	wound	wound
Shine	shone	shone	Wring	wrung	wrung

[1] *Awaked* is less common.

[2] "Beholden" means "indebted."

Group III.—Mixed or Strong-Weak Verbs (28 in number).

Present Tense.	*Past Tense.*	*Past Participle.*
Beat	beat	beaten
Cleave (split)	clave, cleft	*cloven, cleft
Climb	clomb, climbed	climbed
Crow	crew, crowed	crowed, crown (rare)
Do	did	done
Grave	graved	*graven, graved
Hang[1]	hung, hanged	hung, hanged
Heave	heaved, hove	heaved, hove
Hew	hewed	*hewn, hewed
Lade	laded	laden
Melt	melted	*molten, melted
Mow	mowed	mown
Prove	proved	†proven, proved
Rive	rived	riven
Rot	rotted	*rotten, rotted
Saw	sawed	sawn
Seethe	seethed	*sodden, seethed
Sew	sewed	*sewn, sewed
Shape	shaped	†shapen, shaped
Shave	shaved	shaven
Shear	sheared	*shorn, sheared
Show	showed	shown
Sow	sowed	sown
Stave	stove, staved	stove, staved
Strew	strewed	strewn or strown
Swell	swelled	swollen
Thrive	throve, thrived	thriven, thrived
Wash	washed	*washen, washed
Writhe	writhed	†writhen, writhed

Note 1.—The participles marked * are now chiefly used as adjectives, and not as parts of a tense :—

Adjective.	*Part of some Tense.*
A *graven* image.	The image was *engraved* with letters.
A *molten* image.	The image was *melted* with heat.
A *rotten* plank.	The plank was *rotted* by water.
The *sodden* flesh.	The flesh was *seethed* in hot water.
A well-*sewn* cloth.	I have *sewed* or *sewn* it.
Un-*washen* hands.	I have *washed* my hands.
A *shorn* lamb.	The lamb was *sheared* to-day.
A *hewn* log.	The log is *hewed* or *hewn*.

Note 2.—The participles marked † are almost obsolete.

78. Lists of Weak Verbs.—The mode of adding the suffix

[1] The Intransitive verb is conjugated in the Strong form only. The Transitive verb is conjugated in both forms. *Hanged* means "killed by hanging"; as, "The man was *hanged*." *Hung* is used in a general sense; as, "He *hung* up his coat."

of the Past tense is not uniform; and the two rules given below should be observed :—

(1) If the verb ends in *e*, then *d* only is added; as—

Live, lived (not *liveed*).
Clothe, clothed (not *clotheed*).

To this rule there is no exception.

(2) The final consonant is doubled before *ed*, provided—(*a*) that the final consonant is *single;* (*b*) that it is *accented* or *monosyllabic;* (*c*) that it is preceded by a *single vowel;* as—

Fan, fanned (not *faned*)*; drop, dropped* (not *droped*).
Compel, compelled; control, controlled; confer, conferred.

But in a verb like *lengthen*, where the accent is not on the last syllable, the Past tense is *lengthened;* in a verb like *boil*, where the vowel is not single, the Past tense is *boiled;* and in a verb like *fold*, where the last consonant is not single, the Past tense is *folded.*

To this rule there are very few exceptions. One exception occurs in the final *l*. The final *l* is doubled, even when it is not accented; as, travel, trav*elled* (not trav*eled*).

Group I.—Shortening of Inside Vowel: Past tense in t.

Present Tense.	*Past Tense.*	*Past Part.*	*Present Tense.*	*Past Tense.*	*Past Part.*
Creep	crept	crept	Feel	felt	felt
Sleep	slept	slept	Kneel	knelt	knelt
Sweep	swept	swept	Smell	smelt	smelt
Keep	kept	kept	Spell	spelt	spelt
Weep	wept	wept	Lean (lēn)	lĕ*a*nt or leaned	lĕ*a*nt or leaned
Burn	burnt	burnt			
Deal (dēl)	dĕ*a*lt	dĕ*a*lt	Mean (mēn)	mĕ*a*nt	mĕ*a*nt
Dream (drēm)	drĕ*a*mt or dreamed	drĕ*a*mt or dreamed	Spill	spilt	spilt
Dwell	dwelt	dwelt	Spoil	spoilt or spoiled	spoilt or spoiled

Exceptional Verbs.—Make, made, made. Have, had, had. Hear, heard, heard. Leave, left, left. Cleave, cleft, cleft. Lose, lost, lost. Shoe, shod, shod. Flee, fled, fled. Say, said, said. Lay, laid, laid. Pay, paid, paid. Clothe, clothed or clad.

Group II.—Changing of Inside Vowel.

Present Tense.	*Past Tense.*	*Past Part.*	*Present Tense.*	*Past Tense.*	*Past Part.*
Beseech	besought	besought	Work	wrought, worked	wrought, worked
Bring	brought	brought			
Buy	bought	bought	Owe	ought, owed	owed
Catch	caught	caught	Dare	durst or dared	dared
Seek	sought	sought	Can	could	(*Wanting*)
Sell	sold	sold	Shall	should	(*Wanting*)
Teach	taught	taught	Will	would	(*Wanting*)
Tell	told	told	May	might	(*Wanting*)
Think	thought	thought			

Group III.—Verbs ending in **d** *or* **t.**

Verbs ending in *d* or *t* in the Present tense have discarded the suffix of the Past tense, to avoid the repetition of *d* or *t*.

(*a*) Some verbs in this group have the three forms (Present tense, Past tense, and Past Participle) all exactly alike :—

Present Tense.	*Past Tense.*	*Past Part.*	*Present Tense.*	*Past Tense.*	*Past Part.*
Burst	burst	burst	Shut	shut	shut
Cast	cast	cast	Slit	slit	slit
Cost	cost	cost	Spit	spit or spat	spit
Cut	cut	cut	Split	split	split
Hit	hit	hit	Spread	spread	spread
Hurt	hurt	hurt	Sweat	sweat	sweat
Let	let	let	Thrust	thrust	thrust
Put	put	put	Bet	bet	bet
Rid	rid	rid	Quit	quit or quitted	quit or quitted
Set	set	set			
Shed	shed	shed	Knit	knit or knitted	knit or knitted
Shred	shred	shred			

Note.—"Spit" is a Weak verb, although it has a form *spat* for the Past tense. In Anglo-Saxon the Present had two forms also.

(*b*) Other verbs in this group end in *d* in the Present tense, but form the Past tense and Past Participle by changing *d* into *t*. (There are at least nine such verbs in English.)

Present Tense.	*Past Tense.*	*Past Part.*	*Present Tense.*	*Past Tense.*	*Past Part.*
Bend	bent	bent	Rend	rent	rent
Build	built	built	Send	sent	sent
Gild	gilt, gilded	gilt	Spend	spent	spent
Gird	girt, girded	girt	Wend	went	(*Wanting*)
Lend	lent	lent			

Exceptions :—end-ed, mend-ed, blend-ed or blent, defend-ed.

(*c*) Other verbs of this group have the three forms all alike, except that they shorten the vowel in the Past forms :—

Present Tense.	*Past Tense.*	*Past Part.*	*Present Tense.*	*Past Tense.*	*Past Part.*
Bleed	bled	bled	Lead	led	led
Breed	bred	bred	Read	read	read
Feed	fed	fed	Light	lit, lighted	lit, lighted
Speed	sped	sped	Shoot	shot	shot
Meet	met	met			

Exercise 13.

In the following sentences say whether the verb italicised is Strong, Weak, or Mixed :—

1. The ox *fell* into a well. 2. The bubble *burst* as soon as it *was pricked*. 3. We *sought* for him in vain. 4. I *felt* very sorry, when I *heard* that. 5. He *meant* everything that he *said*. 6. The lawn *has been* well *mown*. 7. The cock *crew* at four o'clock. 8. The prisoners *fled* as soon as the door of the jail *was thrust* open. 9. You *could* not *do* that, if you *tried*. 10. A *shorn* lamb *feels* a cold wind. 11. Who *steals* my purse *steals* trash.—SHAKSPEARE. 12. The evil that men *do lives* after them; the good *is* oft *interred* with their bones.—SHAKSPEARE. 13. The wind *blows* cold and fresh from the tops of hills. 14. Never *forget* a kindness. 15. *Owe* no man anything.—*New Test.* 16. *Know* then thyself, and *seek* not God to *scan*.—POPE. 17. What I *have written* I have written.—*New Test.* 18. Solomon *built* him an house.—*New Test.* 19. There is a *hidden* meaning in his words. 20. *Stick* to your point. 21. *Abide* with us; fast *falls* the eventide.—KEBLE. 22. I have *fought* a good fight; I have *kept* the faith.—*New Test.* 23. Men will *reap* as they *sow*. 24. Hope *springs* eternal in the human breast.—POPE. 25. On whomsoever it *shall fall*, it will *grind* him to powder.—*New Test.* 26. There's a divinity that *shapes* our ends, rough *hew* them how we *will*.—SHAKSPEARE.

CHAPTER XII.—AUXILIARY VERBS.

79. Six Auxiliary verbs.—The Auxiliary verbs are *have*, *be*, *shall*, *will*, *may*, *do*. None but these six are rightly called Auxiliary, because none but these are used for *helping other verbs to form those tenses, which cannot be formed by inflection*. Their uses are shown in the forms given in pp. 43-46.

(*a*) Observe that *have* and *be*, when these verbs are used for Auxiliary purposes, are always followed by Participles:—

I have *seen*. I am *seen*. I am *seeing*.

(*b*) Observe that the other four, when they are used for Auxiliary purposes, are always followed by an Infinitive, and that the Infinitive is never preceded by "to":—

I shall *go*. He will *go*. May he *go!* I did not *go*.

The verb that is helped by an Auxiliary, as *seen* or *seeing* in (*a*) and *go* in (*b*), is called the **Principal** verb.

Note.—Auxiliary verbs not only assist Principal verbs, but they assist one another:—

I shall have been going.

Here *shall* (which by rule (*b*) is followed by an Infinitive) helps *have*. *Have* (which by rule (*a*) is followed by a Participle) helps *been*. *Been* (which by rule (*a*) is followed by a Participle) helps the Principal verb *going*.

80. Shall, will.—These are the Auxiliaries used for forming the Future tense; for this tense cannot be formed by inflection, as the Present and Past can.

Take note that the Future tense is formed with **shall** in the *First* person, and with **will** in the *Second* and *Third* persons (see scheme in pp. 43-46):—

	1	2	3
Singular	I *shall* go.	Thou *wilt* go.	He *will* go.
Plural	We *shall* go.	You *will* go.	They *will* go.

If *will* is used in the First person, as "I *will* go," it expresses not merely future time, but intention. Thus "I *will* go" means "I intend to go." Here *will* is a Principal verb (not an Auxiliary), since it expresses a great deal more than future time and is equivalent to the verb "intend."

If *shall* is used in the Second or Third person, as "You *shall* go," "He *shall* go," it expresses not merely future time, but an order or a promise or a threat. Here *shall* is a Principal verb, not an Auxiliary, since it expresses a great deal more than future time.

81. May, might; should, would.—These are the Auxiliaries used for forming the various tenses and expressing the various uses of the Subjunctive mood.

May and *might* are used to express a purpose. If the verb going before is in the Present or Future Indicative, we use *may* to express the Subjunctive. If the verb going before is in the Past Indicative, we use *might* to express the Subjunctive:—

He *has worked* hard (Present) }
He *will work* hard (Future) } that he *may* win a prize.
He *worked* hard (Past) that he *might* win a prize.

May is also used to express a wish or prayer—

May he live long and see not the grave!

Should and *would* (the Past forms of *shall* and *will*) are used to express a condition and its consequence:—

Condition.	*Consequence.*
If he *should* meet me,	he *would* know me.

82. Do, did.—These auxiliaries are used for forming the Present and Past tenses (Indefinite) of a Principal verb in the Indicative mood, whenever the Principal verb is used either (1) with a Negative, or (2) for asking a question:—

I *do* not see this. *Did* he see it?

The verb "*do*" is also used for forming the Imperative of a

Principal verb, whenever the Principal verb is used with a Negative :—

Do not come. *Do* not ask me any questions.

83. Auxiliary and **Principal.**—The verbs *may*, *have*, *be*, *do*, like the verbs *shall* and *will*, are sometimes Auxiliary and sometimes Principal verbs :—

Auxiliary.	*Principal.*
I *have* come.	I *have* a watch (Transitive).
He *was* praised.	The earth *is* round (Intransitive).
He eats that he *may* live.	He *may* go away (Transitive).
He *did* not go.	He *did* his work well (Transitive).
If he *should* come.	He *should* keep his word (Trans.).

Whenever the verbs *may*, *shall*, *will* are used as Principals, not as Auxiliaries, remember (1) that they are in the *Indicative* mood ; (2) that "*may*," "*shall*," "*will*" are *Present* Indicatives ; (3) that "*might*," "*should*," "*would*" are *Past* Indicatives ; (4) that the Infinitive by which they are followed is their object.

Exercise 14.

In the following sentences say whether the verb italicised is Principal or Auxiliary :—

1. I *had* a fine horse to show him ; but he *had* gone away and could not see it. 2. That horse of yours *is* a fine creature, and *is* admired by every one who *has* seen it. 3. You *shall* leave the room, if you *do* not leave off making that noise. 4. Why *did* you refuse to speak? 5. You *may* read that book, if you wish to *do* so ; but *do* not ask me to lend you another. 6. If you take a man's life, you *shall* be hanged. 7. Thou *shalt* not steal. 8. He *shall* receive his prize to-morrow, and I hope that all *will* be satisfied. 9. The spirit of my father grows strong in me, and I *will* no longer endure it. 10. Charles, I thank thee for thy love to me, which thou *shalt* find I *will* most kindly requite.—SHAKSPEARE.

CHAPTER XIII.—DEFECTIVE AND IMPERSONAL VERBS.

84. Defective verbs.—Among the six Auxiliary verbs there are three, namely *have*, *be*, *do*, that have all the forms of moods and tenses complete, whether they are or are not used for Auxiliary purposes.

The remaining three, namely (1) *shall*, *should*, (2) *will*, *would*, and (3) *may*, *might*, have no tenses but the Present and Past just given. These are therefore said to be **Defective** (that is, deficient in some of the forms that belong to other verbs).

Note.—The verb *will*, when it signifies to bequeath by will or testament, is not Defective, but is conjugated in all possible forms throughout. The Past Tense is then *willed*, not *would*.

To these three we must add three more Defective verbs, namely (1) *can*, *could*, (2) *must*, (3) *ought*, –all of which are in common use. Not one of these three verbs is an Auxiliary. They are all Principal verbs (Transitive), and the Infinitive that follows them is their object :—

(i.) I *can* or *could* (Trans. verb) *go* (Infin. object).
(ii.) I *must* (Trans. verb) *go* (Infin. object).
(iii.) I *ought* (Trans. verb) *to go* (Pres. Infin. object).
(iv.) I *ought* (Trans. verb) *to have gone* (Past Infin. object).

Note.—Avoid the common mistake of saying, "*He didn't ought to have gone.*" This is very bad English. The Auxiliary *did* can never be used before *ought;* for it has been shown in § 79 that *did* as an Auxiliary is always followed by an Infinitive. But *ought* is not an Infinitive. It is a Past tense, an older form of "owed." The sentence should therefore be, *He ought not to have gone.*

85. Impersonal verbs.—These take "it" for their Subject, and are followed by some Personal pronoun in the Objective case, which in Personal verbs would be the Subject in the Nominative case :—

It shames *me* to hear this = I am ashamed to hear this.
It repents *me* of my folly = I repent of my folly.
It behoves *me* to do this = I ought to do this.

In the common phrase "methinks" (it seems to me) the "it" is omitted. The verb "thinks" is here an Old English verb signifying "seems," quite distinct from the verb *think* = imagine. The verbs, though now they are both spelt with *i*, were differently spelt in Anglo-Saxon,—the former with a *y* (thync-an), the latter with an *e* (thenc-an).

Note.—Besides the Defective verbs named in § 84, we may mention the following, some of which are now rarely used.

Beware ; a compound of *be* + *ware* (= wary, cautious).

Dight, "adorned," Past Part. for *dighted ;* rare.

Hight, "is or was named." The only Eng. verb in the Passive voice. He *hight* = he is or was named.

Quoth, "says" or "said," used only in the First or Third person. Properly the Past tense of an obsolete verb, Strong Conj., of which the Present form has survived in "be-*queath*."

Wis, wot (Pres.), **wist** (Past), "to know"; nearly obsolete.

Wont, "accustomed." Past Part. of an obsolete verb.

Worth ; as "Woe worth (= befall) the day." Subjunctive mood.

PART III.—PARSING AND SYNTAX.

This Part assumes that the student has thoroughly mastered Parts I. and II. The main points of both, so far as parsing is concerned, are recapitulated below:—

Kinds of Nouns.

Proper: a name given to one particular person or thing, and not intended to denote more than one person or thing at a time; as *John, London, Windsor Castle, the Bible.*

Common: a name that may stand for any number of persons or things of the same kind; as *man, city, castle, book.*

Collective: a name given to a group, collection, or multitude; as *herd, flock, class, library, pack.*

Material: a name denoting some kind of matter or substance; as *mutton, grass, fruit, bread, water, oil, grease, blacking.*

Abstract: a name denoting some quality, state or action, apart from any object or objects; as *hardness, fever, pride, stealth.*

Gender.

Masculine: denotes males, as *father;* **Feminine**, females, as *mother;* **Common**, either sex, as *parent.*

Neuter: neither sex (or things without life), as *book, bread, fever.*

Kinds of Pronouns.

Personal: denotes the First person, as *I, me;* the Second, as *thou, you;* the Third, as *he, she, it, they.*

Demonstrative: points to some noun previously mentioned, and is used instead of it, as "Health is better than wealth; *this* gives less happiness than *that.*" Here *this* stands for *wealth, that* for *health.*

Note.—Such words are *Pronouns*, when they are used **for** some noun; *Adjectives*, when they are used **with** some noun expressed or understood.

Relative or **Conjunctive**: (1) relates to some noun or pronoun going before (which is called the Antecedent), and (2) joins its own sentence to the previous sentence, as "I *whom* you speak of am here."

Interrogative: inquires about some person or thing; as "*Who* spoke? *What* did he say?"

Kinds of Adjectives.

Proper: formed from a proper noun, as *English*, *French*.

Descriptive: showing of what quality or in what state a thing is; as "a *tame* lion," "a *fine* house," "a *thick* forest."

Quantitative: showing how much of a thing is meant, as "*much* bread," "a *whole* holiday," a *half* holiday."

Numeral: showing how many things are meant (*Cardinal*), or in what order a thing stands (*Ordinal*): as "six houses," "the sixth house." If the number is not specified, as in "*many* houses," "a *few* houses," "*all* houses," the adjective is called *Indefinite Numeral*.

Demonstrative: showing which or what thing is meant, as "*this* house," "*that* man." (The articles *a* and *the* are Demon. Adjectives.)

Interrogative: asking which or what thing is meant, as "*which* house?" "*what* man?"

Distributive: showing that things are taken separately or in separate lots, as "*each* person," "*every* word," "*every* six hours," "*either* side." (Every six hours=every space of six hours.)

Degrees of Comparison.

Positive: denotes the simple quality expressed by the adjective, as "a *fat* ox."

Comparative: denotes a higher degree of the quality, when one thing is compared with another of the same kind, as "a *fatter* ox."

Superlative: denotes the highest degree of the quality, when one thing is compared with all other things of the same kind, as "the *fattest* ox."

Kinds of Adverbs.

Simple: modifies the meaning of some verb, adjective, preposition, conjunction, or other adverb, by saying something about the **quality**, as "*badly*"; or the **quantity**, as "*almost*"; or the **number**, as "*thrice*"; or the **time**, as "*then*"; or the **place**, as "*there*"; or any other attendant circumstance.

Interrogative: makes some inquiry about the **quality**, as "*how?*" the **quantity**, as "*how far?*" the **number**, as "*how often?*" the **time**, as "*when?*" or the **place**, as "*where?*"

Relative or **Conjunctive**: (1) modifies the verb of its own sentence, and (2) joins its own sentence to the previous sentence; as, "Tell me *when* you will come."

Kinds of Verbs.

Transitive: denotes an action that is directed towards an object; as "He *shot* a crow."

Intransitive: denotes an action that stops with the doer, and concerns no person or thing except the doer; as "He *fell*."

Auxiliary: assists a Principal verb (which may be either Transitive or Intransitive) to form some tense in the Indicative or Subjunctive mood and in the Active or Passive voice; as "I *have* come."

Conjugations of Verbs.

Weak: forms its Past tense by adding *d* or *ed* or *t* to the Present, and sometimes changes the inside vowel of the Present tense; as *seek, sought; sell, sold.* (Sometimes called Regular.)

Strong: never adds *d* or *ed* or *t* to the Present tense for forming its Past tense, but always changes the inside vowel of the Present tense; as *drink, drank.* (Sometimes called Irregular.)

Mixed: forms its Past tense as a Weak verb does by adding *d* or *ed* or *t*, but forms its Past participle by adding *en* or *n*, as some Strong verbs do; as *mow, mowed, mown.*

Voice.

Active: in this Voice the person or thing denoted by the Subject is said to *do* something; as *I love.*

Passive: in this Voice the person or thing denoted by the Subject is said to *suffer* something; as *I am loved.*

Finite Moods.

Indicative: asserts something as a fact, or as a condition; as "I *came*," "if he *comes*."

Imperative: commands or advises or begs for something; as *come.*

Subjunctive: expresses a doubt, purpose, or wish; as "if he *come*," "that he *may come*," "*may* he *come*."

Tenses in the Finite Moods.

Indefinite: denotes Present, Past, or Future time in its simplest form, making no assertion about the degree of completeness or incompleteness to be ascribed to the event; as "I *come*," "I *came*."

Continuous: denotes that the event (in Present, Past, or Future time) is not yet complete; as "I *am coming*," "I was *coming*."

Perfect: denotes that the event (in Present, Past, or Future time) is in a completed or perfect state; as "I *have come*."

Perfect Continuous: combines the force of the two preceding forms; as "I *have been coming*."

Parts of a Verb not Finite.

Infinitive: names the action without reference to any doer.

Participle: that part of a verb which is used either (*a*) as part of a tense and as such is preceded by an auxiliary verb *be* or *have*, or (*b*) as an adjective to qualify some noun or pronoun.

Gerund: a mixture of noun and verb,—(1) a noun in so far as it can be in the Nominative or Objective case; (2) a verb in so far as it expresses Present or Past time,—is in the Active or Passive voice, and (if Transitive) is followed by an object.

Complement of a Verb.

Complement to an Intransitive, *i.e.* **Copulative**, verb is a word or form of words, which completes what the verb left unsaid about its *Subject*.

Complement to a Transitive, *i.e.* **Factitive**, verb is a word or form of words, which completes what the verb left unsaid about its *Object*.

CHAPTER XIV.—THE PARSING OF NOUNS.

86. What parsing is.—To *parse* a word is to examine it in two different points:—(1) What *part* of speech it is, (2) what *part* it plays in the building of a sentence. (*Parse* is from Latin *pars*, a part.)

Note.—Of the eight parts of speech the only kind of word that cannot be parsed in the second sense is an Interjection. This has been explained already in § 4. So in parsing such a word the only thing we can say is that it is an Interjection.

All the other parts of speech stand in some relation with other words, and must therefore be parsed in the second sense as much as in the first. Thus if we have to parse "*in*" in such a phrase as "a bird in the hand," we say not merely that it is a preposition, but a preposition having "hand" for its object.

In the older forms of our language, when inflectional endings were more numerous, parsing was less difficult than it is now, when we have but few of these left to guide us. Now we have to look chiefly to *the work that a word does in a sentence* (as explained in Chap. I.), and not expect so much help from the form or ending.

87. How to parse Nouns.—To parse a noun you have to show four different things about it:—

(*a*) Of what **kind** it is,—whether Proper, Common, Collective, Material, or Abstract.

(*b*) Of what **gender** it is,—whether Masculine, Feminine, Common, or Neuter.

(*c*) Of what **number** it is,—whether Singular or Plural.

(*d*) In what **case** it is,—whether Nominative, Possessive, or Objective. (On the rules for case, see Chapter XVI.)

Examples.

(1) The master of this class teaches French without a book.

Master—Common noun, Masculine gender, Singular number, Nominative case, Subject to the verb "teaches."

Class—Collective noun, Neuter gender, Singular number, Objective case after the preposition "of."

French—Proper noun, Neuter gender, Singular number, Objective case after the verb "teaches."

Book—Common noun, Neuter gender, Singular number, Objective case after the preposition "without."

(2) The deer in my father's forest nibble the grass with eagerness.

Deer—Common noun, Common gender, Plural number, Nominative case, Subject to the verb "nibble."

Father's—Common noun, Masculine gender, Singular number, Possessive case qualifying the noun "forest."

Forest—Collective noun, Neuter gender, Singular number, Objective case after the preposition "in."

Grass—Material noun, Neuter gender, Singular number, Objective case after the verb "nibble."

Eagerness—Abstract noun, Neuter gender, Singular number, Objective case after the preposition "with."

CHAPTER XV.—THE PARSING OF PRONOUNS.

88. How to parse Pronouns.—To parse a pronoun you have to show five different things about it:—

(*a*) Of what **kind** it is,—whether Personal, Demonstrative, Relative, (*i.e.* Conjunctive), or Interrogative.

(*b*) Of what **gender** it is,—whether Masculine, Feminine, Common, or Neuter.

(*c*) Of what **number** it is,—whether Singular or Plural.

(*d*) Of what **person** it is,—whether first, second, or third.

(*e*) In what **case** it is,—whether Nominative, Possessive, or Objective. (On the rules for case, see Chapter XVI.)

Examples.

(1) I have written down your names in my book.

I—Personal pronoun, Common gender, Singular number, First person, Nominative case, Subject to the verb "have written down."

Your—Personal pronoun, Common gender, Plural number, Possessive case qualifying the noun "names."

My—Personal pronoun, Common gender, Singular number, First person, Possessive case qualifying the noun "book."

(2) Who spoke? and what did he say?

Who—Interrogative pronoun, Common gender, Singular number, Third person, Nominative case, Subject to the verb "spoke."

What—Interrogative pronoun, Neuter gender, Singular number, Third person, Objective case after the verb "say."

He—Personal pronoun, Masculine gender, Singular number, Third person, Nominative case, Subject to the verb "did."

89. Relatives and Demonstratives.—The following rule should be remembered and observed in parsing Relatives and Demonstratives:—

A Relative or Demonstrative pronoun is of the same gender, number, and person as its antecedent; but in case it depends upon its own sentence.

This rule is called a Concord (or Agreement). The following form may be used for putting it into effect:—

Kind of Pronoun.	Name its Antecedent.	Therefore the same in			Case.
		Gender.	Number.	Person.	

Examples.

(1) **I prefer a white horse to a black *one*.**

One—Demonstrative pronoun, having "horse" for its antecedent, and therefore of Common gender, Singular number, and Third person. **Objective case after the preposition "to."**

(2) **The man who was caught turned out to be the thief.**

Who—Relative pronoun, having "man" for its antecedent, and therefore of Masculine gender, Singular number, and Third person. **Nominative case, Subject to the verb "was caught."**

(3) **I whom you suspected of the theft was not guilty.**

Whom—Relative pronoun, having "I" for its antecedent, and therefore of Common gender, Singular number, and First person. **Objective case after the verb "suspected."**

CHAPTER XVI.—CASES OF NOUNS AND PRONOUNS.

90. Nominative.—There are five different conditions under which a noun or pronoun can be in the Nominative case :—

(1) As Subject to a verb :—

I did this. *Rain* is falling. *You* are tired.

(2) As Complement to an Intransitive or Passive verb :—

I am *he*. William I. was surnamed the *Conqueror*.

Note.—Such a Nom. as *he* or *conqueror* is sometimes called a **Complementary Nominative**.

(3) In apposition with some other noun or pronoun in the Nominative case. (One noun is in apposition with another, when it refers to the same person or thing and is mentioned immediately after it.)

John, the *carpenter*, has done well to-day.

Note.—Sometimes a noun is in apposition with a sentence :—

He slew all his prisoners,—a barbarous *act*.

(4) Nominative of address :—

How art thou fallen, O *Cæsar*!

(5) Nominative absolute. (A noun or pronoun is absolute, *i.e.* free and independent, when it is neither the Subject to a verb, nor the Object to a verb or to a preposition. In this construction it goes with some participle or with an Infinitive):—

(*a*) We then started, *he* remaining behind.
(*b*) *We* having given the signal, the guns were fired.
(*c*) The race will be run to-day, *the winner* to receive a silver cup.

In (*a*) the participle expresses present time, in (*b*) the participle expresses past time, in (*c*) the Infinitive expresses future time. We have no participle to express futurity.

91. Possessive.—A noun or pronoun in the Possessive case has the same force as an adjective, and may be used either as qualifying some noun or as complement to some verb:—

My son has come; I am pleased at *his* coming . . (*Qualifying*).
This house is *mine*, not the *barber's* . . (*Complement*).

Note.—When two Possessive nouns are in apposition, the apostrophe *s* is added either to the first or last, but not to both:—

Herod married his *brother* Philip's wife.
For the queen's sake, his *sister*.—BYRON.

92. Objective.—There are seven different conditions, under which a noun can be in the Objective case:—

(1) As Object to a verb: for details see Chapter XVII.

(2) As Complement to a Transitive verb:—

They made him their *leader*.

Note.—Such an Objective as "leader" is sometimes called a **Complementary Object.**

(3) In apposition with another noun or pronoun in the Objective case:—

The Roundheads beheaded Charles I., *the king*.

(4) As Object to a preposition:—

A house built on *sand*. He depends on *me*.

(5) Adverbial objective:—

He lived ten *years* . . . *Time*.
He walked four *miles* . . . *Space*.
This cost or is worth six *shillings* . *Price*.
That box weighs twelve *pounds* . *Weight*.
The air is a *trifle* hotter to-day . *Quantity*.
Bind him *hand and foot* . . *Attendant circumstance*.

(6) Objective after the adjectives *like*, *near*. (This has arisen from the omission of the preposition "to," which is still sometimes expressed.)

No man could ride like *him*.
The house nearest the *grove* is the best.

(7) Objective in exclamation:—

Oh dear *me!* Unhappy *man!*

Exercise 15.

Parse (by the methods shown in §§ 87-89) every noun and pronoun occurring in the following examples, and explain its case by the rules given in Chapter XVI.:—

1. Marius having been defeated returned to Rome. 2. Marius having been defeated, his troops returned to Rome. 3. He needs strong arms, who swims against the tide. 4. If he had remained a soldier, he would probably have received his commission. 5. Here lay Duncan, his silver skin laced with his golden blood. 6. For thy servant David's sake.—*Old Test.* 7. This wall is a hundred feet high. 8. He came to see us every other day. 9. I thought him the cleverest man that I had ever seen. 10. Solomon's temple was built without the noise of axe or hammer; the fabric grew silently like a tall palm. 11. He dwelt two months in the house of one Simon, the Tanner. 12. He grew day by day more and more like his former self. 13. The army of the Canaanites, nine hundred chariots strong, covered the plains of Esdraelon.—MILMAN. 14. Why stand ye here all the day idle? —*New Test.* 15. He, having finished the work, received his pay for the day. 16. He having finished the work, the horse and cart were taken back to the farm. 17. Who is the maker of this watch? 18. My story being done, she gave me for my pains a world of sighs.—SHAKS. 19. Poor man! I wish I could have helped him out of that difficulty. 20. I who speak unto thee am he.—*New Test.* 21. Six shillings were paid for this book; but it was worth only four (shillings). 22. Our country has not produced two Newtons. 23. The rock lies ten fathoms deep under the water. 24. He walked ten miles a day, and never complained of fatigue. 25. Ye mariners of England, who guard our native seas, whose flag has braved a thousand years the battle and the breeze.—CAMPBELL.

CHAPTER XVII.—VERB AND OBJECT.

93. **Direct and Indirect Objects.**—There are some Transitive verbs that take two objects, one of which (called the *Direct*) expresses the **thing** towards which the action of the verb is directed, and the other (called the *Indirect*) expresses the **person** or **persons** for whom the action is done:—

{ The master teaches *French* . . . *Direct Object.*
{ The master teaches *me* French . . *Indirect Object*

Let *me* (Indir. Object) *see* (Dir. Object, Infinitive).

Note.—The Indirect object always comes first, that is, immediately after the verb. If it is not put first, it has some preposition placed before it:—

The master teaches French *to me.*

94. **Retained Object.**—A verb that takes two objects in the Active voice can retain one in the Passive. Hence such an object is called the "Retained object":—

Active. The master teaches me French.

Passive. { I was taught *French* by the master.
French was taught *me* by the master.

95. Cognate Object.—An object can be placed after an Intransitive verb, if its meaning is cognate or kindred with that of the verb, that is, implied more or less in the verb itself.

The horse ran a *race*.
The clock struck one (*stroke*).
The illness must run its *course*.
At the time of that battle the river ran *blood*.

In the last example *blood* really means "a bloody or blood-stained course," and "course" is the implied Cognate object. We cannot place any *outside* object after the Intransitive verb "run," that is, any object that has no connection with the meaning of the verb itself:—"The horse ran a wall." This is nonsense.

96. Reflexive Object.—An object, placed after an Intransitive verb, and consisting of a pronoun in the same person as the subject, is called a Reflexive object. Such objects, however, are not common.

John overslept *himself*.

This means "John overslept or slept too long for himself." "Himself" is here a kind of Indirect object, because it names the person for whom the action is done.

Summary.—There are thus five different kinds of objects that can be placed after verbs,—the Direct after a Transitive verb, Active; the Indirect after a Transitive verb, Active; the Retained after a Transitive verb, Passive; the Cognate after an Intransitive verb; the Reflexive after an Intransitive verb.

Observe further that these various objects are placed not merely after Finite verbs, but after Participles, Gerunds, and Infinitives.

Note.—The Complementary object described in § 92 (2) is merely a continuation of the Direct object.

Exercise 16.

Point out the object to the verb in each of the following sentences, and say what kind of object it is:—

1. He lived a life of industry, and died the death of the righteous. 2. I was asked a question, which I could not answer. 3. Teach me, O Lord, the way of thy statutes.—*Old Test.* 4. I was promised that post, but it was given to another. 5. I have fought a good fight; I have kept the faith.—*New Test.* 6. O thou invisible spirit of wine, if thou hast no name to be called by, let us call thee devil! SHAKSPEARE. 7. They sat them down on the grassy bank of the river. 8. She busied herself with gathering the wild flowers of the forest. 9. He went away gloomy and sad, meditating revenge. 10. He always

looked puzzled on being asked an unusual question. **11.** The fever kept him ill for two or three weeks before it had run its full course. 12. He was taught reading by one master, and writing by another. 13. Ask me no more questions: I have no desire to answer one of them. 14. Old mother Hubbard she went to the cupboard, to fetch her poor dog a bone. 15. Fare thee well. 16. To save one's country from ruin is an honour that few men have been able to acquire. 17. Pure religion and undefiled before God is this, To visit the fatherless and widows in their affliction, and to keep himself unspotted from the world.—*New Test.* 18. The wind blew a cold blast from the north.

CHAPTER XVIII.—THE PARSING OF ADJECTIVES.

97. How to parse Adjectives.—To parse an Adjective you have to show three different things about it:—

(*a*) Of what **kind** it is,—whether Proper, Descriptive, Quantitative, Numeral, Demonstrative, Interrogative, or Distributive:—

(*b*) In what **degree** it is,—whether Positive, Comparative, or Superlative:—

(*c*) What its **use** is,—whether Attributive or Predicative; and if Attributive, what word it qualifies.

Note 1.—An adjective is used **attributively**, when it *directly* qualifies some noun or pronoun; as "A *large* house."

It is used **predicatively**, when it is part of the predicate, that is, when it is the complement to some verb (see § 63), and qualifies *indirectly* the noun or pronoun that stands as Subject to the verb; as—

This house (*Subject*) | is *large* (*Predicate*).

Note 2.—In poetry, and sometimes in prose, an adjective is used to qualify a verb, as if it were an adverb:—

And *furious* every charger neighed.—CAMPBELL.

Examples.

(1) A fine horse has just been bought.

A—Demonstrative adjective (Indefinite article).

Fine—Descriptive adjective, Positive degree, used attributively to qualify the noun "horse."

(2) This house is larger than that.

This—Demonstrative adjective, used attributively to qualify the noun "house."

Larger—Descriptive adjective, Comparative degree, used predicatively as complement to the verb "is."

That—Demonstrative adjective, used attributively to qualify the noun "house" understood.

(3) The three men had each a gun, and the tallest of them seemed young.

The—Demonstrative adjective (Definite article).

Three—Numeral adjective (cardinal), used attributively to qualify the noun "men."

Each—Distributive adjective, used attributively to qualify the noun "man" understood.

Tallest—Descriptive adjective, Superlative degree, used attributively to qualify the noun "man" understood.

Young—Descriptive adjective, Positive degree, used predicatively as complement to the verb "seemed."

98. A noun or Verbal noun placed before another noun is sometimes used as an adjective; that is, it qualifies the noun as an adjective would do:—

A *bathing* place; *summer* heat; *drawing* room; *dining* room; *winter* cold; a *gold* chain; *sailing* ship; an *apple* tart; a *Bath* bun; an *oyster* shop; an *evening* fire; a *morning* breeze, etc.

When the two nouns are joined by a hyphen, the noun formed by the junction is called a Compound:—

The battle-field; tool-shed; oak-tree; cotton-mill; hand-mill.

Sometimes the two nouns are joined together without any hyphen:—

Bathroom; eyelid; eyebrow; watchword; moonlight, etc.

CHAPTER XIX.—FINITE VERB AND SUBJECT.

99. How to parse Finite verbs.—The points to be explained in the parsing of a Finite verb are shown in their proper order in the two following tables:—

Kind of Verb.	Conjug.	Voice.	Mood.	Tense.	Form of Tense.
Transitive Intransitive	Strong Weak Mixed	Active Passive	Indic. Imper. Subjunc.	Present Past Future	Indefinite Continuous Perfect Perf. Contin.

Number.	Person.	Agreement.
Singular Plural	First Second Third	Agreeing in Number and Person with its subject or subjects, expressed or understood.

(1) James has been fishing all the morning.

Has been fishing Intransitive verb, Weak conjugation, Active voice, Indicative mood, Present-Perfect-Continuous tense, having "James" for its subject, and therefore in the Singular number and Third person.

(2) James and I will be promoted next term.

Will be promoted—Transitive verb, Weak conjugation, Passive voice, Indicative mood, Future-Indefinite tense, having "James and I" for the two subjects, and therefore in the Plural number and First person. (See Rules I. and II. in § 100.)

(3) He worked hard that he might win a prize.

Worked—Intransitive verb, Weak conjugation, Active voice, Indicative mood, Past-Indefinite tense, having "he" for its subject, and therefore in the Singular number and Third person.

Might win—Transitive verb, Strong conjugation, Active voice, Subjunctive mood, Past-Indefinite tense, having "he" for its subject, and therefore in the Singular number and Third person.

(4) You will have got to your house by that time.

Will have got—Transitive verb used Intransitively, Strong conjugation, Active voice, Indicative mood, Future-Perfect tense, having "you" for its subject, and therefore in the Plural number and Second person.

(5) The jury were puzzled and would have been divided in their opinions, if the judge had not known well how to guide them.

Were puzzled—Transitive verb, Weak conjugation, Passive voice, Indicative mood, Past-Indefinite tense, having "jury" for its subject (a noun that implies more persons than one), and therefore in the Plural number, Third person. (See Rule IV. in § 100.)

Had known—Transitive verb, Strong conjugation, Active voice, Indicative mood, Past-Perfect tense, having "judge" for its subject, and therefore in the Singular number and Third person.

(6) So be it.

Be—Intransitive verb, Subjunctive mood, Present tense, having "it" for its subject, and therefore in the Singular number, Third person.

100. Agreement of Verb with Subject.—The rule relating to the agreement between a Finite verb and its Subject is called a Concord:—

A verb must be in the same number and person as its Subject or Nominative.

The following special rules for working out this general Concord or Agreement should be also noted and observed:—

Rule I.—When two or more singular Subjects are connected by *and*, the verb is plural:—

Time and tide *wait* for no man.

Rule II.—When two or more Subjects connected by *and* differ in person, the verb takes the first person in preference to the second, and the second in preference to the third:

James and I (=we) *have* been promoted . (*First person.*)
James and you (=you) *were* both absent . (*Second person.*)
James and John (=they) *are* great friends . (*Third person.*)

Rule III.—When two nouns connected by *and* express a single person or thing, the Subject is singular in sense, and hence the verb is singular also :—

Truth and honesty *is* the best policy.
The poet and statesman *is* dead.

Note.—If the article were repeated before "statesman," this would show that two different persons were intended : the verb would then of course be plural :—

The poet and *the* statesman *are* dead.

Rule IV.—When the Subject is a noun of Multitude, *i.e.* singular in form but plural in sense, the verb is Plural :—

The jury (=the men who were on the jury) *were* divided in their opinions . . . (*Plural in sense.*)
The regiment *is* encamped at Aldershot . . (*Singular in sense.*)

Rule V.—When two or more singular Subjects are connected by *either* . . . *or*, *neither* . . . *nor*, the verb is Singular :—

Either James or John *is* to be promoted.

Note.—Thus Rule V. is the opposite to Rule I. The conjunction *and* (in Rule I.) unites the sense of the two subjects, and therefore the verb is Plural. But the conjunction *or* (in Rule V.) disunites the sense of the two subjects. It means "one or the other, not both." Hence the verb is Singular.

Rule VI.—When one of the Subjects connected by *or*, *nor*, etc., is Singular and the other Plural, the Plural subject should be placed next to the verb so as to make the verb plural :—

Neither the cock nor the hens *are* in the yard.

Rule VII.—When the Subjects connected by *or*, *nor*, etc., are of different persons, the verb agrees with the one mentioned last :—

Either James or I *am* to get the prize.

But it is better to repeat the verb :—

Either James *is* to get the prize, or I *am*.

Rule VIII.—When two or more Singular subjects are connected by *as well as*, the verb is Singular :—

A box as well as a book *has* been stolen.

Rule IX.—When the Subjects connected by *as well as* differ in number or person or both, the verb takes the number and person of the subject that stands first :—

My partners as well as I *were* at fault.
I as well as they *am* ruined.

Rule X.—When two or more Singular nouns are qualified by a Distributive adjective, the verb is Singular :—

Every leaf, every twig, every drop of water *teems* with life.

Exercise 17.

In the following sentences parse each Finite verb on the method shown in § 99, *and according to the rules given in* § 100 :—

1. He had been gone two hours, before we received notice that he was to stop. 2. Go, where glory awaits thee. 3. The horse was taken to the stable. 4. The man and his friend walked into the field. 5. I have long been absent from home. 6. Were I in his place, I should pay the debt. 7. He will have walked about three miles, since he left the house. 8. Murder, though it have no tongue, will yet speak. 9. If I were he, I should start at once. 10. He would have started at once, if he had known better. 11. The committee were all agreed that A. had done good work. 12. Either Albert or I am to be promoted. 13. The hens as well as the cock have been lost. 14. Youth and experience seldom exist together. 15. Let me speak for once. 16. By the time the clock strikes six, I shall have been working eight full hours. 17. God save the queen ; long live the king. 18. Pride and poverty make no one happy. 19. Greater love hath no man than this, that a man lay down his life for his friends.—*New Test.* 20. No sooner had he got into bed, than he fell asleep. 21. It is I who am asked, not you. 22. Jack and Jill went up the hill. 23. A carriage and pair costs a large sum.

Exercise 18.

Correct any errors that you may find in the agreement of Subject and Finite verb :—

1. James with his friend have come to-day. 2. A large number of holiday-makers were present on that day. 3. A boy as well as a man were caught trespassing. 4. Two apples as well as a pear was given me to-day. 5. Neither he nor she were present that day. 6. Either you or your brother are blamed for this, not I. 7. The jury consist of twelve persons. 8. The scene and the foliage is very beautiful. 9. A carriage and pair have just entered the coachman's yard. 10. A man with his dog have just come into the street.

CHAPTER XX.—THE PARSING OF INFINITIVES.

101. **How to parse Infinitives.**—To parse an Infinitive you have to show two different things about it :—

(*a*) Of what **form** it is,—whether Indefinite, as *to see ;* or Present-Continuous, as *to be seeing ;* or Perfect, as *to have seen ;* or Perfect-Continuous, as *to have been seeing.*

(*b*) What is its **use**,—whether it is used as a Noun-Infinitive or as a Qualifying Infinitive.

Note.—The Qualifying Infinitive is also known as the "Gerundial Infinitive."

102. **The Noun-Infinitive.**—In this capacity the Infinitive

does the work of—(*a*) Subject to a verb, (*b*) Object to a verb, (*c*) Complement to a verb, (*d*) Object to a preposition.

(*a*) *Subject to a verb*:—

To sleep is necessary to health.
To work hard is the way to success.

(*b*) *Object to a verb*:—

We desire *to improve.*

Note.—The "to" is not used after the Auxiliary verbs *shall*, *will*, *may*, *do*, nor after *must*, *can*, *dare not*, *need not*. To all of these verbs the Infinitive is the Object:—

I shall *go*, I did not *go*, He dare not *go*, etc.

Here *go* is the object first to "shall," then to "did," and then to "dare."

(*c*) *Complement to a verb*:—

I saw him *come.* I ordered him *to go.*

Note.—The student will remember (see § 71) that the "to" is not used after the verbs *hear*, *see*, *feel*, *make*, *let*, *bid*, *watch*, *behold*, *know*, to all of which the Infinitive is used as complement.

(*d*) *Object to a preposition*:—

He did nothing but *laugh.*

Here the Infin. *laugh* is the object of the preposition *but*.

103. The Qualifying Infinitive.—In this capacity the Infinitive does the work of (*a*) an adverb to a verb, (*b*) an adverb to an adjective, (*c*) an adjective to a noun.

(*a*) *Adverb to a verb*:—

He came *to see* the sport.

Here *to see* qualifies the verb "came," as if it were an adverb.

(*b*) *Adverb to an adjective*:—

Quick *to hear* and slow *to speak.*

Here *to hear* qualifies the adjective "quick," and *to speak* qualifies "slow." Each Infinitive therefore does the work of an adverb.

(*c*) *Adjective to a noun*, either attributively or predicatively (§ 97, *Note* 1):—

A house *to let.* This house is *to let.*

Here *to let* qualifies the noun "house" attributively in the first example, and predicatively in the second. In each case, therefore, it does the work of an adjective.

Examples.

(1) He intended *to have seen* you to-day.

Perfect in form, noun in function, object to the Transitive verb "intended."

(2) I came *to see* you, but you did not *appear*.

To see—Indefinite in form, adverb in function, qualifying the verb "came."

Appear—Indefinite in form, noun in function, object to the verb "did."

Exercise 19.

Parse every Infinitive that you can find in the following sentences:—

1. We saw the ship leave the docks at four o'clock. 2. We came to see it start and say good-bye to one of the passengers. 3. We hope to see him back soon. 4. He did not come back in time to spend Christmas with us. 5. We watched the cat steal silently towards the mouse and then suddenly seize it in its claws. 6. I was very much pleased to see you. 7. I will see you again shortly. 8. The boys dare not speak, when the master tells them to be silent. 9. Being quick to forgive and slow to avenge an injury, he made no one dislike him. 10. I shall be glad to see you whenever you desire to come here. 11. There are many houses to let in this street. 12. That the injustices of the present world will be amended in the world to come is a thing to be hoped for by the good and feared by the evil. 13. Let me see the ship sail by. 14. We must work while it is day; for the night cometh, when no man can work. 15. Make the horse step out a little faster. 16. Did you see that shooting star? 17. To err is human; to forgive, divine. 18. I am ashamed to say that he let the man go without paying him. 19. Have you finished all the work that you had to do? 20. I am sorry to find that your feelings have been hurt. 21. I am to blame, not you.

CHAPTER XXI.—THE PARSING OF PARTICIPLES.

104. How to parse Participles.—To parse a Participle you have to show four different things about it:—

(*a*) In what **form** it is,—whether Present, as *fading*; or Past Indefinite, as *faded*; or Past Perfect, as *having faded*.

(*b*) What **kind** of verb it is,—whether Transitive or Intransitive.

(*c*) In what **voice** it is,—whether Active or Passive.

(*d*) What the **use** of the Participle is,—whether Attributive, Predicative, or Absolute.

Note 1. If the Participle given is part of a tense, it should be parsed as part of the tense, and not as a separate word. Thus in "I have *come*," we should parse *come*, not as a separate word, but as part of a Present Perfect tense.

Note 2.—The Attributive and Predicative uses of participles are the same as those of adjectives, which have been explained in *Note* 1 to § 97. The Absolute use has been explained in § 90 (5).

Examples.

(1) He appeared *tired* after his work.

Past Indefinite participle, Transitive verb, Passive voice, used predicatively as complement to the verb "appeared."

(2) *Believing* himself to be right, he stuck to his opinion.

Present participle, Transitive verb, Active voice, used attributively to qualify the pronoun "he."

(3) The sun *having risen*, we can now set off.

Past Perfect participle, Intransitive verb, used absolutely with the noun "sun."

Note.—When no noun or pronoun is placed before a participle used absolutely, the participle is practically a preposition. Such a participle is sometimes called an *Impersonal* Absolute.

He plays well, *considering* his age.

Exercise 20.

Parse every Participle in the following sentences:—

1. Having finished all the work given him to do, he seemed more pleased with himself than usual. 2. The sun, having set at six o'clock, left us in the evening twilight. 3. The sun having set at six o'clock, we had scarcely enough daylight left to get home. 4. A faded rose is not so pleasing as a blooming daisy. 5. The rose in your hand is more faded than the one in mine. 6. Having been convicted of more than one theft, he left the country. 7. He seemed contented with his lot. 8. A contented mind is a continual feast. 9. It is not enough for a house to be well built; it ought also to be well planned. 10. The trees having cast their leaves, we are now on the verge of winter. 11. The trees, having cast their leaves, look bare.

CHAPTER XXII.—THE PARSING OF GERUNDS AND VERBAL NOUNS.

105. Gerund.—A Gerund is a mixture of verb and noun. To parse it you have to show three different things about it in its verb-character, and one thing about it in its noun-character.

Verb.
- (*a*) In what **form** it is,—whether Present, as *going*, or Past, as *having gone*.
- (*b*) What **kind** of verb it is,—whether Transitive or Intransitive.
- (*c*) In what **voice** it is,—whether Active or Passive.

Noun.
- (*d*) In what **case** it is,—whether Nominative, Possessive, or Objective.

Examples.

(1) He is fond of ***swimming*** in the sea, and was pleased with himself for ***having swum*** out far from the shore.

Swimming—(1) as Verb, Present form, Intransitive verb; (2) as Noun, Objective case after the preposition "of."

Having swum—(1) as Verb, Past form, Intransitive verb; (2) as Noun, Objective case after the preposition "for."

(2) *Deceiving* others amused him, but he disliked ***being deceived*** himself.

Deceiving—(1) as Verb, Present form, Transitive verb, Active voice; (2) as Noun, Nominative case, Subject to the verb "amused."

Being deceived—(1) as Verb, Present form, Transitive verb, Passive voice; (2) as Noun, Objective case after the verb "disliked."

106. Verbal noun.—The form ending in *-ing* is called a Verbal noun, either (*a*) when it is followed by the preposition "of"; or (*b*) when it is used in the plural number. This is a *pure noun*, and should be parsed like any other noun (§ 75). It has no verb-character whatever; and hence it is qualified by an *adjective*, while a gerund is qualified by an *adverb*.

(1) The second ***hearing*** of the case was postponed.

Verbal noun, Abstract, Neuter gender, Singular number, Nominative case, Subject to the verb "was postponed."

(2) I am much pleased with my ***surroundings***.

Verbal noun, Common, Neuter gender, Plural number, Objective case after the preposition "with."

107. Summary of forms ending in "-ing." The grammatical uses of such forms may be summed up as follows:[1]

I. *Participial*	Part of a tense		1
	Adjective	Attributive / Predicative	2
	Absolute	With noun or pronoun / Without noun or pronoun	3
II. *Gerundial*	Gerund Proper, noun and verb mixed		4
	Verbal noun, pure noun		5

1. *Part of tense:* I am *coming;* he has been *coming;* he will be *coming.*

2. *Adjective:* A ***disappointing*** result. (***Attrib. use.***)
The result is *disappointing* to all of us. (***Predic. use.***)

---

[1] It is sometimes said that a verb ending in *-ing* may be either I. a participle (as shown above), or II. a gerund (as shown above), or III. *an inflected form of infinitive.* The third is a mistake. The form ending in *-ing* was never anything else than either a participle or a gerund (verbal noun). It was never an Infinitive at any time in the history of English.

3. *Absolute:* We all set off, the clock *striking* one. (*With noun.*)
Opinions differ *regarding* this point. (*Without noun.*)

(Here *regarding*, though a participle in origin, is practically a preposition.)

4. *Gerund (noun and verb mixed)*: I am tired of *warning* you.
5. *Verbal noun (pure noun)*: I do not require your *warnings*.

Exercise 21.

Parse every word ending in **-ing** *in the following sentences:—*

1. We have been *working* hard *during* the whole of the past week. 2. It is of no use *questioning* him *regarding* this matter. 3. *Owing* to the long drought, every plant is *beginning* to fade. 4. Great things sometimes result from small *beginnings*. 5. I was much pleased on *hearing* of your success. 6. *Seeing* is *believing*. 7. There is some talk of his *returning* before long. 8. *Deepening* his voice with the *deepening* of the darkness, he continued *humming* a tune. 9. I hope to be *returning* home at this time to-morrow. 10. The shades of night are *falling* fast. 11. The journey was soon finished, the one *walking* and the other *riding* in turns. 12. The *ending* of a word is called in grammar an inflection. 13. Do you think of *giving* a new name to your house, or do you prefer *leaving* the name as it is? 14. I am tired of *swimming*: I have been *swimming* for the last hour or more.

CHAPTER XXIII.—THE PARSING OF ADVERBS, PREPOSITIONS, AND CONJUNCTIONS.

108. How to parse Adverbs.—To parse an adverb you must show four different things about it:—

(*a*) Of what **kind** it is,—whether Simple, Conjunctive, or Interrogative.

(*b*) If Simple, in what **degree** of comparison it is,—whether Positive, Comparative, or Superlative.

(*c*) What its **use** is,—whether Attributive or Predicative; and if Attributive, what word it qualifies.

Note.—An adverb is used **attributively**, when it directly qualifies some adjective, verb, preposition, conjunction, or other adverb; as—

This boy is *remarkably* clever . . . . (*Adjective.*)
A snake moves *silently* through the grass . (*Verb.*)
His cleverness is *decidedly* above the average (*Preposition.*)
He is despised *merely* because he is poor . (*Conjunction.*)
He sings *unusually* well . . . . . (*Adverb.*)

An Adverb is used **predicatively**, when it is part of the predicate, that is, when it is the complement to some verb:—

The results are *out*.

Examples.

(1) He works *more industriously* than you.

Simple adverb of the Descriptive class, Comparative degree, used attributively to qualify the verb "works."

(2) I have not seen the house *where* you live.

Conjunctive adverb qualifying the verb "live" in its own sentence, and joining its own sentence "you live" to the sentence "I have not seen the house."

(3) *When* the cat is *away*, the mice play.

When—Conjunctive adverb qualifying the verb "is" in its own sentence, and joining its own sentence "the cat is away" to the sentence "the mice play."

Away—Simple adverb of Place, used predicatively as complement to the verb "is."

109. How to parse Prepositions and Conjunctions.[1]—Care must be taken to distinguish prepositions and conjunctions from each other and from adverbs. The way to distinguish them is to ask yourself, *What work does the word do in the sentence?*

(i.)	I have seen this man *before* . .	(*Adverb.*)
(ii.)	He stood *before* the door . . .	(*Preposition.*)
(iii.)	The rain fell *before* we reached home .	(*Conjunction.*)

In (i.) *before* is a Simple adverb of Time qualifying "have seen."
In (ii.) *before* is a Preposition having "door" for its object.
In (iii.) *before* is a Conjunction joining its own sentence "we reached home" to the sentence "The rain fell."

In parsing a Conjunction say what words or what sentences it joins together:—

Exercise 22.

Parse the words printed in Italics in the following sentences:—

1. He walked *about* the house. 2. He is walking *about*. 3. The *above* named book was lost. 4. The sky is *above* the earth. 5. He was *all* covered with mud. 6. We walked *along* the bank of the river. 7. He is going *along* at a great pace. 8. We must rest *before* going *any* farther. 9. Men will reap *as* they sow. 10. *As* rain has fallen, the grass will soon look green. 11. He came *after* a few days. 12. He came a few days *after*. 13. He will go *after* he has dined. 14. He stood *below* me in the class. 15. There is a world *below* and a world *above*. 16. You are working *better* to-day. 17. There is *but* one man present. 18. Who could have done this *but* him? 19. He is a man of common-sense, *but* not learned in books. 20. We could not do anything *else*. 21. He has some real cause for sorrow; *else* he would not weep as he does. 22. He has worked hard *enough* for

[1] The distinction between Co-ordinative and Subordinative conjunctions does not belong to Parsing, but to Analysis; see below, § 116 and § 126.

anything. 23. Whom was this done *by?* 24. The horse is going *by.* 25. All *except* one agreed to this. 26. It was at York that I *first* saw him. 27. He has been ill *for* a long time past. 28. He was much missed; *for* he was a really good man. 29. He was *half* dead with fear. 30. Come *in* and take a seat. 31. You will find him *in* the house. 32. I love Cæsar *less* than Rome. 33. I saw him once *more.* 34. I liked him *most* of all. 35. *Neither* you *nor* I can do that. 36. He must *needs* know the reason of this. 37. Who comes *next?* 38. He stood *next* me in class. 39. I can do *no* more. 40. He fell *off* the saddle. 41. The robber ran *off.* 42. I heard of this *only* yesterday. 43. Take what you like; *only* keep silence. 44. He is *over* ten years of age. 45. The holidays are now *over.* 46. The secret is *out.* 47. I have not seen him *since* Monday last. 48. I took this house four weeks *since.* 49. We must trust you *since* you say so. 50. The men are all *together.* 51. Rocks are *ahead.*

OXFORD PRELIMINARY EXAMINATIONS.

July 1898.

A.

1. Parse fully each word in the following passage:—

Southward, from Surrey's pleasant hills, flew these bright warriors forth.

2. Make short sentences containing—

Over (*a*) as an Adverb, (*b*) as a Preposition.
Show (*a*) as a Noun, (*b*) as a Verb.
But (*a*) as a Preposition, (*b*) as a Conjunction.

3. Write in columns the present tense and past participle of each verb in the following passage:—

I laid down the buck, and unslung my double gun, and threw a stick at the nest, when out shot a large pine-martin, and like a squirrel sprang from tree to tree.

B.

4. What is a Pronoun? Write down in a column the pronouns in the following sentence, and opposite each state what kind of pronoun it is:—

One of these is mine: are there any that belong to you?

5. Give the Comparative degree of the following adjectives:—*red, curious, little, lively.*

6. Write in your own words the meaning of the following lines:—

And there was mounting in hot haste: the steed,
The mustering squadron, and the clattering car,
Went pouring forward with impetuous speed,
And swiftly forming in the ranks of war;
And the deep thunder peal on peal afar;
And near, the beat of the alarming drum
Roused up the soldier ere the morning star.

July 1899.

A.

1. Parse fully the verbs and pronouns in the following sentence:—

Thrice is he armed that hath his quarrel just.

2. Define a Noun. State to what class each noun in the following sentence belongs:—

Farmer John had a good crop of wheat last summer, but it was badly harvested through the laziness of a crowd of reapers.

3. Write down the past tense (1st person sing.) and the past participle of the following verbs:—*set*, *buy*, *do*, *spread*, *arise*, *lie* (down).

B.

4. Make short sentences in which—

(*a*) the verb "to be" shall have the meaning of "to exist."
(*b*) the verb "to be" shall be merely copulative.
(*c*) the verb "to tell" shall have a direct and an indirect object.
(*d*) the verb "to make" shall be used actively with two objects.
(*e*) the verb "to make" shall be used passively with two nominatives.

5. Write down the Superlative of the following adverbs:—*well*, *fast*, *boldly*, *little*, *much*.

6. Write in your own words the meaning of the following lines:—

But Sir Richard cried in his English pride,
"We have fought such a fight for a day and a night
As may never be fought again!
We have won great glory, my men!
And a day less or more,
At sea or ashore,
We die—does it matter when?
Sink me the ship, Master Gunner—sink her, split her in twain!
Fall into the hands of God, not into the hands of Spain!"

CAMBRIDGE PRELIMINARY EXAMINATIONS.

December 1896.

1. Write a sentence containing at least five different parts of speech. Point out in this sentence an example of each of the five, naming the part of speech to which it belongs.

2. Give the feminines corresponding to *governor*, *lad*, *mayor*, and give the possessive case plural of the feminine forms corresponding to *drake*, *earl*, *nephew*, *lord*.

State the number of each of the following words:—*them*, *son's*, *me*, *men's*, *men*, *whose*, *she*, *us*. State also the case or cases in which each may be.

3. What are the Comparatives and Superlatives of *lazy*, *red*, *beautiful*, *cruel*, *much*, *grave*?

Write short sentences containing the word "that" used (*a*) as a

Demonstrative pronoun, (*b*) as a Demonstrative adjective, (*c*) as a Relative pronoun.

What is the meaning of "demonstrative"?

Would you put *a* or *an* before *aim*, *heir*, *help*, *hour*, *year?*

4. Parse fully the words in Italics in the following passage :—

Unbending *'midst* the *wintry skies*,
Rears the firm oak *his* vigorous *form*,
And stern in rugged strength *defies*
The *rushing* of the storm.

5. Give in two columns the past tense indicative and the past participle of the following verbs :—*arise*, *dwell*, *do*, *get*, *lay*, *lean*, *thrive*.

Which of these verbs may be used transitively? What is the meaning of "Transitive"?

6. What are Subjects in the following sentences?

(*a*) His money being spent, he left the country.
(*b*) There is no help for it.
(*c*) Where is he?
(*d*) Riding is a healthy exercise.

7. Write a short sentence in which *by* is used as an adverb, and another sentence in which it is used as a preposition. Do the same with the words *behind*, *near*, *since*. Which of these four words can be used as a conjunction? Write a sentence in which it is so used.

December 1897.

1. Name the parts of speech to which the words in Italics in the following sentence belong :—

She sleeps, *nor dreams*, but *ever* dwells
A *perfect* form in perfect *rest*.

2. Give the feminine forms corresponding to *bachelor*, *lord*, *sultan*, *testator*.

Write down the possessive cases, singular and plural, of *singer*, *monkey*, *thief*, *mistress*, *he*.

3. Form adjectives from *worth*, *south*, *quarrel*, *glory*, and attach each adjective to a suitable noun.

Give the other degrees of comparison of *dim*, *famous*, *shy*; and of *farther*, *inner*, *less*.

Combine in one sentence the following pair of sentences :—

The tree was cut down. The tree was a poplar.

Do the same with the sentences :—

They did not see the Queen. They went to see the Queen.

4. Parse fully the words in Italics in the following passage :—

I *saw* thee *smile*: the sapphire's *blaze*
Beside thee ceased to shine;
It could not match the *living* rays
That filled *that* glance of thine.

5. Give in two columns the first person singular of the past tense indicative and the past participle of the following verbs :—*cast*, *eat*,

lean, *lend*, *lie* (to lie down), *swell*, *weave*. Which of these verbs can be used intransitively?

Correct the following where necessary:—

I left the hammer laying on the table.
The captive lay in the dungeon.
We laid down to rest.

6. Point out the *subjects* and *objects* in the following passage:—

For you these cherries I protect,
To you these plums belong:
Sweet is the fruit that you have picked,
But sweeter far your song.

7. Write a sentence in which the word *but* is used as a conjunction, a second in which it is used as a preposition, and a third in which it is used as an adverb.

December 1898.

1. Give one instance of a Common noun, one of a Proper noun, and one of a Collective noun.

Write down the plurals of *fox*, *ox*, *cliff*, *life*, *key*, *negro*, *piano*.

2. Give the possessive cases, singular and plural, of *empress*, *lady*, *woman*.

What are the masculine forms corresponding to *witch*, *vixen*, *hind*.

3. Give the comparatives and superlatives of *free*, *hot*, *neat*, *well*, *courteous*.

Form adjectives from *disaster*, *two*, *wheat*, and adverbs from *gay*, *holy*, *other*, *south*, *week*.

Correct the following, if necessary:—

I know who I like, it is her who gave me this knife.
Whom do you believe him to be?
Let you and I the battle try.

4. Parse fully the words in Italics in the following passage:—

All *along* the valley, *stream that flashest* white,
Deepening thy *voice* with the *deepening* of the night,
All along the valley, where thy waters flow,
I walked with one I loved two and thirty years *ago*.

5. Give in two columns the first person singular of the past tense indicative and the past participle of the following verbs:—*bite*, *choose*, *lie* (to lie down), *ride*, *sing*, *sit*, *steal*, *swear*, *swim*.

What are the transitive verbs corresponding to *lie* and *sit*?

Give the negative and the interrogative forms of—

The cat purrs. The tide is ebbing. I will speak.

6. Point out the subjects and objects in the following:—

Alas, how light a cause may move
Dissension between hearts that love,
Hearts that the world in vain had tried,
And sorrow but more closely tied!

7. How do you decide whether a word is a preposition or an adverb? Write a sentence containing a word used as an adverb.

Parse the words *for* and *until* wherever they occur in the following sentence :—

I will do your work *for* you *until* Tuesday or *until* you return, *for* I promised to do so.

CENTRAL WELSH BOARD, JUNIOR CERTIFICATE EXAMINATIONS.

July 1898.

1. Give the plural form of the following nouns :—*ox, church, wharf, tooth, genius, chief, leaf, brother, penny;* and the comparative form of the following adjectives :—*holy, fair, tender, little, good, many, old, far.*
2. How do we form the Possessive case of the English noun ?
3. Define (giving two examples in each case) Proper noun, Relative pronoun, Passive voice, Compound sentence.
4. Write sentences illustrating the various uses of the following words :—*the, but, as, such, much.*
5. What tenses and moods occur in the conjugation of the English verb ? Which of these are expressed by the help of Auxiliaries ?
6. Correct, giving in each case your reason for correction :—
   (*a*) He is taller than me.
   (*b*) Who were you speaking to ?
   (*c*) Neither the king nor his minister were at fault.
   (*d*) Neither of them were remarkable for precision.
7. Tabulate the different forms of the Personal pronoun.
8. Parse fully every word in the following sentence :—

   Into the street the Piper stept,
   Smiling first a little smile,
   As if he knew what magic slept
   In his quiet pipe the while.
9. Analyse :—
   (*a*) Into the street the Piper stept.
   (*b*) How pregnant sometimes his replies are !
   (*c*) Reading maketh a full man, conference a ready man, and writing an exact man.

July 1899.

1. How are nouns inflected for the plural ? Give some examples of nouns that form the plural irregularly, and also of nouns that change their meaning in the plural.
2. Define, giving in each case an example : — Cognate Object, Antecedent, Verb of Incomplete Predication, Nominative Absolute, Perfect tense.
3. How are adjectives compared ? Give some examples of defective comparison.
4. Mention the various uses of the Infinitive.

5. Show by means of examples the difference between (*a*) Relative and Interrogative pronoun, (*b*) Preposition and Conjunction, (*c*) Transitive and Intransitive verb, (*d*) Adjective and Adverb, (*e*) Active and Passive voice.

6. Amend the following phrases and sentences:—

(*a*) How sourly these apples taste.
(*b*) Here is a capital novel, which I am going to sit on the ground and read.
(*c*) It is not merely necessary to observe but to meditate.
(*d*) However fine a sight the fleet was by day, it was certainly eclipsed by night.
(*e*) The powers they possess, but cannot make use of them.
(*f*) Colonel Sandys a hot man, and who had more courage than judgment.
(*g*) There were three alternatives open.
(*h*) There was not a shadow of a whisper heard.
(*i*) What do you think of me learning French.
(*k*) He is a tall man, like his father was.

7. Distinguish between a Strong and a Weak verb. Give the Preterite tense[1] (1st person singular) and Preterite Participle of the following, stating also in each case whether the verb is Strong or Weak:—*shake, buy, shut, tell, take, sting, put, catch, ring, feel.*

8. Analyse the following passage:—

A man *who* has *been* brought up *among* books, and is able *to talk* of nothing *else*, is a *very* indifferent *companion*, and *what* we *call* a *pedant*. But, *methinks*, we should *enlarge* the title, and give it *to* every one that does not know *how* to think out of his profession and *particular* way of life.

9. Parse the words italicised in the above passage.

COLLEGE OF PRECEPTORS, CERTIFICATE EXAMINATIONS, THIRD CLASS.

Midsummer 1897.

I have just done somewhat for Ned, which he could not do for himself: I have bound up his hand which he had badly cut. Wiping away some natural tears, he must needs say—"I am ashamed, aunt, that you should see me cry; but the worst of it is that all this pain is for no good; whereas when my uncle beats me for misconstruing my Latin, though I cry at the time, all the while I know it is for my advantage."

1. Say what parts of speech the following words are, and give the reason for your answer in each case:—*somewhat, Ned, worst, all, good, whereas, beats, Latin.*

2. Parse fully each of the words in the clause—"aunt, that you should see me cry."

---

[1] "Preterite" is another name for Past Indefinite. Pluperfect is a name sometimes used for Past Perfect.

3. Give the subjects of *could do*,[1] *had cut*, *beats*, *know*, and the direct objects of *have done*, *could do*,[1] *wiping*, and *misconstruing*. Explain what you mean by the terms *subject* and *object*.

4. The conjunction *that* occurs twice in the above passage. What pairs of sentences are connected by it? What sentences are connected by the conjunction *though?*

5. What are the following words ending in *ing?—wiping*, *misconstruing*. Which of them can be replaced by a clause and a conjunction? Make the change.

6. Point out the words modified by the adverbs *badly*, *away*, *needs*.

7. What auxiliary verbs do you find in the given passage? To what principal verbs are they respectively auxiliary? Explain what is meant by an *Auxiliary verb*.

8. Write with proper capitals, stops, inverted commas, etc.:—the pass of thermopylæ was favourable to the greeks for the persians could not avail themselves of their superior numbers xerxes sent messengers to leonidas king of sparta bidding him give up his arms he replied come and take them lands were then offered to the defenders of the pass on condition that they should become allies of the great king but the lacedæmonians answered it was their custom to win lands by valour not by treachery.

Christmas 1897.

"Friend Sancho," said Don Quixote to him, "I find the approaching night will overtake us ere we can reach Toboso, where I am resolved to pay my vows, receive my benediction, and take my leave of the peerless Dulcinea; for nothing in this world inspires a knight-errant with so much valour as the smiles of his mistress."

1. Name the parts of speech to which the following words belong, giving in each case the reason for your answer:—*ere*, *where*, *peerless*, *for*, *knight-errant*, *as*.

2. Parse as fully as you can:—"I find the approaching night will overtake us."

3. Write down the *subject*, and where possible the *direct object*, of each of the verbs given below. *Tabulate your answer thus:*—

VERB.	SUBJECT.	DIRECT OBJECT.
said		
can reach		
am resolved		
inspires		

4. Give, in a tabulated form, the Past Indefinite of the Indicative (first person singular only) and the Perfect Participle of all the verbs in the passage.

5. How do you distinguish between a *Personal* pronoun and a *Relative* pronoun? Write two sentences in illustration.

6. Construct short sentences to show the difference in meaning

---

[1] This assumes the existence of a Potential mood, formed by *can* or *could*. This mood, however, is not now generally recognised. *Can* is regarded as a Principal, not an Auxiliary verb; and the Infinitive following is its object; see § 83.

between the following words, and in each case name the part of speech to which each of these words belongs :—(1) *some* and *sum*, (2) *vain* and *vein*.

7. Name the different ways in which the subject of a sentence may be enlarged, and write two sentences as examples.

8. In the following passage supply the necessary capital letters and put in the stops and inverted commas where necessary :—you are mad said the curate starting up astonished is thy master such a wonderful hero as to fight a giant at two thousand leagues distance then they heard don quixote bawling out stay villain since i have thee here thy scimitar shall but little avail thee.

Midsummer, 1898.

Bramble took the glass off the top of the compass-box, lifted up the card, and then showed me the needle below, which pointed due north. He also showed me the north point above, and then the other points, and made me repeat them as he touched each with his finger.

1. What determines the part of speech a word is? Point out what each of the following words does in the above passage, and name the part of speech which it is :—*up, and, then, he, also, other.*

2. Parse fully :—"off the top of the compass-box," and "which pointed due north."

3. Write down all the *direct objects* of verbs in the given passage, and also the *verbs* which govern them, and the *subjects* of those verbs. *Arrange your answer in a tabular form thus :—*

DIRECT OBJECT.	VERB.	SUBJECT.
The escape	Helped	The captain

4. Give the present and the past participles of the verbs *took, lifted, showed, pointed, made, touched.*

5. Write two sentences, each containing a *Relative* pronoun, a *Personal*, and an *Interrogative* pronoun. Draw a single line under the Relative pronoun, two lines under the Personal pronoun, and three under the Interrogative pronoun.

6. In passing from one form of a word to another, when is the final consonant doubled? Give three instances.

7. Correct or justify the following sentences, giving your reasons :—

(i.) He told me to go and lay down on the bed.
(ii.) Who are you calling for? Is it me?
(iii.) Your gold and silver is cankered.
(iv.) The boys have a dozen tennis balls.

8. Write with proper capitals, stops, inverted commas, etc. :—i opened the boxes and to andersons surprise i counted out gold coin to the amount of four hundred pounds not a bad legacy said mr. wilson then you knew of this of course i answered i have known it some time ever since the attempt to rob her but what are these papers said the lawyer

Christmas, 1898.

Columbus was the first one of the Europeans who set foot in the New World which he had discovered. His men soon followed, and kneeling down they all kissed the ground which they had so long desired to see. They then took solemn possession of the country.

1. Point out what each of the following words does in the above passage, and name the part of speech to which it belongs :—*Columbus, first, on, discovered, soon, solemn.*

2. Parse as fully as you can : — "And kneeling down they all kissed the ground."

3. Write down the *subject*, and where possible the *object*, of each of the verbs given below. *Tabulate your answer thus :—*

VERB.	SUBJECT.	DIRECT OBJECT.
was		
set		
had desired		
took		

4. Make a list of all the pronouns in the passage, and opposite each write what kind of pronoun it is.

5. Give the meanings of the following prefixes, and two instances of the use of each :—*in, per, dis, re.*

6. Write short sentences containing :—

Jump (*a*) as a noun, (*b*) as a verb.
Up (*a*) as an adverb, (*b*) as a preposition.
That (*a*) as a pronoun, (*b*) as a pronoun of another kind.

7. State clearly the reasons for the corrections made in the following sentences :—

(*a*) "Neither John nor James were there."—*Were* should be *was.*
(*b*) "I am sure it was not him."—*Him* should be *he.*
(*c*) "He resembles one of those men who is always hesitating."—*Is* should be *are.*

8. Write with proper capitals, stops, inverted commas, etc. :— the traveller made three quick steps towards the jail then turning short tell me said he has that unnatural captain sent you nothing to relieve your distress call him not unnatural replied the other gods blessing be upon him he sent me a great deal of money but i made a bad use of it.

Exercise 23.

Correct or justify the following. Give the reason of every correction that you make.

(*a*) 1. Let each see to their own. 2. Nobody can talk like he can. 3. Soldiers are tried by court-martials. 4. Neither he nor John say this. 5. These kind are the best. 6. Who do you think I saw yesterday? 7. Neither he nor I are expected. 8. Time and tide waits for no man. 9. Each of you in their turn will enjoy the benefits to which they are entitled. 10. Every leaf, every twig, every drop of water teem with life. 11. Do you know who you are speaking to? 12. Neither of them seem to have any idea of their ignorance. 13. They, which do their best, are most likely to succeed. (*Oxford Junior.*)

(*b*) 1. Bacon's "Essays" are the most important of these two books. 2. Do you remember my cousin, whom we thought had settled in Australia? There is some talk of him returning. 3. Somebody called; I could not at first tell whom; but afterwards I found out it was her. 4. They had awoke him, as they said, to tell him that the river had overflown its banks. 5. Travelling along the line, the towers of the castle came in sight. 6. If this be him we mean, let him beware. 7. I saw the pickpocket and policeman on opposite sides of the street. 8. Who did you see at the regatta? 9. It is unfair to argue like you do. 10. For ever in this humble cell, | Let you and I, my fair one, dwell. 11. The number of failures were very great. 12. My lawyer is a man whom I know is trustworthy. 13. A thousand weary miles now stretch | Between my love and I. (*Cambridge Junior.*)

(*c*) 1. No sound but their own voices were heard. 2. He is a boy whom I think likely to do well. 3. The phenomena of nature is wonderful. 4. Is she older or younger than him? 5. No one saw him leave the house, but me only. 6. Neither of the opponents were inclined to submit. 7. Each of these classes of men has wishes peculiar to itself. 8. When will we start? 9. I saw a young and old man sitting together. 10. She was the worst of the two. 11. They that backbite their neighbours stealthily, take care to rebuke sharply. 12. If I had not broke your stick, you would never have run home. 13. I saw a black and white man walking together. 14. I am neither an ascetic in theory or practice. 15. Of these mistakes none are very serious. 16. I don't know who he has gone with. (*Preceptors' Third Class.*)

(*d*) 1. On the garden seat was his book and pencil. 2. Who can it be from? 3. The ship with all the passengers were destroyed. 4. No one expressed their opinion so clearly as him. 5. At the club dinner the usual loyal toasts were drank first of all. 6. The steam-engine as well as the telegraph were still unknown. 7. He sings better than ever. 8. Stouter hearts than a woman have quailed in this terrible trial. 9. He has appointed as commander nobody knows who. 10. It is not me he injures so much as himself. 11. Having failed in this experiment, no further trial was made. (*Preceptors' Third Class.*)

(*e*) 1. It is sometimes said that the Nile is longer than all the rivers of the eastern and western hemispheres. During the past week it has overflown its right and left banks. 2. Each of the three last were expected to have stopped and voted. 3. Judging from the time taken, the race was rowed quicker than in all previous years. 4. More than one swimming-prize is to be given for boys of thirteen years old. 5. Whom do you think I met to-day? Both your cousins! The oldest had on a new and a most fashionable pair of boots, like you saw Henry wearing yesterday. 6. I don't believe you have got a better bicycle or even as good as me. 7. He must decide between you and I going to him or him coming to us. 8. There goes John with both his dogs on either side of him. 9. When Nelson was ill, he complained of "the servants letting me lay as if a log, and take no notice." 10. I have now the perfect use of all my limbs except the left arm, which I can hardly tell what is the matter with it. 11. From my shoulder to my fingers' ends are as if half dead. (*Cambridge Senior.*)

(*f*) 1. He carried a jaunty sort of stick. 2. They demanded a fair day's wage for a fair day's work. 3. It is not that offends. 4. Now either spoke as hope or fear impressed | Each their alternate triumph in his breast. 5. Your betters have endured me say my mind. 6. After doing the work, his face brightened. 7. Three parts of him is ours already. 8. The wealth of London is greater than Oxford. 9. This is a dress of my mother's. 10. He said that he will soon be back. 11. Nothing but rough games please the boys. 12. 'Twas Love's mistake who fancied what it feared. 13. She suffers hourly more than me. 14. He comes; nor want nor cold his course delay. (*Oxford Senior.*)

(*g*) 1. You and her will be too late without you start soon. 2. Me and he can manage it without you interfering. 3. Let who will say no, you shall go with Will and I. 4. Each of these cathedrals were founded in the two-hundredth and first year after the death of Alfred. 5. Good order, and not mean savings, produce great profit. 6. The literary and commercial value of a book are not necessarily the same. 7. Neither James nor John were there. 8. I fully approve of your going. 9. Let you and I take our own course. 10. Who are going with? 11. The Palmer (or De Wilton, whom he really was). 12. The idle and industrious men came together. 13. He won't go, I don't believe. 14. If William goes to-morrow, will I go to? 15. He said he will give the book to whoever he pleased. 16. A certain portion of auxiliaries were allotted to each legion. 17. To be sold, the stock of Mr. Smith's left-off business. 18. If I had been there, you would not have attempted to have done that. 19. You know that I am, not less than him, a despiser of the multitude. (*Preceptors' Second Class.*)

(*h*) 1. Whom did you say the man was who spoke to you just now. 2. He ran so fastly up the hill that neither Jean or me could overtake him. 3. Will you allow my brother and I to finish what we have begun? 4. Adversity both teach men to think and to feel. 5. At the bottom of the road lay a stream to wide to jump. 6. Who do you think was there? 7. Whom are you going with? 8. They gained nothing by it, and neither did you. 9. They walked by two's and three's. 10. It was my own stupid pride prevented me going. 11. We sorrow not as them that have no hope. 12. I think I will be gone by the time you come. 13. I cannot tell if it be wise or no. 14. Land is not thought to be so good a security as formerly. 15. He was one of the noblest men that has appeared in this century. 16. I should have liked to have been shown to-day the full cost of this war. 17. Anybody may go for the key: I care not who. 18. A few hours' consideration are quite enough. 19. This is the man whom I believed rescued the dog. 20. Nelson was greater than any sailor of his time. 21. He cannot run faster than neither me or John. 22. My partner was a much greater gainer than me by this arrangement. 23. I had ought to be punctual. 24. The attack of the enemy upon our left was foiled: they then endeavoured to outflank the Egyptians with the bulk of their forces. 25. Men of greatest learning have spent their time in finding out the dimensions, and even weight, of the planets. (*Preceptors' Second Class.*)

Exercise 24.—*On the Order of Words.*

The great rule to be observed in fixing the order of words is this:—*Things which are to be thought of together must be mentioned together.* So a word or phrase should always be placed as close as the context allows to the word or phrase that it is meant to go with.

Thus an adjective or adjective-equivalent must be kept as close as possible to its noun or pronoun; a verb to its object or to its complement; an adverb or adverb-equivalent to the word that it is intended to qualify; a preposition to its object; a relative pronoun to its antecedent.

The sense of a sentence very often depends upon the order of the words, as in the following examples:—

Books authorised by teachers as fit for use.
Books authorised as fit for use by teachers.

Improve, if necessary, the order of words in the following sentences:—

(*a*) 1. The experiment of entrusting lodgers with keys has only failed in a few instances. 2. Ellen went with me too. 3. In thirty-seven wrecks only five lives were fortunately lost. 4. The one was nearly dressed in the same way as the other. 5. She was only allowed to occupy the smaller room. 6. The following verses were written by a young man who has long since been dead for his own amusement. (*Oxford, Cambridge, Preceptors'.*)

(*b*) 1. He was shot by a secretary who was under notice to quit and with whom he was finding fault, fortunately without effect. 2. You have already been informed of the sale of Ford's theatre, where Mr. Lincoln was assassinated, for religious purposes. 3. The Moor, seizing a bolster, full of rage and fury, smothers her. 4. Being early killed, I sent a party in search of his mangled body. (*London Matriculation.*)

(*c*) 1. The chair cost ten shillings on which he sat. 2. A gang of robbers entered the house at night armed from head to foot. 3. He repeated those lines after he had read them once with perfect accuracy. 4. They found the house on the top of a hill where they wished to spend the night. 5. The general ordered indignantly the deserters to be shot. 6. An unquestioned man of genius. 7. He cannot be said to have died prematurely whose work was finished, nor does he deserve to be lamented, who died so full of honours (*Southey*). 8. I never remember to have felt an event more deeply than Horner's death. 9. The death occurred last week in Madrid of Mr. W. Macpherson, formerly British vice-consul at Seville (*Times Weekly*, 11th Feb. 1898). 10. No one is entitled to form or express an opinion on the relations between Nelson and Lady Hamilton, or on the parentage of Horatia, who has not carefully studied the letters to be found in this invaluable collection (*Times Weekly*, 4th March 1898).

Exercise 24A. (Could be done orally in class.)

Construct short sentences or phrases exemplifying the uses of the following words in different grammatical relations :—

A.—(1) Indefinite article ; (2) disguised preposition.
After.—(1) adv. ; (2) prepos. ; (3) conjunc. ; (4) in composition.
All.—(1) adj. of quantity ; (2) adj. of number ; (3) noun ; (4) adv.
Any.—(1) adjective ; (2) adverb.
As.—(1) Relative pron. ; (2) Relative adv. denoting (*a*) time, (*b*) manner, (*c*) state, (*d*) extent, (*e*) reason ; (3) in elliptical phrases.
Awake.—(1) verb ; (2) adverb.
Back.—(1) noun ; (2) adverb ; (3) verb ; (4) in composition.
Before.—(1) adverb ; (2) preposition ; (3) conjunction.
Behind.—(1) adverb ; (2) preposition.
Better.—(1) adjective ; (2) adverb ; (3) noun ; (4) verb.
Both.—(1) adjective ; (2) conjunction.
But.—(1) prep. ; (2) adv. ; (3) co-ord. conj. ; (4) subord. conj.
By.—(1) adverb ; (2) preposition ; (3) in composition.
Calm.—(1) adjective ; (2) noun ; (3) verb.
Chief, cold, common.—(1) adjective ; (2) noun.
Clear, correct, corrupt.—(1) adjective ; (2) verb.
Close.—(1) adjective ; (2) adverb ; (3) noun ; (4) verb.
Compact, compound, content.—(1) adjective ; (2) noun ; (3) verb.
Dainty, dark, dead, deep, due.—(1) adjective ; (2) noun.
Damp, desert, double, dread.—(1) adjective ; (2) noun ; (3) verb.
Direct, dull.—(1) adjective ; (2) verb.
Down.—(1) noun ; (2) adverb ; (3) preposition.
Early.—(1) adjective ; (2) adverb.
Either.—(1) adjective ; (2) conjunction.
Elect.—(1) verb ; (2) adjective ; (3) noun.
Elder, English, evil, extreme.—(1) adjective ; (2) noun.
Else.—(1) adverb ; (2) conjunction.
Empty, equal.—(1) adjective ; (2) verb.
Enough.—(1) adverb ; (2) adjective ; (3) noun.
Faint.—(1) adjective ; (2) verb.
Far, fast.—(1) adverb ; (2) adjective.
Few.—(1) adjective ; (2) noun.
Firm.—(1) adjective ; (2) noun.
First.—(1) adjective ; (2) adverb.
Fit.—(1) adjective ; (2) noun ; (3) verb.
For.—(1) preposition ; (2) conjunction.
Four.—(1) adjective ; (2) noun ; (3) in composition.
Further.—(1) adjective ; (2) adverb ; (3) verb.
Gold, good, Greek.—(1) noun ; (2) adjective.
Half.—(1) adjective ; (2) noun ; (3) adverb.
Hard.—(1) adjective ; (2) adverb.
Ill.—(1) adjective ; (2) adverb.
Invalid.—(1) adjective ; (2) noun.
Late, last, little, less, least.—(1) adjective ; (2) adverb.
Light (luminous).—(1) adjective ; (2) noun ; (3) verb.

Long.—(1) adjective ; (2) adverb ; (3) verb.
Loose.—(1) adjective ; (2) verb.
Many.—(1) adjective ; (2) noun.
Marble, mean (middle), **middle.**—(1) noun ; (2) adjective.
Might.—(1) verb ; (2) noun.
Model.—(1) noun ; (2) adjective ; (3) verb.
More.—(1) adjective ; (2) adverb ; (3) noun.
Most.—(1) adjective ; (2) adverb ; (3) noun.
Narrow.—(1) adjective ; (2) verb.
Native, new, novel, nuptial.—(1) adjective ; (2) noun.
Near.—(1) adjective ; (2) adverb ; (3) preposition ; (4) verb.
Needs.—(1) verb ; (2) adverb ; (3) noun.
Neither.—(1) adjective ; (2) conjunction.
Next, no.—(1) adjective ; (2) adverb.
None.—(1) Negative pronoun ; (2) adverb.
Odd.—(1) adjective ; (2) noun.
Off, on.—(1) preposition ; (2) adverb.
One.—(1) adjective ; (2) pronoun.
Only.—(1) adjective ; (2) adverb ; (3) conjunction.
Open.—(1) adjective ; (2) noun ; (3) verb.
Other.—(1) adjective ; (2) noun.
Over.—(1) preposition ; (2) adverb.
Own.—(1) adjective ; (2) verb.
Past.—(1) adjective ; (2) preposition ; (3) adverb
Patent.—(1) adjective ; (2) noun ; (3) verb.
Perfect.—(1) adjective ; (2) verb.
Public.—(1) adjective ; (2) noun.
Quack, quiet.—(1) verb ; (2) noun ; (3) adjective.
Quick.—(1) adjective ; (2) noun.
Rapid.—(1) adjective ; (2) noun.
Right, rival.—(1) adjective ; (2) noun ; (3) verb.
Round.—(1) adj. ; (2) prep. ; (3) adverb ; (4) verb ; (5) noun.
Salt, set.—(1) adjective ; (2) noun ; (3) verb.
Save.—(1) verb ; (2) preposition.
Since.—(1) preposition ; (2) adverb ; (3) conjunction.
So.—(1) adverb ; (2) conjunction.
Some.—(1) adjective ; (2) adverb.
Somewhat.—(1) adverb ; (2) noun.
Still.—(1) adjective ; (2) adverb ; (3) verb.
Such.—(1) adjective ; (2) pronoun.
Than.—(1) conjunction ; (2) preposition.
That.—(1) adj. ; (2) Dem. pron. ; (3) Rel. pron. ; (4) conjunction.
The.—(1) Def. article ; (2) adverb.
Through, to, under, up.—(1) preposition ; (2) adverb.
Till.—(1) preposition ; (2) conjunction.
Trim.—(1) adjective ; (2) noun ; (3) verb.
Well.—(1) adverb ; (2) conjunction ; (3) noun.
What.—(1) Interrog. pron. ; (2) Rel. pron. ; (3) adverb.
While.—(1) noun ; (2) conjunction.
Yet.—(1) conjunction ; (2) adverb.

PART IV.—ANALYSIS AND CONVERSION OF SENTENCES: SEQUENCE OF TENSES.

CHAPTER XXIV.—SENTENCES SIMPLE, COMPOUND, AND COMPLEX.

110. Simple Sentence.—A Simple sentence (Lat. *simplex*, single-fold) is one that has *only one* **Finite** *verb* expressed or understood.

Subject.	*Predicate.*
The merchant, having much property to sell,	*caused* all his goods to be conveyed on camels, there being no railway in that country.

In this sentence there are five different verbs, "having," "to sell," "caused," "to be conveyed," "being." Of these only one, viz. "caused," is *finite*. The sentence is therefore Simple.

111. Compound Sentence.—A compound sentence is one made up of two or more *Co-ordinate* clauses.

Clauses are said to be Co-ordinate, when one can be separated from the other so that each makes an independent sentence and gives an independent sense.

The sun rose with power, *and* the fog dispersed.
He called at my house, *but* I was not at home.

Note.—Observe the difference between **Sentence, Clause,** and **Phrase.** (1) A sentence is a combination of words that contains at least one subject and one predicate. (2) A sentence which is *part of a larger sentence* is called a clause. (3) A phrase is a combination of words that *does not contain a predicate* expressed or understood; as "turning to the left" (participial phrase), "on a hill" (adjectival or adverbial phrase).

112. Complex Sentence.—A Complex sentence consists of a Principal clause (*i.e.* the clause containing the main *verb* of the sentence) with one or more Subordinate or dependent clauses.

Complex { A merchant, who had much property to sell, *caused* all his goods to be conveyed on camels, as there was no railway in that country.

Simple { A merchant, having much property to sell, *caused* all his goods to be conveyed on camels, there being no railway in that country.

The two sentences mean precisely the same thing, and both have a Finite verb in common, "caused." But in other respects they are very different. In the latter there is but *one* Finite verb, "caused," and therefore the sentence is Simple. In the former, besides the Finite verb "caused," there are two more Finite verbs, "had" and "was," and therefore the sentence must be either Complex or Compound. Which is it?

It is not Compound, but Complex, because—(1) the clause "who had much property to sell" is connected with the noun *merchant*, which it qualifies as an adjective would do; and (2) the clause "as there was no railway in that country" is connected with the verb *caused*, which it qualifies as an adverb would do. Neither of these clauses can stand alone; and neither of them gives an independent sense without reference to some outside word. So there is one Principal or Containing clause and two Subordinate or Contained clauses.

113. There are three kinds of Subordinate clauses—the Noun-clause, the Adjective-clause, and the Adverb-clause; and these are defined as follows:—

I. *A Noun-clause is one which does the work of a noun in relation to some* **word** *in some other clause.*

II. *An Adjective-clause is one which does the work of an adjective in relation to some* **word** *in some other clause.*

III. *An Adverb-clause is one which does the work of an adverb in relation to some* **word** *in some other clause.*

Note.—The same clause may be a Noun-clause in one context, an Adjective-clause in another, and an Adverb-clause in another.

Where Moses was buried is still unknown.

—Noun-clause, subject to the verb "is."

No one has seen the place *where Moses was buried.*

—Adj.-clause, qualifying the noun "place."

Without knowing it the Arabs encamped *where Moses was buried.*

—Adverb-clause qualifying the verb "encamped."

I. *The Noun-clause.*

114. A Noun-clause is subject to all the liabilities and duties of a noun proper. It may therefore be the subject to a verb, the object to a verb, the object to a preposition, the complement to a verb, or in apposition with a noun:—

That he will come back soon is certain . . .	*Subj. to verb.*
I shall be glad to know *when you will return* .	*Obj. to verb.*
This will sell for *what it is worth*	*Obj. to prep.*
This is exactly *what I expected*	*Comp. to verb.*
The rumour *that he is sick* is false	*App. to noun.*

Note 1.—From the above examples it will be seen that a Noun-clause can be introduced either by the Conjunction "*that*" or by a Conjunctive pronoun or by a Conjunctive adverb. Sometimes, however, the Conjunction *that* is left out :—

It seems (that) he is not clever.

Note 2.—A clause containing the very words used by a speaker is another form of Noun-clause :—

All that he said was, "*I have seen you before.*"

Here the italicised clause is the complement to the verb "was."

Exercise 25.

Pick out the Noun-clause in each of the following examples, and say whether it is the Subject to some verb, or the Object to some verb, or the Object to some preposition, or the Complement to some verb, or in Apposition to some noun expressed. Supply the Conjunction "that" *whenever it has been left out :—*

1. No one knows when he will come, or whether he will come at all, or whether he is even alive.
2. How this came to pass is not known to any one.
3. What is sauce for the goose is sauce for the gander.
4. It is quite evident rain will fall to-day.
5. The Equator shows where days and nights are of equal length.
6. What is one man's meat is another man's poison.
7. You must know that the air is never quite at rest.
8. I think I shall never clearly understand this.
9. We heard the school would open in ten days' time.
10. The name "Volcano" indicates the belief of the ancient Greeks, that the burning hills of the Mediterranean were the workshops of the divine blacksmith, Vulcan.
11. Even a feather shows which way the wind is blowing.
12. Whatever faculty man has is improved by use.
13. The fool hath said in his heart, "There is no God."
14. "Know thyself," was the advice given us by a Greek sage.
15. He did not know that his father had been shot.
16. The fact that you have not signed your name to a letter shows that you lack moral courage.
17. It will be easily understood how useful even the simplest weapons were to the first dwellers on the earth.
18. The question first occurring to the mind of a savage is how is fire to be made.
19. Common sense soon taught him that fire could be produced by rubbing two sticks together.
20. In chipping their flint weapons men must have seen that fire occasionally flashed out.

21. We learn from travellers that savages can produce fire in a few seconds.
22. He shouted out to the thief, "Leave this house."
23. We cannot rely on what he says.
24. It is quite evident you have made a mistake.
25. It was very unfortunate that you were taken ill.
26. He was a man of fine character except that he was rather timid.

II. *Adjective-clause.*

115. An Adjective-clause has but one function, viz. to qualify some noun or pronoun belonging to some other clause. In doing this it simply does the work of an adjective proper. An Adjective-clause is introduced by a Relative pronoun or by a Relative adverb. The noun or pronoun that stands as antecedent to the Relative pronoun or Relative adverb, is the *word* (§ 113, II.) qualified by the Adjective-clause.

A man *who* has just come inquired after you.
This is not the book *that* I chose.
This is not such a horse *as* I should have bought.
We found it in the place *where* we had left it.

Note.—The Relative pronoun (when the case would be Objective) is sometimes left out. (It is never left out when the case is either Nominative or Possessive):—

The food (that or which) he needed was sent.

Exercise 26.

Pick out the Adjective-clause or clauses in each of the following examples, and point out the noun or pronoun qualified by it in some other clause. If the Relative pronoun has been omitted anywhere, supply it:—

1. Man has the power of making instruments, which bring into view stars, whose light has taken a thousand years to reach the earth.
2. The first thing that man needed was some sharp-edged tool.
3. The exact time when the theft was committed was never found out.
4. The man by whom the theft was committed has been caught.
5. The house we lived in has fallen down.
6. This is the same story that I heard ten years ago.
7. It's an ill wind that blows no one any good.
8. This is not such a book as I should have chosen.
9. He made his living by the presents he received from the men he served.
10. All that glitters is not gold.
11. In ponds, from which but a week before the wind blew clouds of dust, men now catch the re-animated fish.
12. A river is joined at places by tributaries that swell its waters.

13. Of what use is a knowledge of books to him who fails to practise virtue?

14. Fortune selects him for her lord, who reflects before acting.

15. Springs are fed by rain, which has percolated through the rocks or soil.

16. Nuncoomar prepared to die with that quiet fortitude with which the Bengalee, so backward, as a rule, in personal conflict, often encounters calamities for which there is no remedy.

17. I have seen the house where Shakspeare was born.

18. The plan you acted on has answered well.

19. They accepted every plan we proposed.

20. Surely the story you are telling me is not true.

21. Thrice is he armed that hath his quarrel just.

22. The night is long that never finds the day.

III. *The Adverb-clause.*

116. An Adverb-clause does the work of an adverb to some verb, adjective, or adverb belonging to some other clause.

Those conjunctions or conjunctive adverbs, which are used for introducing an adverb-clause or any other kind of dependent clause, are called Subordinative.

Principal Clause.	*Adverb-Clause.*	*Adverbial Relation.*
He will succeed,	*because* he works hard	*Cause.*
He worked *so* hard,	*that* he was quite tired	*Effect.*
He took medicine	*that* he might get well	*Purpose.*
I will do this,	*if* I am allowed	*Condition.*
He is honest,	*although* he is poor	*Contrast.*
He likes you *more*	*than* (he likes) me	*Comparison.*
Men will reap	*as* they sow	*Extent or Manner.*
The tooth stopped aching	*when* the dentist came in	*Time.*

Note.—Conjunctions like *because, that, if, though, than, as* may be called **Simple**. Those which are formed from the Relative pronoun, such as *when, where, why, how, whether, whither,* are known as **Relative** or **Conjunctive** adverbs. See § 59.

117. After the conjunctions *though, when, unless, till, if, whether . . . or,* and *while,* the Predicate-verb "**to be**" is often understood. This must be supplied in the Analysis.

Though (*he was*) much alarmed, he did not lose all hope.
He sprained his foot, while (*he was*) walking in the dark.
His opinion, whether (*it is*) right or wrong, does not concern me.

118. When an adverb-clause is introduced by "**than,**" its Predicate-Verb is not usually expressed; it must therefore be borrowed from the clause to which it is subordinate:—

He loves you better than (he loves) me.
He loves you better than I (love you).

Exercise 27.

Pick out the Adverb-clause or clauses in the following. Show what word or phrase is qualified by every such clause, and what Adverbial relation is denoted thereby :—

1. He will succeed, because he has worked hard.
2. Men engage in some work, that they may earn a living.
3. He threatened to beat him, unless he confessed.
4. He was always honest, although he was poor.
5. This is not true, so far as I can tell.
6. He likes you as much as I do.
7. He tried for a long time before he succeeded.
8. Let us go to bed, as it is now late.
9. He walked with care, lest he should stumble.
10. I agree to this, provided you sign your name.
11. Though he punish me, yet will I trust in him.
12. He returned home, after he had finished the work.
13. Prove a friend, before you trust him.
14. When the cat's away, the mice play.
15. He persevered so steadily, that he succeeded at last.
16. I will let off this man, who has been well punished already.
17. He sees very well, considering that he is sixty years of age.
18. I gave him a prize, that he might work harder next year.
19. They deserted their former associate, who had become poor and unfortunate.
20. As the tree falls, so will it lie.
21. Ever since we left the house, it has not ceased raining.
22. I should be glad to lend you that money, if I had as much in my own pocket.
23. Murder, though it have no tongue, will yet speak.
24. Unless you leave the house at once, I will send for a policeman.
25. A jackal, while prowling about the suburbs of a town, slipped into an indigo tank ; and not being able to get out he laid himself down, so that he might be taken for dead.
26. Ambassadors were sent from Sparta, who should sue for peace.

CHAPTER XXV.—THE METHOD OF ANALYSIS.

119. Form of Analysis.—The following form will be sufficient for the purposes of this chapter. The fourth example is a Complex sentence ; the other three are Simple sentences :—

A man convinced against his will is of the same opinion still.
He made himself mean and of no reputation.
The second master of the school has been teaching my sons Euclid since Thursday last.
Whom the gods love die young.

I. Subject.		II. Predicate.			
			Completion of Finite Verb.		
Nominative or Equivalent. 1	Enlargement of Nominative. 2	Finite verb. 3	Object. (1) Direct. (2) Indirect. 4	Complement. 5	Extension of Finite Verb. 6
man	(1) A (2) convinced against his will	is	...	of the same opinion	still.
He	...	made	himself	mean and of no reputation.	
master	(1) The (2) second (3) of the school	has been teaching	(1) *Direct* Euclid (2) *Indirect* my sons	...	since Thursday last.
Whom the gods love	...	die	...	...	young.

120. Nominative or its equivalent: see heading to col. 1. This is the chief part of the Subject, and when there is no enlargement, it is the only part. It is this that fixes the number and person of the Finite verb. Its most typical form is that of a noun or pronoun in the Nominative case. The following is a list of the various forms in which a Nominative or its equivalent can be expressed :[1]—

(1) **Noun.**—A *ship* went out to sea yesterday.
(2) **Adj. used as Noun.**—The *brave* are always respected.
(3) **Pronoun.**—*He* (some one previously named) has gone.
(4) **Noun-Infinitive.**—*To walk* regularly is good for health.
(5) **Gerund or Verbal noun.**—*Reading* is good for the mind.
(6) **Noun-phrase.**—*How to do this* is a difficult question.
(7) **Noun-clause.**—*Whom the gods love* die young.

Note 1.—Sometimes a sentence begins with "it," and the Nominative or its equivalent is mentioned after the verb: "*It* is easy to do this." Here the "it" is redundant, and may be left out in the analysis :—"To do this is easy."

[1] There is no need to commit this list of forms to memory. They are enumerated merely to show what the student may expect to find. The same remark applies to the lists in §§ 121-125.

Note 2. When the Finite verb is in the Imperative mood, the Nominative is understood, as, *go!* Here *go* is the Finite verb, and *thou* is the Nominative.

121. Enlargement: see heading to col. 2. The most typical form is an Adjective. We call this "*enlargement*," because an adjective, according to the definition given, is a word that adds to or *enlarges* the meaning of a noun or pronoun.

The following is a list of the various forms in which an "enlargement" can be expressed:—

(1) **Adjective.**—*Just* men deserve to prosper.
(2) **Participle.**—A *fertilising* shower fell to-day.
(3) **Qualifying Infin.**—Water to *drink* is scarce in this place.
(4) **Possessive noun or pronoun.**—*Your* teacher has come.
(5) **Noun used as Adj.** (§ 98).—The *village* school opens to-day.
(6) **Verbal noun used as Adj.**—*Drinking* water is scarce here.
(7) **Prep. with object.**—A man *of virtue* does not tell lies.
(8) **Adverb with Def. article.**—*The then* king died suddenly.
(9) **Noun in Apposition.**—Charles, my *son*, has come.
(10) **Noun-clause in Appos.**—The rumour *that he was dead* is false.
(11) **Adjective-clause.**—The house *in which we live* has been sold.

122. Finite verb: see heading to col. 3. This is the chief part of the predicate, and, when the verb is Intransitive and requires no Complement, it can be the only part; as, "Hogs *grunt*."

If the tense or mood of the Finite verb is formed, not by inflection, but by the help of one or more of the six Auxiliary verbs (see § 79), remember that the Auxiliary verb or verbs and the Principal verb together make up the "Finite verb," and *must be mentioned together* in column 3.

Subject.	Finite verb.	Object.
I	have been examining	the pictures.

But if the previous verb is not Auxiliary, as "*will*," for instance, when it occurs in the *first* person of the Future tense (§ 80), in such a sentence *will* alone makes the Finite verb, and the Noun-Infinitive that follows is its Object:—

Subject.	Finite verb.	Object.
I	will	see him to-morrow.

123. Object, direct or indirect: see col. 4. The different forms in which a *Direct* object can be expressed are the same as those in which the Nominative can be expressed (§ 120).

(1) **Noun.**—The snake bit the *man*.
(2) **Adj. used as Noun.**—He satisfied the *public*.
(3) **Pronoun.**—My friend will not deceive *me*.
(4) **Noun-Infinitive.**—He deserves *to succeed*.
(5) **Gerund or Verbal noun.**—He likes *riding*.
(6) **Noun-phrase.**—We did not know *how to do it*.
(7) **Noun-clause.**—We do not know *who he is*.

There are only two forms in which an *Indirect* object can be expressed, viz. a noun denoting some person or other animal, or some personal pronoun:—

He gave *James* a book . . . . (*Trans. verb.*)
He overslept *himself* . . . . (*Intrans. verb.*)

124. Complement: see heading to col. 5. The following are the various forms in which a Complement can be expressed. The student will no doubt remember from what he has learnt in § 63 that a Transitive verb followed by a Complement is called Factitive, while an Intransitive verb followed by a Complement is called Copulative:—

(1) **Noun**	The citizens made him their *king* .	(*Fact.*)
	That beggar turned out a *thief* . .	(*Cop.*)
(2) **Possessive**	She made A.'s quarrel *her own* . .	(*Fact.*)
	This book is *mine*, not *James's* . .	(*Cop.*)
(3) **Adjective**	The judge set the prisoner *free* . .	(*Fact.*)
	The prisoner is now *free* . . .	(*Cop.*)
(4) **Participle**	They found her *weeping* . . .	(*Fact.*)
	He seemed much *pleased* . . .	(*Cop.*)
(5) **Prep. with object**	I prefer a dog *to a cat*	(*Fact.*)
	He is *in a sad plight*	(*Cop.*)
(6) **Qualifying Infinitive**	I like a thief *to be punished* . .	(*Fact.*)
	This house is *to let*	(*Cop.*)
(7) **Adverb**	That noise sent him *asleep* . . .	(*Fact.*)
	The man has fallen *asleep* . . .	(*Cop.*)
(8) **Noun-clause**	We have made him *what he is* . .	(*Fact.*)
	The result is *what we expected* . .	(*Cop.*)

125. Extension: see heading to col. 6. The most typical form is an Adverb. We call this "*extension*," because an adverb, according to the definition given, is a word that adds to or *extends* the meaning of the word with which it is connected.

Two points should be noticed: (1) In the analysis of sentences (not in parsing, which is a different kind of operation), extension applies *only to the Finite verb* of its own clause: if an adverb or adverb-equivalent belongs to any part of a sentence except the Finite verb, it must not be placed in column 6. (2) "Extension" means the same thing as "enlargement." But as one relates to the Finite verb, and the other to the Nominative or its equivalent, it is convenient in analysing sentences to give them separate names.

Enlargement and Extension are sometimes called **Adjunct**, the former being of course adjectival, the latter adverbial.

(1) **Adverb.**—He slept *soundly*.
(2) **Prep. with object.**—He slept *for six hours*.
(3) **Adjective.**—He went away *sad*.
(4) **Participle.**—He went away *disappointed*.
(5) **Qualifying Infin.**—He came *to see* the horse.
(6) **Adverbial objective.**—Bind him *hand and foot*.
(7) **Absolute phrase.**—We all set off, *he remaining behind*.
(8) **Adverb-clause.**—We all set off, *while he remained behind*.

Note.—The student must not be surprised that in (3) an *adjective* is included among forms of extension, the typical form of which is an *adverb*. The word "sad," though an adjective in *form*, is nevertheless adverbial here in *function*. In what manner or in what state of mind did he go away? In a sad state. The word "sad" therefore qualifies the verb "went away" in just the same way as if it were expressed in the form "sadly." The same remark applies to the participle "disappointed" in the fourth sentence. See § 97, *Note* 2.

Analyse each of the following sentences, using the model given in § 119, p. 98, *and say whether it is Simple or Complex.*

1. He was the only son left to his widowed mother.
2. The sun is darting its rays from the edge of that cloud.
3. The king himself was willing to surrender.
4. The firm sent him out on a voyage of discovery.
5. Who steals my purse steals trash.
6. He deserves all the success that he can get.
7. The earnest endeavour of the Czar was to secure peace.
8. He called them up to explain to them his decision.
9. What to say or do at such a time was a puzzle.
10. Sir Isaac Newton explained the ebb and flow of the tides.
11. He that hath ears to hear, let him hear.
12. This is what they call a very modest request.
13. The thief was ordered to be locked up.
14. The night being now far spent, we must go no farther.
15. Thy father and I sought thee sorrowing.
16. It is easy to be wise after the event.
17. Whatever he says is right in his own opinion.
18. I cannot foresee what the consequences will be.
19. They sat themselves down on the bank to rest.
20. Fare thee well!—*Byron*.

21. Why is there so much wailing on board your ship?
22. They found the soldiers encamped on Salisbury Plain.
23. There are very few houses to let in this town.
24. They questioned him eagerly about the voyage.
25. It is never too late to mend.
26. The righteous shall be had in everlasting remembrance.
27. He gave his eldest son the first choice.
28. Praising a man is not always to his benefit.
29. He told me with much sorrow what he had done.
30. I hope soon to take up the study of history.
31. He who complies against his will
Is of the same opinion still.
32. Being so far from her own country, she begged me to take her back in my ship.
33. The above remarks are well worthy of attention.
34. I prefer riding a bicycle to riding a horse.
35. The old woman told him the sad story weeping.
36. One day he went to work in the garden.
37. His father died when he was ten years old.
38. He failed to fulfil his engagement punctually.
39. To place pleasure before duty is the mark of a fool.
40. I never knew any one so difficult to manage.
41. What puzzles me most is his quickness of hand.
42. My friend the carpenter's health has improved since yesterday.
43. The life of a hunter has no attractions for me.
44. He told me how, when, and where to find the thief.
45. I am not able to satisfy your curiosity.
46. Shortly after, he fitted out another ship for himself.
47. Youth and experience seldom exist together.
48. Digging is a very healthy form of exercise.
49. His jealousy for the honour of his calling is commendable.
50. How to answer such a question is beyond me.
51. I will tell you when I feel better.
52. I begin to feel better already.
53. The hope that he will soon recover is groundless.
54. That tree is above a hundred feet high.
55. I cannot satisfy your curiosity.
56. He walked ten miles without once sitting down.
57. What you have still to learn is perseverance.
58. The poor are always amongst us.
59. He ought not to have left his friend in the lurch.
60. How much do these poor men owe you?
61. The sailors overslept themselves next morning.
62. A thief should not go unpunished.
63. We were afloat on the river by 4 o'clock.
64. The result that we had so long waited for is out at last.
65. Though all his friends deserted him, he stood firm.
66. Why are all these men in such a hurry?
67. The innocent often suffer for the guilty.
68. Many of us had no sleep last night.
69. My son has learnt how to ride a bicycle.
70. The proof of the pudding is in the eating.

71. You cannot make a silk purse out of a sow's ear.
72. Two hundred workmen have gone on strike.
73. What you offer to do is not what I want.
74. They appointed him trustee of the estate.
75. The ship having anchored, we can go ashore.
76. Alexander the Great, the son of Philip, conquered the king of Persia.
77. A man to carry my box must be sent for.
78. How he could have made such a mistake is a mystery.
79. There is no happiness without health.
80. A resting place could not be found.
81. What has made him so down-hearted is unknown to us.
82. To work and rest alternately is the common lot of man.
83. He loved nothing but vain and foolish pursuits.
84. He does not deserve to be more liberally treated.
85. Jonathan, the friend of David, refused the kingdom.
86. The excuse he made was not accepted.
87. God's ways are different from ours.
88. All men think all men mortal but themselves.
89. Those days have passed never to return.
90. However much you may try you will not deceive me.
91. He went away meditating on what he had heard.
92. To start in business without capital is almost impossible.
93. The firm have taken me into partnership.
94. On the completion of his schooling he was sent out to one of the colonies.
95. The last voyage of Sir Walter Raleigh was to the Orinoco river.
96. What we have seen is not what we expected.
97. The evil which men do lives after them.
98. The good is oft interred with their bones.

CHAPTER XXVI.—COMPOUND SENTENCES.

126. A **Compound** *sentence is one made up of two or more* **Co-ordinate** (*that is, equal or independent*) *clauses.* See § 111.

Those conjunctions which are used for binding together the different clauses, of which a Compound sentence is made up, are called Co-ordinative.

These conjunctions are distinguished into I. **Cumulative** (adding); II. **Alternative** (offering a choice); III. **Adversative** (contrasting); IV. **Illative** (drawing an inference). The following examples will suffice :—

(1) The sun rose with power, *and* the fog dispersed (*Cumulative.*)
(2) Either he must leave the house *or* I (must leave the house) . . . . (*Alternative.*)
(3) He called at my house, *but* I did not see him . (*Adversative.*)
(4) He came back tired ; *for* he had walked all day (*Illative.*)

127. Co-ordinate clauses can also be joined together by a Relative pronoun or Relative adverb, provided it is used in a co-ordinative or merely continuative sense, and not in a restrictive or qualifying sense.

He met John, *who* was in London at that time . (*Contin.*)
He met the brother, *who* was in London at that time (*Restrict.*)

128. Contracted Sentences.—Compound sentences often appear in a contracted or shortened form, so as to avoid the needless repetition of the same word :—

(*a*) When there are *two Finite verbs to the same Nominative*, the Nominative is not usually mentioned more than once, but it must be repeated in the Analysis :—

(1) The sun *rose* and (the sun) *filled* the sky with light.
(2) He *called* at my house, but (he) *left* soon after.

(*b*) When there are *two Nominatives to the same Finite verb*, the Finite verb is not usually mentioned more than once, but it must be repeated in the Analysis :—

(1) *He* as well as *you* is guilty (=He is guilty as well as you are guilty).
(2) Either *this man* sinned or his *parents* (sinned).
(3) He is poor, but (he is) honest.
(4) He is diligent, and therefore (he is) prosperous.

129. Omission of the Conjunction "and."—The "*and*" can be left out, when the aim of the writer is to give a string of sentences, all bearing upon one central fact. Only the last sentence or the last verb should have "*and*" prefixed to it in such a case.

The uses and power of steam have been thus described, one single word standing as subject to no less than twenty-six Finite verbs :—

What will not the steam-engine do? It propels, elevates, lowers, pumps, drains, pulls, drives, blasts, digs, cuts, saws, planes, bores, blows, forges, hammers, files, polishes, rivets, cards, spins, winds, weaves, coins, prints, *and* does more things than I can think of or enumerate.

Examples of compound sentences analysed.

(1) His greatest enemy as well as his best friends declared him to be innocent of the fault laid to his charge.
(2) Either you or your son will sign his name at once on that paper.
(3) He, not I, is certainly the author of that plan.

The Clauses.	Connective.	I. Subject.		II. Predicate.			
		Nominative or Equivalent.	Enlargement of Nominative.	Finite Verb.	Completion of Finite Verb.		Extension of Finite Verb.
					Object.	Complement.	
His greatest enemy repeatedly declared him to be innocent of the fault, etc.		enemy	his greatest	declared	him	to be innocent of the fault laid to his charge	repeatedly.
His best friends declared him to be innocent of the fault, etc.	as well as	friends	his best	declared	him	to be innocent of the fault, etc.	repeatedly.
You will sign your name at once on that paper.	either	you	*nil*	will sign	your name	*nil*	(*a*) at once (*b*) on that paper.
Your son will sign his name at once on that paper.	or	your son	*nil*	will sign	his name	*nil*	(*a*) at once (*b*) on that paper.
He is certainly the author of that plan.		He	*nil*	is	*nil*	the author of that plan	certainly.
I am not the author of that plan.	[illegible]	I	*nil*	am	*nil*	the author of that plan	not

Exercise 28.—*Compound sentences to be analysed.*

First write out each simple sentence in full (*supplying all the omitted words*), *and then analyse according to the model*:—

1. The Lord knoweth the way of the righteous, but the way of the ungodly shall perish.
2. Little Bo-peep has lost her sheep, and can't tell where to find them.
3. She found them indeed, but it made her heart bleed; for they had left their tails behind them.
4. The hornet is our declared enemy, and a very troublesome one it is; however, it is well to make its acquaintance; for by doing so we shall be forced to admire it, and even to admire the instrument used by it for wounding us.
5. The life of some insects is brief, but very active; the female lives for two or three weeks, lays its eggs, and dies.
6. In wet weather the water rises and floats the eggs of the musquito, producing an abundant harvest; whereas in dry seasons many eggs fail to reach the water, and so dry up and perish.
7. The barbers of Singapore have to shave heads and clean ears; for which latter operation they have a great array of tweezers, picks, and brushes.
8. Others carry a portable cooking-apparatus and serve up a meal of fish, rice, and vegetables for two or three halfpence; while porters and boatmen waiting to be hired are seen on every side.
9. In this way the spider lived in a precarious state for more than a week, and nature seemed to have fitted it for such a life; otherwise it could not have subsisted upon a single fly for so long a time.
10. Howard was then led to inquire into the condition of more distant jails; for which purpose he visited every large jail in England, and many of those in Scotland and Ireland.
11. At Venice he went with the greatest cheerfulness into the sick-house, where he remained as usual for forty days, and thus exposed his life for the sake of his fellow-creatures.
12. The diver, on descending into the water, seizes the rope with the toes of his right foot, and takes hold of the bag with those of his left; nor does he expect to remain under water for less than two minutes.
13. The astrologers promise success to the divers; for they expect a liberal gift of pearls as a reward for the happy sense of confidence imparted by them to those men.
14. Sir Ralph the Rover tore his hair,
And beat his breast in his despair;
The waves rush in on every side,
And the ship sinks down beneath the tide.
15. We had a boat at our stern just before the storm, but she was staved by dashing against the ship's rudder.
16. The ranger in his couch lay warm
And heard him plead in vain;
But oft amid December's storm
He'll hear that voice again.

CHAPTER XXVII.—ANALYSIS OF COMPLEX AND MIXED SENTENCES.

130. Degrees of Subordination.—In complex sentences it often happens that one Subordinate clause is dependent on another Subordinate clause. To show how this works it will be best to give an example :—

(1) The unfortunate man had not long lain in the cavern (*a*) before he heard a dreadful noise, (*b*) which seemed to be the roar of some wild beast, and frightened him very much.

(2) A merchant, who had much property to sell, caused all his goods to be conveyed on camels, as there was no railway in that country.

In sentence (1) the clause "before he heard a dreadful noise" is an adverb-clause qualifying the Finite verb "had lain," which occurs in the Principal clause : it is therefore Subordinate to the Principal clause in the *first* degree, as indicated by a *single* line drawn under it. In the same sentence the clauses "which seemed to be the roar of some wild beast, and frightened him very much," are adjective-clauses qualifying the noun "noise," which occurs in a Subordinate clause : they are therefore Subordinate to the Principal clause in the *second* degree, as indicated by the *two* lines drawn under them. The student will thus understand that what is directly Subordinate to the *Principal* clause is Subordinate in the first degree, and what is Subordinate to a *Subordinate* clause is Subordinate to the Principal clause in the second degree, and so on.

Now take sentence (2). The clause "who had much property to sell" is an adjective-clause qualifying the noun "merchant," which occurs in the Principal clause. It is therefore Subordinate to the Principal clause in the first degree, as indicated by the single line drawn under it. In the same sentence the clause "as there was no railway in that country" is an adverb-clause qualifying the Finite verb "caused," which occurs in the Principal clause. It is therefore Subordinate to the Principal clause in the first degree, as indicated by the single line drawn under it.

The two sentences may be analysed in the following form :—

Clause.	Kind of Clause.	Connective.	I. SUBJECT.		II. PREDICATE.			
			Nominative or Equivalent.	Enlargement of Nominative.	Finite Verb.	Completion of Finite Verb. Object. (1) *Direct.* (2) *Indirect.*	Completion of Finite Verb. Complement.	Extension of Finite Verb.
(1) The unfortunate man had not lain long in the cavern	Principal clause.	..	man	(1) the (2) unfortunate	had lain	..	..	(1) not long (2) in the cavern (3) before he heard, etc.
(*a*) before he heard a dreadful noise	Adv.-clause qualifying "had lain."	before	he	..	heard	a dreadful noise, which, etc.	..	..
(*b*) which seemed to be the roar of some wild beast	Adj.-clause qualifying "noise" in (*a*).	which	which	..	seemed	..	to be the roar of some wild beast	..
and frightened him very much.	Co-ordinate with clause (*b*).	and	(which)	..	frightened	him	..	very much
(2) A merchant caused all his goods to be conveyed on camels,	Principal clause.	..	merchant	(1) a (2) who had much property, etc.	caused	all his goods	to be conveyed on camels,	as there was no railway, etc.
who had much property to sell,	Adj.-clause qualifying "merchant."	who	who	..	had	much property to sell	..	..
as there was no railway in that country.	Adv.-clause qualifying "caused."	as	railway	no	was	..	..	in that country.

131. Mixed Sentences.—We often meet with a sentence which consists of two Co-ordinate clauses, and is therefore compound: but each Co-ordinate clause contains one or more Subordinate clauses. Such sentences are mixed, partly compound and partly complex.

What is obvious is not always known, and what is known is not always present.—JOHNSON.

Here we have *four* Finite verbs, and therefore four clauses. The sentence as a whole is compound, the two parts being combined co-ordinately by the conjunction *and*. But each part contains a Subordinate clause. "What is obvious" is a Noun-clause in the first part, and "what is known" is a Noun-clause in the second part.

Exercise 29.

Miscellaneous sentences to be analysed.

1. Blessed is the man that walketh not in the counsel of the wicked, nor standeth in the way of sinners, nor sitteth in the seat of the scornful.—*Psalm* i. 1.

2. Nothing can describe the confusion of thought which I felt when I sank into the water.—*Robinson Crusoe.*

3. At four o'clock P.M. we reached York, which is a fine old town dating back to the time of the Romans, though they called it by a different name that I cannot now remember.

4. If you put the end of an iron rod in the fire and hold it there, you not only heat the end, but the whole of the rod up to the end that you hold in your hand.—TYNDALL.

5. The elections proved that since the spring the distrust and hatred with which this Government was regarded had made fearful progress.—MACAULAY.

6. These men, than whom I have never known men more unwilling, have suddenly left me, merely because I asked them to work a little overtime on account of certain orders that I unexpectedly received this morning from the Admiralty.

7. Sir Isaac Newton, after deep meditation, discovered that there is a law in nature called attraction, by virtue of which every particle of matter in the world draws towards itself every other particle of matter with a force that is proportionate to its mass and distance.—*Evenings at Home.*

8. Everywhere there is a class of men who cling with fondness to whatever is ancient.

9. When she I loved was strong and gay
And like a rose in June,
I to her cottage bent my way
Beneath the evening moon.—WORDSWORTH.

10. After his schooling was finished, his father desiring him to be a merchant like himself, gave him a ship freighted with various sorts of merchandise, so that he might go and trade about the world, and become a help to his parents who were now advanced in age.

11. I heard a thousand blended notes,
While in a grove I sat reclined
In that sweet mood when pleasant thoughts
Bring sad thoughts to the mind.—WORDSWORTH.

12. Content is a pearl of great price, and whoever procures it at the expense of ten thousand desires, makes a good purchase.

13. The rocks that first meet the eye of the traveller, as he enters the Suez Canal, are a part of the breakwater that extends out into the sea for two miles on either side of the canal.

14. This poor widow hath cast in more than they all: for they cast in of their abundance; but she of her want hath cast in all that she had, even all her living.—*New Test.*

15. Air, when it is heated, expands, or in other words the particles of which it is composed are driven farther and farther apart from one another; and so the air being less dense, less compact, or less solid, becomes proportionately lighter.

16. Our deeds shall travel with us from afar,
And what we have been makes us what we are.—G. ELIOT.

17. Foul deeds will rise,
Though all the earth o'erwhelm them, to men's eyes.—SHAKS.

18. An anonymous letter signifies that the writer lacks moral courage to affix his name, and either cannot or dare not face the contents.

19. Just so we have heard a baby, mounted on the shoulders of its father, cry out, "How much taller I am than papa!"

20. I like a rascal to be punished, when I am quite sure that his guilt has been proved before a jury who had no prejudice against him, before they began hearing his case.

21. The electricity of the air stimulates the vegetation of the trees, and scarcely a week passes before the plants are covered with the larvæ of butterflies, the forest is murmuring with the hum of insects, and the air is harmonious with the voices of birds.—TENNENT'S *Ceylon.*

22. As a goddess she had whims and fancies of her own; and one of these was that no woman was permitted to touch the verge of her mountain or pluck the berries of a certain bush that grew upon the sides.—*Volcano of the Hawaians.*

23. I shun a friend who pronounces my actions to be good when they are bad; but I like a simple and sincere friend, who holds my faults as he would a looking-glass before my face, and compels me to see them.

24. He that bullies those who are not in a position to resist him may be a snob, but cannot be a gentleman.—SMILES.

25. When the eggs have been transformed into the state of larva or caterpillar, they change their skin three times in the course of two or three weeks, each change being preceded by a period of repose and succeeded by one of activity and voracity.

26. Every one who is not blind has seen a butterfly,—that light and happy insect, which flies from flower to flower in fields and gardens, adding brightness and beauty wherever it goes.

27. A time there was, ere England's griefs began,
When every rood of ground maintained its man.—GOLDSMITH.

CHAPTER XXVIII.—CONVERSION OF SENTENCES.

132. From Simple to Compound.—Simple Sentences can be converted into Compound ones of equivalent meaning, by expanding words or phrases into Co-ordinate clauses.

Simple. *Besides making* a promise, he kept it.
Compound. He *not only made* a promise, *but also* kept it.

Simple. He must confess his fault *to escape being fined.*
Compound. He must confess his fault, *or he will be fined.*

Simple. Notwithstanding his sorrow, he is hopeful.
Compound. He *is sorrowful, but yet* hopeful.

Simple. *Owing to* bad health, he could not work.
Compound. *He was* in bad health, *and so* he could not work.

Exercise 30.

Convert from Simple to Compound:—

1. Seeing a bear coming, he fled.
2. Besides myself, every one else declares him to be guilty.
3. Before retiring, he must first serve twenty-five years.
4. After making a great effort, he at last gained his end.
5. In addition to advising them, he helped them liberally.
6. The agreement having been signed, all were satisfied.
7. Drawing his sword, he rushed at the enemy.
8. The judge believes with me in his innocence.
9. The sun having risen, the fog dispersed.
10. He will be dismissed in the event of his doing such a thing again.
11. You must take rest, on pain of losing your health.
12. He fled away, to escape being killed.
13. He escaped punishment by confessing his fault.
14. Approach a step nearer at peril of your life.
15. You must walk two hours a day to preserve your health.
16. For all his riches he is not contented.
17. Notwithstanding all his efforts, he failed to gain his end.
18. In spite of the opposition of all men, he never swerved.
19. In spite of our search, we could not find the book.
20. He had every qualification for success, except quickness of understanding and decision of character.
21. He hated every one but himself.
22. He persevered, in spite of all men being against him.
23. He stuck to his point against every one.
24. Notwithstanding his recent failure, he is still hopeful.
25. He was honoured in virtue of his wealth.
26. He worked night and day, being desirous to excel.
27. He was taken ill through grief at the loss of his son.
28. By means of his great wealth, he was able to build himself a fine house.
29. He spoke the truth from fear of the disgrace of falsehood.
30. The letter, having been addressed to the wrong house, never reached me.
31. To our great disappointment, we failed to carry out our purpose.
32. To add to his difficulties, he lost his health.

33. The fog being very dense, we were forced to halt.
34. St. Paul continued preaching at Rome, no man forbidding him.

133. From Compound to Simple, as in the following:—

(*a*) By substituting a Participle for a Finite verb:—

Compound. The sun rose, and the fog dispersed.
Simple. The sun having risen, the fog dispersed.

(*b*) By substituting a Preposition, etc., for a clause:—

Compound. He not only made a promise, but kept it.
Simple. Besides making a promise, he kept it.

(*c*) By substituting a Gerundial Infinitive for a clause:—

Compound. He must confess his fault or he will be fined.
Simple. He must confess his fault to escape being fined.

Exercise 31.

Convert from Compound to Simple:—

1. An ass accidentally found a lion's skin, and put it on to frighten the other beasts.
2. He was fatigued with walking, and so he sat down to take a little rest.
3. Turn to the left and you will find the house of your friend.
4. Not only the tank, but even a part of the river was frozen over with ice.
5. The judge, as well as the jury, believed the prisoner to be guilty.
6. You must work hard the whole term, and then you will get promotion.
7. He was the son of poor parents, and therefore he had to encounter many trials and difficulties at the outset of his career.
8. He was a poor man, and yet he was of an independent spirit at all times.
9. I advised him to make the best use of his time, but he paid no heed.
10. He was much frightened, but not much hurt.
11. Every effort was made to check the spread of cholera; yet a large number of persons died.
12. He was well fitted for that post by character and attainments; only he was rather too young and inexperienced.
13. He did his best to be punctual, but still he was occasionally behind time.
14. He is well versed in books, but wanting in common sense.
15. You must work hard, or you will not get promotion.
16. Give us some clear proofs of your assertion, otherwise no one will believe you.
17. A certain fowler fixed his net on the ground, and scattered a great many grains of rice about it.
18. The pigeons flew down to pick up the rice grains; for they were all hungry.
19. The old man frequently begged his sons to live together in peace, but he was disregarded.

134. From Simple to Complex.—Simple sentences can be converted to complex ones, by expanding words or phrases into subordinate clauses.

(*a*) *Noun-Clause.*

Simple. I am certain *of giving* you satisfaction.
Complex. I am certain *that I shall give* you satisfaction.

(*b*) *Adjective-Clause.*

Simple. He paid off *his father's debts.*
Complex. He paid off the debts *which his father had contracted.*

(*c*) *Adverb-Clause.*

Simple. *On reaching manhood* you will have to work for your living.

Complex. *As soon as you have reached manhood,* you will have to work for your living.

Exercise 32.

Convert from Simple Sentence to Complex:—

1. I was glad to hear of your having succeeded so well.
2. He is generally believed to have died of poison.
3. No one can tell the time of his coming.
4. He shouted to his neighbours to come to his help.
5. We can place no confidence in any of his words.
6. The usefulness of even the simplest weapons to men in the savage state will easily be understood.
7. We must hope for better times.
8. Tell me the time and place of your birth.
9. The verdict of the judge was in favour of the accused.
10. Our present house suits us exactly.
11. This rule, the source of all our troubles, is disliked by every one.
12. The diamond-field is not far from here.
13. He and his friend entered into a partnership binding themselves to incur equal risks.
14. Their explanation cannot be true.
15. The king took refuge in the fortress, being determined to make a last attempt in that place to save his kingdom.
16. He was a man of irreproachable conduct.
17. The snow-line in India is about 20,000 feet high.
18. The troubles besetting him on all sides did not daunt him.
19. In the absence of any other helper, we must accept his aid.
20. The two chief points having been gained, success is now certain.
21. The problem was too difficult to be solved.
22. He worked very well, to the astonishment of every one.
23. Every precaution was taken against the failure of the plan.
24. They proceeded very cautiously for fear of being caught.
25. He started by night to escape being seen by any one.
26. He would be very thankful to be relieved of all this trouble.
27. With or without his leave, I shall leave the room.
28. Notwithstanding the heat of the sun we must go out.
29. In spite of all his riches, he is never contented.

135. From Complex to Simple.

I. *Noun-clause.*

(*a*) By substituting a noun for the Noun-clause introduced by the Conjunction "that":—

Complex. It is sad that he died so young.
Simple. His death at so young an age is sad.

(*b*) By substituting a noun for the Noun-clause introduced by a Conjunctive adverb:—

Complex. Tell me when and where you were born.
Simple. Tell me the time and place of your birth.

(*c*) By substituting a noun for the Noun-clause introduced by a Conjunctive pronoun:—

Complex. We need not disbelieve what he said.
Simple. We need not disbelieve his word.

Exercise 33.

1. What he spoke on that occasion was unworthy a man of his age and experience.
2. That the rose is the sweetest and most beautiful of flowers is admitted by almost every one.
3. They are now ready to confess that the charge against my friend was groundless.
4. Even his friends admitted that what his enemies complained of was just and reasonable.
5. What we have learnt already is a step towards learning what we do not at present know.
6. They admit that Milton was a great poet, but deny that he was a good man.
7. What seemed most strange in the battle of Plassey was that the Nawab's immense army should have been defeated by so small a force, and that the victory on the English side should have been so decisive.
8. I should like to be informed what character in English history you most admire.
9. I will now be bold enough to confess what my heart desires and how I shall obtain it.
10. From what you have read in this book, you have become acquainted with the state in which the Saxons were living, when the Normans arrived under William the Conqueror.
11. You will easily understand from what you have been told how much this book has displeased me by its bad teaching.

II. *The Adjective-clause.*

(*a*) By using some adjective or participle:—

Complex. Such pupils as work hard may win a prize.
Simple. Hard-working pupils may win a prize.

(*b*) By using a noun or pronoun in the Possessive case ;—

Complex. They soon forgot the labours they had endured.
Simple. They soon forgot *their* past labours.

(*c*) By using a noun in apposition :—

Complex. This rule, from which all our troubles have come, is much disliked.
Simple. This rule, the source of all our troubles, is much disliked.

(*d*) By using a Preposition with its object :—

Complex. The benefits that he derived from his early training were soon lost.
Simple. The benefits of his early training were soon lost.

(*e*) By using a Gerundial Infinitive :—

Complex. I have no money that I can spare.
Simple. I have no money to spare.

(*f*) By using a Compound noun :—

Complex. That is the place where my father was buried.
Simple. That was my father's burial-place.

Exercise 34.

1. The explanation he gave was not to the point.
2. The year in which the school was opened was 1884.
3. Let us take a walk into the grove that adjoins my father's house.
4. The army that Hannibal led against Rome was the most formidable that the Romans had up to that time encountered.
5. He was not fully aware of the extent of the dangers by which he was surrounded.
6. Mary Queen of Scots was the most unfortunate of all the sovereigns of that part of the century in which she lived.
7. The whole plan was upset by the course which affairs took after the 24th of May.
8. We decided on building a cottage in the vale that is watered by a streamlet which flows from a perennial fountain.
9. The people of Israel mourned in the land to which they had been taken captive.
10. The temple of Solomon was built on the site which David had taken from the Jebusites who were its former masters.
11. There was no rope whereby the boat might be tied to the river's bank.
12. The intelligence that the lower animals display in the search for food, and in the preservation of their young, is something very different from what is called a blind instinct.
13. You are not the kind of man who would tell an untruth for the sake of an advantage that would be merely temporary.
14. This is a rule that must not be violated by any one, and admits of no variation.

III. *Adverb-clause.*

(*a*) By using a preposition or prepositional phrase :—

Complex. The boy was pleased that he had won a prize.
Simple. The boy was pleased at having won a prize.

(*b*) By using a participle :—

Complex. As the main point has been gained, success is certain.
Simple. The main point having been gained, success is certain.

(*c*) By using a Gerundial (or Qualifying) Infinitive :—

Complex. They were surprised, when they heard him confess.
Simple. They were surprised to hear him confess.

Exercise 35.

1. He drew the plan of the building more skilfully than any one else could have done it.
2. They were much alarmed, when they saw that their position was hopeless.
3. The king or queen cannot impose taxes, unless the Parliament consents or approves.
4. If a man puts on the appearance of honesty, he can sometimes pass for honest.
5. Though he is a man of years and experience, he is still apt to be imprudent and thoughtless when some sudden emergency occurs.
6. The speaker declared he had changed his mind on that subject, so that the audience were much surprised and distressed.
7. As the sun has set, we had better start for home.
8. These men suspect that I am a swindler.
9. When the fire was put out and the inmates of the house rescued, the firemen removed the pumps, so that they might take a little rest.
10. As the judge has already decided the case, further defence is useless.
11. His mother will be much consoled, when she sees that her son has escaped from so many dangers.
12. I should be indeed sorry, if I were the cause of your ruin or stood in the way of your advancement.
13. He spoke so rapidly that we could not clearly understand him.
14. There is no branch of knowledge so difficult that it cannot be conquered by perseverance.
15. The rope in your hand is so long, that it will touch the bottom of the well, if a stone is tied to the end of it.
16. He was not so courageous, that he was willing to ride that spirited horse.
17. The moment I saw how industriously and patiently he worked, I decided that I would secretly give him some pecuniary help that very day.
18. He made such an excellent speech in defence of his friend, that every one admired and respected him.

136. From Compound to Complex.—In a Compound sentence the second of two co-ordinate clauses is the one that completes the sense, and is therefore the more important of the two.

Hence it follows that in transforming a Compound sentence to a Complex one, the *second* must be made the *Principal* or *Containing* clause, and the *first* the *Dependent* or *Contained* clause.

Compound. Speak the truth, *and* you need have no fear.
Complex. *If* you speak the truth, you need have no fear.

Compound. Leave this room, *or* I will compel you to do so.
Complex. *Unless* you leave this room, I will compel you to do so.

Compound. He was a poor man, *but* he was always honest.
Complex. He was always honest, *although* he was poor.

Compound. He was very tired, and *therefore* he fell sound asleep.
Complex. He fell sound asleep, *because* he was very tired.

Exercise 36.

Convert from Compound to Complex:—

1. Hand over the prisoner to me, and I will examine him.
2. Take care of the pence, and the pounds will take care of themselves.
3. Only hold your tongue, and you can hold anything else.
4. He stands up to speak, and every one is at once silent.
5. Is any man sick? let the elders pray for him.
6. I go to this place and that, and the same thought pursues me everywhere.
7. He confessed his fault, or he would have been punished.
8. Sign your name, or I shall not agree to this.
9. You must be careful of your money, or you will soon lose it.
10. Conquer thy desires, or they will conquer thee.
11. He is sixty years old, and yet he still has good sight.
12. Murder has no tongue, but it will some day speak.
13. All men were against him; nevertheless he persevered.
14. He might be ever so rich; yet he was greedy for more.
15. Go wherever you like, only you must not stay here.
16. In the discharge of duty he was a strict, but just man.
17. I thoroughly dislike that man, and therefore I cannot admire him.
18. It is now late; so we had better go to bed.
19. My son's health was bad last year, and hence he was not promoted at the end of the term.
20. Food is raised by agriculture, which is therefore the foundation of all wealth.
21. My son has never done such a thing before: he should therefore be pardoned.

137. From Complex to Compound.—In a Complex sentence the Principal or Containing clause is, as its name implies, of more importance than the Subordinate or Contained clause.

Hence it follows that in transforming a Complex sentence to Compound, the Principal clause must be placed last, and the

Subordinate (which now becomes a Co-ordinate) clause must be placed first.

Complex.	I am certain that he will not recover.
Compound.	He will not recover, and of this I am certain.
Complex.	I have found the sheep that I had lost.
Compound.	I had lost a sheep, but I have found it again.
Complex.	He is more a fool than a knave.
Compound.	He is something of a knave, but still more a fool.

Exercise 37.

Convert from Complex to Compound:—

1. You may keep this book, since you have earned it as a prize.
2. He will pay off all his debts in time, if only his creditors will have patience.
3. The enemy fled as soon as our guns came in sight.
4. Every man howled with pain, as he took his turn of the lash.
5. When you have worked out this sum, you may go out to play.
6. Could I but see that wonderful object, I would believe in its existence.
7. As soon as the trumpet sounded, the battle commenced.
8. He left for home yesterday as soon as he received that letter.
9. We selected this boy as the best in the class, after we had examined all of them.
10. He could do this, if he tried.
1. If our king should be slain on the battlefield, we still have his son to lead us against our enemies.
12. Though you may not be able to conquer, I exhort you to fight bravely to the last.
13. Brave as he is, he has few men around him, and may be defeated.
14. Grievous words stir up anger, though a soft answer turneth away wrath.—*Old Testament.*
15. Though the waves dash ever so high, the ship will not be lost.
16. If you do not hold your peace, you will be fined.
17. Unless he speaks the truth in your behalf, you will not be acquitted.
18. If we had helped him in the time of need, he would now be ready to give help to us.
19. If I had known the extent of his demand, I would not have promised to pay him.
20. Unless he works hard and in earnest, he will be certainly plucked.
21. If he buys that house, he will run into debt.
22. I must begin my book with a preface as other writers do.
23. Now that every one is convinced of your honesty, you are free to go.
24. Those bags should be carefully guarded, as every one is trying to steal them.
25. He worked hard, as he had an object to work for.
26. He was taken very ill, because he had lost his only son.
27. He spoke the truth, because he feared the disgrace of falsehood.

CHAPTER XXIX.—SEQUENCE OF TENSES: DIRECT AND INDIRECT SPEECH.

138. Sequence of Tenses.—There are two main rules :—

I. A Past tense in the Principal sentence must be followed by a Past tense in the Dependent sentence :—

He *would* come, if you *wished* it.
He *succeeded*, because he *worked* hard.
He *worked* hard, that he *might* succeed.

Exceptions.—(1) If the verb in the Dependent sentence expresses some *universal* or *habitual* fact, it is in the Present tense :—

They *did* not know, that the earth *moves* round the sun.

(2) After "than" the verb can be in the Present or Future tense; in fact, in any tense that expresses the sense intended :—

He *liked* you better than he *likes* me.
He *liked* you better than he *will like* me.

II. A Present or Future tense in the Principal sentence can be followed by any tense whatever in the Dependent sentence :—

I *know* that he *was* angry.
I *shall* soon get the letter that he *posted* yesterday.

Excercise 38.

(*a*) *Correct or justify the following* :—

1. I was informed that he *had been reading* a book. 2. He did not say when he *will come*. 3. No one knew whether he *intended* to come or not. 4. He concealed from me what his plans *are*. 5. I fear that you *were* displeased with me yesterday. 6. I shall soon find out why you *were* so displeased. 7. His face was so changed that I *do* not know him again. 8. The teacher gave me a prize that I *may work* hard next year. 9. The teacher has given me a prize that I *may work* hard next year. 10. You will be pleased to hear that I *have won* a prize. 11. He asked me why I *wish* to go away so soon. 12. No one understood how he *can* do so much work. 13. He had come that he *might* help me to finish the task. 14. You did not tell me when you *intend* to return home. 15. I was sorry to find that I *have displeased* you. 16. I hope that you *will pardon* me soon. 17. I did not know why you *give* me this order. 18. We shall soon know what progress he *has made*. 19. We heard to-day what progress he *has made*. 20. You never told us that honesty *was* the best policy.

(*b*) *Supply the tense and voice of the verbs enclosed in brackets.*

1. I hope that you (return) soon. 2. If you (foresee) the consequences of idleness, you (be) more industrious than you were last term. 3. He tried how many miles he (can) walk in an hour. 4. He (go)

away for a change, as soon as the holidays begin. 5. He not (go) away till the work of the term was over. 6. The oxen (low) so loud, that the thieves (can) not prevent us from finding out the place where they had hidden them. 7. He is so disappointed with the result that he (decide) to give up all further trial. 8. I went to his house that I (see) him and tell him all that (happen). 9. It was very unlikely that he (reach) before six o'clock P.M. 10. There was a rumour that he (perished) in the fire, which (break) out in the village yesterday. 11. I am sorry that you (keep) waiting so long last night. 12. I signed my name on the understanding that you (keep) your engagement with me; but I am sorry to see that you not (do) so. 13. Your son has turned out more industrious than I (expect) he (will). 14. To-morrow you (do) what I (do) to-day, and to-day you (do) what I (do) yesterday. 15. We never (see) such fine batting before, and perhaps we never (see) the like again. 16. Though he (gain) one prize already, he is willing to begin working for another. 17. The tradesman's voice trembled so much that my suspicions (arouse). 18. I gave him no answer lest I (make) him more angry than ever. 19. The more money he made, the more he (want). 20. Though he is a poor man, he never (resort) to anything dishonest. 21. He came upon me as suddenly as if he (drop) from the sky. 22. I hope you (make) up your mind that such a thing never (happen) again. 23. It made no difference to him how we (carry) on our business; for he (be) not one of our partners, and we (will) not take him into partnership, if he (ask) us.

139. Direct and Indirect Speech.—A speech is said to be in *Direct* Narration, when the very words used by the speaker are repeated without any change; in *Indirect*, when the words are given with some change of construction.

In Indirect Narration the verbs are bound by the same rules as those given in § 138 for the Sequence of Tenses.

Thus by Rule I., when the reporting or principal verb is in the Past tense, the Present tense in the reported speech must be changed into its corresponding Past form. Thus we change—

Shall	into	*should*	*See*	into	*saw*
Will	,,	*would*	*Is seeing*	,,	*was seeing*
May	,,	*might*	*Has seen*	,,	*had seen*
Can	,,	*could*	*Has been seeing*	,,	*had been seeing*

Observe also that when the Present tense is changed into the Past by Rule I., an adjective or adverb expressing *nearness* is similarly changed into one expressing *distance*. Thus we change:—

Now	into	*then*	*To-day*	into	*that day*
This or *these*	,,	*that* or *those*	*To-morrow*	,,	*next day*
Hither	,,	*thither*	*Yesterday*	,,	*the previous day*
Here	,,	*there*	*Last night*	,,	*the previous night*
Hence	,,	*thence*	*Ago*	,,	*before*
Thus	,,	*so*			

Direct.—"What *is this* strange outcry?" said Socrates; "I *sent* the women away mainly in order that they might not offend in *this* way; for I *have heard* that a man should die in peace. *Be* quiet then and *have* patience."

Indirect.—Socrates *inquired* of them what *that* strange outcry *was*. He *reminded* them that he *had sent* the women away mainly in order that they might not offend in *that* way; for he *had heard* that a man should die in peace. He *begged* them therefore *to be* quiet and *have* patience.

Exercise 39.

(*a*) *Convert from Direct to Indirect*:—

1. He said, "I have been very ill, but am now better."

2. Pilate replied to the Jews, "What I have written, I have written."

3. He said to me, "You are guilty, and I am innocent."

4. They said, "The boy is hiding in the place where we left him."

5. They said, "The boy will soon be found; and we will bring him."

6. "What do you mean?" asked the man; "how can a rope be used for binding flour?" "A rope may be used for anything," said the other, "when I do not wish to lend it."

7. A rich man once said to his poorer brother, "Why do you not enter the service of the king, so that you may be relieved of the baseness of labour?"

8. Finding no remedy, he said to himself, "It is better to die than to live in such misery as I am compelled to suffer from a master who treats me and always has treated me so unkindly."

9. And they said one to another, "We are verily guilty concerning our brother, in that we saw the anguish of his soul, when he besought us, and we would not hear: therefore is this distress come upon us."—*Old Testament.*

10. The violent man said, "What violence have I done? What anger have I been guilty of?" Then the others laughed and said to him, "Why should we speak? You have given us ocular proof of your violent temper."

11. The robber said to Alexander, "I am thy captive: I must hear what thou art pleased to say, and endure what thou art pleased to inflict. But my soul is unconquered; and if I reply at all to thy reproaches, I will reply to thee like a free man."

12. "You are old, Father William," the young man cried,
"The locks that are left you are grey;
You are hale, Father William, a hale old man;
Now tell me the reason, I pray."

13. "I am sorry indeed," replied the king, "that my vessel is already chosen; and I cannot therefore sail with the son of the man who served my father."—DICKENS.

14. He cried to them in agony, "Row back at any risk! I cannot bear to leave her behind to be drowned."—DICKENS.

15. He made a promise to the king's surgeon, saying:—"Bleed

the king to death with this lancet, and I will give you a thousand pieces of gold; and when I ascend the throne, you shall be my chief minister."

(*b*) *Convert from Indirect to Direct:—*

1. My brother told me that he had been reading all day.
2. My father told me that I was wrong and would be fined.
3. I replied that if my fault was proved I would pay the fine.
4. I admitted that I had acted foolishly in what I had done.
5. Damon, before his execution, requested but one favour from Dionysius, which was that he might be permitted to visit his wife and children, who were at that time a considerable distance from him, and he promised faithfully to return on the day appointed.
6. This Dionysius refused to grant, unless some person could be found who would consent to suffer death in his stead, if he did not perform his promise and return by the appointed time.
7. In a short speech Pythias told the surrounding multitude that his dear friend, Damon, would soon arrive; but he hoped not before his own death had saved a life so dear as Damon's was to his family, his friends, and his country.
8. He sent his compliments to Francis, Clavering, and Monson, and charged them to protect Raja Guru Das, who was about to become the head of the Brahmins of Bengal.
9. The governor of the town then called out with a loud voice, and ordered Androcles to explain to them how a savage and hungry lion could thus in a moment have forgotten its innate disposition, and be converted all of a sudden into a harmless animal.
10. Androcles then explained to them that that very lion, which was standing before them, had been his friend and partner in the woods, and had for that reason spared his life, as they then saw.
11. Socrates then suggested to Glaucon that the entire abolition of the guards which he (Glaucon) recommended could not remedy the evils which he desired to remove, and he inquired of Glaucon whether he knew by personal examination that the guards did their work as badly as he imagined.
12. When he reached home, his father asked him where his ship was and what had become of his merchandise. The son in reply told him what had happened,—how he had given up his vessel with its cargo, and had taken in exchange the slaves and set them free, and how he had consented to take this girl back with him and make her his wife.
13. When they asked Thales what thing in the world was more universal than anything else, he replied that Hope was the most universal thing, because Hope remained with those who had nothing else left.
14. When Solon and Periander were sitting together over their cups, Periander, finding that Solon was more silent than usual, asked him whether he was silent for want of words or because he was a fool. Solon told him in reply that no fool could be silent over his cups.

PART V.—ANALYSIS AND DERIVATION OF WORDS: SOUNDS AND SPELLINGS.

CHAPTER XXX.—COMPOUND WORDS.

140. Simple words.—A word that is not combined with any other word or syllable is called a Simple or Primary word; such as *buy, walk, come* (verbs); *bench, fire, name* (nouns); *hot, cold, stiff* (adjectives).

141. Compounds, Derivatives.—Most of our words, however, are not Simple, but either Compounds or Derivatives.

When one *word* is added to another, the combination is called a **Compound**; as *man-kind.*

When a *particle* (*i.e.* a syllable which does not make a complete word, or is not *now* used as one) is added to a word, the combination is called a **Derivative**; as *man-ly.*

If one Simple word is formed from another by means of some internal change, as *graze* from *grass, bleed* from *blood, raise* from *rise*, this is called a **Primary** Derivative; but a Derivative formed by adding a particle to the beginning or end of a word, as "man-*ly*," "*un*-man-*ly*," is called **Secondary**.

142. Compounds.—Such words fall into four main classes:—

(1) *Noun Compounds.*

(1) *Adjective + Noun:* blue-bell, mid-day, sweet-heart, noble-man.
(2) *Noun + Noun:* noon-tide, plough-man, sports-man, rail-road.
(3) *Pronoun + Noun:* he-goat, she-goat, she-ass.
(4) *Verb + Noun:* tell-tale, dare-devil, pick-pocket, break-fast.
(5) *Verb + Adverb:* keep-sake, break-down, stand-still, draw-back.
(6) *Adverb + Verb:* out-come, off-spring, out-lay, in-come.
(7) *Adverb + Noun:* by-path, after-life, up-land, in-land, over-coat.

(2) *Adjective Compounds.*

(1) *Noun + Adject.:* sky-blue, blood-red, foot-sore, air-tight.
(2) *Adject. + Adject.:* red-hot, high-born, blue-green, ready-made.
(3) *Prep. + Noun:* over-land, under-hand, over-hand.

(3) *Verb Compounds.*

(1) *Noun + Verb:* back-bite, way-lay, hen-peck, brow-beat.
(2) *Adject. + Verb:* white-wash, rough-hew, safe-guard, rough-shoe (chiefly seen in the participial form "rough-shod").
(3) *Adverb + Verb:* back-slide, over-awe, up-set, with-hold.
(4) *Verb + Adverb:* doff (do off), don (do on), turn out, put on.

(4) *Adverb Compounds.*

(1) *Adject. + Noun:* mean-time, other-wise, mid-way, yester-day.
(2) *Adverb + Prep.:* here-in, forth-with, there-for(e), here-upon.
(3) *Noun + Noun:* length-ways, side-ways.

CHAPTER XXXI.—DERIVATIVES.

143. Root, Stem, Prefixes, Suffixes.—A word reduced to its simplest etymological form, is called a **Root**.

A **Stem** is the change of form (if any) assumed by the root, before a suffix is added to it. Thus in the word "fals-i-ty" the root is *fals* (Lat. *fals*-us); the stem is *falsi;* and the suffix is *ty*. The stem and the root, however, often coincide; as in *man* (root or stem) + *ly* (suffix).

Particles added to the *end* of a stem are called **Suffixes**. Those added to the *beginning* are called **Prefixes**. The name "Affix" stands for either, though more commonly used for Suffix.

As a general rule Prefixes alter the meanings of words, while Suffixes show to what Part of Speech they belong. Thus there is a very radical difference of meaning between "*pre*-scribe," to order, and "*pro*-scribe," to prohibit. Again "dark-*ness*" is a noun, "dark-*ly*" is an adverb, "dark-*en*" is a verb.

144. Sources of Prefixes and Suffixes.—The three sources from which our Prefixes and Suffixes have come are:—

I. Teutonic (Anglo-Saxon, with a few Norse and Dutch). These are sometimes, but wrongly, called "English."

II. Romanic (Latin or French, with a few Spanish and Italian).

III. Greek (borrowed either directly or through French).

145. Hybrids.—The name "hybrid" (which means "of mixed origin") is applied to any Compound or Derivative word, whose parts have come from different sources, *i.e.* are neither purely Teutonic, nor purely Romanic, nor purely Greek. Hybrids are very common in our language.

Thus in *en-dear* the prefix is Romanic, the stem is Teutonic. In *starv-ation* the stem is Teutonic, the suffix is Romanic. In *be-siege* the stem is Romanic, the prefix is Teutonic. In *false-hood* the stem is Romanic, the suffix is Teutonic. In *bi-cycle* the stem is Greek, the prefix is Romanic. In *art-ist* the stem is Romanic, the suffix is Greek.

SECTION 1.—SUFFIXES: TEUTONIC, ROMANIC, GREEK.

146. Noun-forming.—We may classify the principal suffixes under the following headings:—

(*a*) Denoting agent, doer, or one appointed to act:—

Teutonic:—

-er, **-ar**, **-or** (modern forms of A.S. *-ere*): bak-*er*, do-*er*, li-*ar*, tail-*or*, London-*er*, law-y-*er*, saw-y-*er*.

-ther, **-der** (A.S. *-ther*, *-der*): fa-*ther*, bro-*ther*, daugh-*ter*, spi(n)-*der*.

Romanic:—

-or, **-eur** (Latin *-or*, *-ator*, French *-eur*): aggress-*or*, doct-*or*, amat-*eur*, emper-*or*, cens-*or*, specul-*ator*.

-ary, **-aire**, **-ar**, **-eer**, **-ier** (Latin *-arius*, *-aris*): secret-*ary*, million-*aire*, schol-*ar*, volunt-*eer*, cash-*ier*, brigad-*ier*.

-an, **-ain**, **-en**, **-ian**, **-on** (Latin *-anus*): public-*an*, capt-*ain*, citiz-*en*, guard-*ian*, sext-*on*.

-ant, **-ent** (Latin *-antem*, *-entem*): merch-*ant*, tru-*ant*, ten-*ant*, combat-*ant*; stud-*ent*, rod-*ent*, cli-*ent*.

-ate (Latin *-atus*, *-atem*): candid-*ate*, magistr-*ate*, prim-*ate*.

-ee, **-ey**, **-y** (French *-é*, from Latin *-atus*): deput-*y*, jur-*y*, attorn-*ey*, grand-*ee*, employ-*é*.

-ive, **-iff** (Latin *-ivus*, Fr. *-if*): fugit-*ive*, mot-*ive*; plaint-*iff*, bail-*iff*.

Greek:—

-ist, **-ast** (Greek *-ist-es*, *-ast-es*): soph-*ist*, art-*ist*, psalm-*ist*, botan-*ist*, nihil-*ist*; enthusi-*ast*.

-ot (Greek *-ot-es*): patri-*ot*, zeal-*ot*, idi-*ot*, Iscari-*ot*.

-ite, **-it** (Greek *-it-es*): Israel-*ite*, erem-*ite*, herm-*it*, Jesu-*it*.

(*b*) Marking the Feminine gender:—

Teutonic:—

-ster (A.S. *-es-tre*), **-en** (A.S. *-en*): spin-*ster*, vix-*en* (Fem. of "fox").

Romanic:—

-ess (Latin *-ix*, French *-esse*): testatr-*ix*, shepherd-*ess*.

Note.—"Sultan-*a*," "donn-*a*." Here the *a* is Italian.

Greek:—

-ine (Greek *in-e*, French *-ine*): hero-*ine*, czar-*ina*.

(*c*) Diminutives (denoting smallness, endearment, contempt):—

Teutonic:—

-en (A.S. *-en*): maid-*en*, chick-*en*.

-ing, **-ling** (A.S. *-ing*, *-el+ing*); farth-*ing*, tith-*ing*; hire-*ling*, duck-*ling*.

-kin (Dutch *-ken*): fir-*kin*, nap-*kin*.

-ock, **-k** (A.S. *-uc*, *-c*): bull-*ock*, hill-*ock*, stir-*k* (little steer).

-y, **-ey**, **-ie** (A.S. *-ig*): bab-*y*, Tomm-*y*, Charl-*ey*, bird-*ie*, lass-*ie*.

-el, **-le**, **-l** (A.S. *-el*): hov-*el*, bund-*le*, freck-*le*, gir-*l*.

-erel, **-rel** (A.S. *-er+el*): cock-*erel*, mong-*rel*, dogg-*erel* (?).

-ster (A.S. *es-tre*): trick-*ster*, pun-*ster*, young-*ster*, rhyme-*ster*.

Romanic:—

-aster (Lat. *-aster*, cf. A.S. *-estre*): ole-*aster*, pil-*aster*, poet-*aster*.

-ule, **-le** (Lat. *-ulus*): pill-*ule*, sched-*ule*; circ-*le* (hence circ-*ul*-ar).

-cule, **-cle** (Lat. *-cu-lus*, Fr. *-cle*): animal-*cule*, pinna-*cle*.

-el, **-le**, **-l**, **-elle** (Lat. *-ellus*): dams-*el*, cast-*le*, vea-*l*, bagat-*elle*, vermi-c-*elli*, umbr-*ella*, violon-c-*ello* (Ital.).

-et, **-ot**, **-ette** (Fr. *-et*, fem. *-ette*; Ital. *-etto*): lock-*et*, lanc-*et*; ball-*ot*; brun-*ette*, cigar-*ette*; stil-*etto*.

-let (Double suffix, *-el+et*): brook-*let*, rivu-*let*, ham-*let*, cut-*let*.

-ito (Span. *-ito*): negr-*ito*, mosqu-*ito*.

Greek:—

-isk (Gr. *-iscos*): aster-*isk*, obel-*isk*.

(*d*) Augmentatives (denoting greatness, or excess to a fault):—

Romanic:—

-ard, **-art** (Low Lat. *-ardus*): drunk-*ard*, wiz-*ard*, bragg-*art*.

-oon, **-on**, **-one** (Fr. *-on*, Ital. *-one*): ball-*oon*, flag-*on*, tromb-*one*.

(*e*) Abstract suffixes (denoting act, state, quality, etc.):—

Teutonic:—

-dom (A.S. *dóm*): free-*dom*, martyr-*dom*, earl-*dom*.

-hood, **-head** (A.S. *hád*): man-*hood*, priest-*hood*, maiden-*head*.

-lock, **-ledge** (A.S. *lác*): wed-*lock*, know-*ledge*.

-red (A.S. *réd*): hat-*red*, kind-*red*.

-ric (A.S. *rice*): bishop-*ric*.

-ness (A.S. *-nis*, *-nes*): dark-*ness*, aloof-*ness*, holi-*ness*.

-ship (A.S. *scipe*): friend-*ship*, wor-*ship*, owner-*ship*.

-t, **-th** (A.S. *-ith*): leng-*th*, tru-*th*, heigh-*t*, ligh-*t*, sigh-*t*.

-ter, **-der** (A.S. *-ther*, *-der*): slaugh-*ter*, laugh-*ter*, mur-*der*.

Romanic:—

-age (Fr. *-age*): cour-*age*, hom-*age*, umbr-*age*, bond-*age*.

-al (Fr. *-aille*): refus-*al*, tri-*al*, surviv-*al*, bestow-*al*.

-ance, **-ence**, **-ancy**, **-ency** (Lat. *-antia*, *-entia*): dist-*ance*, prud-*ence*, guid-*ance*, const-*ancy*, urg-*ency*.

-cy, **-acy** (Lat. *-tia*): cur-*acy*, prel-*acy*, secre(t)-*cy*, idiot-*cy*.

-ice, **-ise**, **-ess** (Lat. *-itia*, Fr. *-esse*): serv-*ice*, exerc-*ise*, prow-*ess*.

-ion (Lat. *-ionem*): relig-*ion*, fash-*ion*, suspic-*ion*, relat-*ion*.

-ment (Lat. *-mentum*): enjoy-*ment*, fer-*ment*, attach-*ment*.

-mony (Lat. *-monia*, or *-monium*): parsi-*mony*, matri-*mony*.
-or, -our, -eur (Lat. *-or*, Fr. *-eur*): err-*or*, fav-*our*, grand-*eur*.
-ry, -ery (Fr. *-rie, -erie*): slave-*ry*, trick-*ery*, brave-*ry*.
-tude (Lat. *-tudo*): forti-*tude*, longi-*tude*, magni-*tude*.
-ty (Lat. *-tas*, Fr. *-té*): cruel-*ty*, certain-*ty*, frail-*ty*.
-ure (Lat. *-ura*): seiz-*ure*, cult-*ure*, capt-*ure*, us-*ury*.
-y (Lat. *-ia, -ium*): infam-*y*, stud-*y*, perjur-*y*.

Greek:—

-ism, -asm (Gr. *-ismos, -asmos*): optim-*ism*, euthusi-*asm*.
-y (Gr. *-ia*): monarch-*y*, energ-*y*, sympath-*y*.

(*f*) Collective (denoting a collection, or the place of one):—

Romanic:—

-ade (Fr. *-ade*): arc-*ade*, colonn-*ade*, balustr-*ade*.
-age (Fr. *-age*): foli-*age*, plum-*age*, vill-*age*, cott-*age*.
-ry, -ery (Fr. *-rie, -erie*): tenant-*ry*, rook-*ery*, gent-*ry*.
-ory (Lat. *-orium*): dormit-*ory*, fact-*ory*, invent-*ory*.
-ary (Lat. *-arium*): gran-*ary*, libr-*ary*, gloss-*ary*.

(*g*) Miscellaneous suffixes, not included in the above:—

Teutonic:—

-m, -om (A.S. *-m, -ma*): bloo-*m* (from *blow*), doo-*m* (from *do*), bes-*om*.
-nd, -and (A.S. Pres. Part. ending): frie-*nd*, wi-*nd*, husba-*nd*.
-ow, -w (A.S. *-u, -we*): mead-*ow*, shad-*ow*, stra-*w*, de-*w*.

Romanic:—

-ace (Lat. *-atio, -atium*; Fr. *-ace*): popul-*ace*, terr-*ace*, pal-*ace*.
-ine, -in (Lat. *-inus*): libert-*ine*, cous-*in* (Lat. consobr-*inus*).
-me, -m (Lat. *-men*): cri-*me*, char-*m*, real-*m* (Lat. regali-*men*).
o (Lat. *-us, -um*; Span. *-o*): studi-*o*, grott-*o*, incognit-*o*.
-cre, -chre (Lat. *-crum*): sepul-*chre*, lu-*cre*.

Greek:—

-on (Gr. *-on*): criteri-*on*, skelet-*on*, col-*on*, phenomen-*on*.
-ic, -ics (Gr. *-ikos, -ika*): log-*ic*, mus-*ic*, phys-*ics*, eth-*ics*.

147. II. **Adjective-forming**:—

(*a*) Possessing a quality of any kind:—

Teutonic:—

-ed (A.S. *-d*): wretch-*ed*, gift-*ed*, fabl-*ed*, money-*ed*.
-en (A.S. *-en*): wheat-*en*, gold-*en*, heath-*en*, op-*en*.
-ly (A.S. *-lic*): god-*ly*, woman-*ly*, man-*ly*.
-some (A.S. *-sum*): toil-*some*, hand-*some*, whole-*some*, bux-*om*.
-y, -ey (A.S. *-ig*): might-*y*, wood-*y*, clay-*ey*, drear-*y*, an-*y*.

Romanic:—

-al (Lat. *-alis*): vit-*al*, parti-*al*, mort-*al*, comic-*al*.
-an, -ane, -ain (Lat. *-anus*): pag-*an*, hum-*an*, hum-*ane*, cert-*ain*.
ant, -ent (Lat. *-antem, -entem*): dist-*ant*, abs-*ent*, pres-*ent*.

-ar, -ary, -arious (Lat. *-aris, -arius*): lun-*ar*, contr-*ary*, vic-*arious*.
-esque (Lat. *-iscus*, Fr. *-esque*): pictur-*esque*, grot-*esque*.
-ile, -il, -eel, -le, -el (Lat. *-ilis*): frag-*ile*, fra-*il*, gent-*eel*, gent-*le*, hum(b)-*le*, cru-*el*.
-ic, -ique (Lat. *-icus, -iquus*): rust-*ic*, com-*ic*, un-*ique*, obl-*ique*.
ine (Lat. *-inus*): div-*ine*, clandest-*ine*, infant-*ine*.
-lent (Lat. *-lentem*): pesti-*lent*, corpu-*lent*, vio-*lent*.

(*b*) Possessing a quality in a high degree:—

Teutonic:—

-ful (A.S. *-ful*, Eng. *-full*): plenti-*ful*, beauti-*ful*, master-*ful*.

Romanic:—

-ous, -ose (Lat. *-osus*): numer-*ous*, fam-*ous*, verb-*ose*.

(*c*) Possessing a quality in a slight degree; hence sometimes used in a depreciative sense:—

Teutonic:—

-ish (A.S. *-isc*): pal-*ish*, redd-*ish*, woman-*ish* (fit for a woman, but not fit for a man), snapp-*ish*, upp-*ish*, slav-*ish*, baby-*ish*.

Note.—The prefix *sub-* (Latin) sometimes means "slightly"; as, *sub*-acid, *sub*-tropical (not quite tropical).

(*d*) Conveying an Active sense:—

Romanic:—

-ive (Lat. *-ivus*): recept-*ive*, act-*ive*: (capt-*ive* is exceptional).
-ory, -orious (Lat. *-orius*): illus-*ory*, cens-*orious*.
-fic (Lat. *-ficus*): terri-*fic*, honori-*fic*, beati-*fic*.

(*e*) Conveying a Passive sense:—

Romanic:—

-able, -ible (Lat. *-bilis*): laugh-*able*, eat-*able*, ed-*ible*.

(*f*) Describing nation, sect, creed, etc.:—

Teutonic:—

-ish, ch (A.S. *-isc*): Engl-*ish*, Ir-*ish*, Span-*ish*, Fren-*ch*.

Romanic:—

-an (Lat. *-anus*): Rom-*an*, Austri-*an*, Belgi-*an*, Christi-*an*.
-ese (Lat. *-ensis*): Chin-*ese*, Siam-*ese*, Portugu-*ese*.

Greek:—

-ite (Gr. *-it-es*): Israel-*ite*, Irving-*ite*, Carmel-*ite*.

(*g*) Miscellaneous suffixes, not included in the above:—

Teutonic:—

-teen, -ty (A.S. *-tén, tig*, ten): thir-*teen* (3 + 10), thir-*ty* (3 × 10).
-ern (A.S. *irn*-an, to turn): north-*ern*, north-*er*(n)-ly.
-ther (A.S. *ther*, Comp. degree): o-*ther*, fur-*ther*, whe-*ther*, ne-*ther*.

Romanic:—

-ior (Lat. comp. degree): exter-*ior*, pr-*ior*, super-*ior*.
-monious (Lat. *-monius*): cere-*monious*, sancti-*monious*.
-ple, -ble (Lat. *-plex*, Fr. *-ple*, fold): tri-*ple*, tre-*ble*.

Greek:—

-astic, -istic (Gr. *-astikos*, *-istikos*): dr-*astic*, art-*istic*.

148. III. **Verb-forming**:—

(*a*) Causative; hence forming Transitive verbs:—

Teutonic:—

-en (A.S. *-en* or *-n*): dark-*en*, sweet-*en*, length-*en*, height-*en*.

Romanic:—

-fy (Lat. *facio*): magni-*fy*, terri-*fy*, stupe-*fy*.

Greek:—

-ise (through French *-iser*): galvan-*ise*, brutal-*ise*, fertil-*ise*.

Note.—Some Prefixes are also used for the same purpose:—*Teutonic* **be-**, as *be*-friend, *be*-calm, *be*-numb; *Romanic* **im-**, **en-**, as *im*-peril, *en*-dear.

(*b*) Frequentative, denoting frequency or continuance:—

Teutonic:—

-el, -le, -l: cack-*le*, jost-*le*, sniv-*el* (sniff), draw-*l* (draw).
-er, -r: batt-*er* (beat), sputt-*er* (spout), glimm-*er* (gleam).
-k: har-*k* (hear), hear-*k*-en, lur-*k*, tal-*k* (tell).

(*c*) Other verb-forming suffixes.—

Romanic:—

-ate (Lat. *-atum*): captiv-*ate*, gradu-*ate*, filtr-*ate*.
-ish (Lat. *-isc*, Fr. *-iss*): pun-*ish* (pun-*ch*), per-*ish*, flour-*ish*.
-esce (Lat. *-esco*, inceptive): coal-*esce*, acqui-*esce*.

149. IV. **Adverb-forming**:—

Teutonic:—

-ly (A.S. *lic-e*, in a like way): on-*ly*, bad-*ly*, dark-*ly*, open-*ly*.
-ling, -long (A.S. *linga*): head-*long*, dark-*ling*, side-*long*.
-meal (A.S. *mǽl*, a time): piece-*meal*, inch-*meal* (Shakspeare).
-ward, -wards (A.S. *weard*, direction): back-*ward*, back-*wards*.
-wise (A.S. *wís-e*, manner): like-*wise*, other-*wise*.
-way, -ways (A.S. *weg*, way): straight-*way*, al-*ways*.
-s, -ce (sign of Possessive): need-*s*, twi-*ce*, back-ward-*s*, some-time-*s*.
-n: whe-*n*, the-*n*, the-*n*-*ce*. (The *n* in *often* is an intruder.)
-re: whe-*re*, the-*re*.
-om (old Dative ending; cf. who-*m*, the-*m*, hi-*m*): whil-*om*, seld-*om*.
-ther (direction): whit-*ther*, hi-*ther*, hi-*ther*-to.

Note.—We have no Romanic or Greek suffixes for forming Adverbs.

SECTION 2.—PREFIXES: TEUTONIC, ROMANIC, GREEK.

150. Teutonic Prefixes.—These have been distinguished into (*a*) Separable, and (*b*) Inseparable:—

(*a*) *Separable; i.e.* capable of being used as separate words; such as *after*-life, *by*-path, *fore*-cast, *forth*-coming, *off*-shoot, *on*-set, *out*-let, *through*-ticket, *up*-start, *wel*-fare. Such words might be called Compounds (§ 141). These do not require further explanation. The few mentioned below are somewhat peculiar.

Out-.—This gives certain verbs the sense of surpassing; as *out*-live (to live beyond), *out*-vote (to defeat by votes), *out*-run, *out*-shine.

Over-.—This denotes excess; as *over*-eat (eat too much), *over*-sleep (sleep too long), *over*-worked (worked too much).

Under-.—This denotes deficiency, too little; as *under*-fed, *under*-paid, *under*-valued, *under*-cooked.

With-.—This denotes "back," "against"; as *with*-stand, *with*-hold, *with*-draw. ("Drawing-room" means "with-drawing-room.")

(*b*) *Inseparable; i.e.* not used as separate words:—

A- (*on, in*): *a*-bed, *a*-shore, *a*-jar, *a*-stir, *a*-sleep, etc.

A- (*of, from*): *a*-down (off a down or hill), *a*-fresh, *a*-kin, *a*-new.

A- (Intensive): *a*-rise, *a*-waken, *a*(f)-fright, *a*(c)-cursed.

Al- (*all*): *al*-one, *l*-one, *al*-most, *al*-ready, *al*-together.

Be- (*by*): (1) Transitive force; as *be*-calm. (2) Intensive force; as *be*-smear. (3) Forming adverbs or prepositions; as *be*-sides, *be*-fore. (4) Privative force in *be*-head.

For- (not the prep. "for"): (1) Intensive; as *for*-bear, *for*-lorn. (2) Privative; as *for*-bid, *for*-get, *for*-swear, *fore*-go (a bad spelling for *for*-go. The prefix *fore* is quite distinct from *for*).

Gain (A.S. *gegn*, against): *gain*-say, *gain*-strive (out of use).

N- (Indef. article "a," the *n* being wrongly detached): *n*-ewt (for *an ewt*), *n*-ugget (for *an ingot*), *n*-ickname (for *an eke-name*).

N- (Negative prefix): *n*-or, *n*-either, *n*-ay.

Mis- (*miss*): *mis*-take, *mis*-hap, *mis*-deed, *mis*-trust.

Twi- (A.S. *twi*, double): *twi*-light, *twi*-n, *twi*-ce, *twi*-st.

Un- (A.S. *un*-): (1) Negative: *un*-wise. (2) Reversal: *un*-twist. (In "*un*-loose" the *un*- is merely Intensive.)

151. Romanic Prefixes.—The following are of frequent occurrence:—

A-, **ab**-, **abs**- (*from*): *a*-vert, *ab*-use, *ab*-normal, *abs*-tain.

Ad- (*to*): *ad*-vice, *ab*-breviate, *ac*-cent, *af*-fable, *ag*-gressor, *al*-lude, *an*-nex, *ap*-pear, *ar*-rears, *as*-sert, *at*-tain.

Ambi- (*on both sides, around*): *amb*-iguous, *amb*-ition.

Ante-, **anti**-, **ant**- (*before*): *ante*-cedent, *anti*-cipate, *ant*-ique.

Bene- (*well*): *bene*-fit, *bene*-volent, *ben*-ison.

Bis-, **bi**-, **bin**- (*twice*): *bis*-cuit, *bi*-ped, *bi*-cycle, *bin*-ocular.

Circum-, **circu**- (*around*): *circum*-stance, *circu*-it, *circum*-ference.

Cis- (*on this side*): *cis*-Alpine, on this side of the Alps.

Con- (*with*), **coun**- (Fr.): *con*-tend, *col*-lege, *com*-pete, *cor*-rect, *coun*-sel, *con*-temporary.

Contra- (*against*), **counter** (Fr.): *contra*-dict, *contra*-st, *counter*-act.

De- (*down, from, astray*): *de*-grade, *de*-part, *de*-viate.

" (Reversal): merit, *de*-merit; *en*-camp, *de*-camp.

" (Intensive): *de*-liver, *de*-clare, *de*-file, *de*-fraud.

Dis-, di- (*asunder*) : *dis*-tract, *dis*-miss, *dis*-member, *di*-vulge.
,, (**Intensive**) : *dis*-sever, *dis*-annul, *di*-minish.
,, (Reversal) : en-chant, *dis*-enchant ; illusion, *dis*-illusion.
,, (Negative) : ease, *dis*-ease ; honour, *dis*-honour ; *dif*-ficult.
Ex-, e-, extra- (*out*) : *ex*-ample, *e*-lapse, *extra*-vagant.
,, (*loss of office*) : *ex*-king, *ex*-empress.
In-, en-, em- (*in*) : *in*-ject, *im*-pute, *ir*-ritate, *en*-close, *em*-ploy.
In- (*not*) : *in*-firm, *il*-literate, *im*-pious, *ir*-regular, *i*-gnorance.
Inter-, enter- (*among*) : *inter*-est, *intel*-lect, *enter*-prise.
Intro-, intra- (*within*) : *intro*-duce, *intra*-tropical, *intr*-insic.
Male-, mal- (*badly*) : *male*-volent, *male*-factor, *mal*-ady.
Mis- (Lat. *minus*, badly) : *mis*-chance, *mis*-chief, *mis*-nomer.
Non-, ne-, neg- (*not*) : *non*-sense, *ne*-uter, *neg*-lect.
Ob- (*against*) : *ob*-ject, *oc*-cur, *of*-fer, *op*-press, *os*-tensible, *o*-mit.
Pen- (Latin *pæne, almost*) : *pen*-insula, *pen*-ultimate.
Per- (*through*) : *per*-form, *per*-haps, *pel*-lucid.
,, (*wrong direction*) : *per*-vert, *per*-jury, *per*-fidy, *per*-ish.
Post- (*after*) : *post*-script, *post*-pone, *post*-ern.
Pre- (Latin *præ, in front, before*) : *pre*-occupy, *pre*-tend, *pre*-dict.
Preter- (Latin *præter, beyond*) : *preter*-natural, *preter*-ite.
Pro-, por-, pur- (Latin *pro, for, before*) : *pro*-fess, *pour*-tray, *por*-trait, *pur*-pose.
Re-, red- (*back*) : *re*-fer, *re*-new, *red*-eem, *red*-undant.
Retro- (*backwards*) : *retro*-cession, *retro*-grade.
Se-, sed- (*apart*) : *se*-cret, *se*-cure, *se*-parate, *sed*-ition.
Semi-, demi- (*half*) : *semi*-circle, *demi*-god.
Sub- (*under*) : *sub*-ject, *suc*-cour, *suf*-fice, *sug*-gest, *sum*-mon, *sup*-pose, *sur*-render, *sus*-pend, *sub*-marine, "under the sea."
,, (*slightly*) : *sub*-acid, *sub*-tropical.
,, (*of lower rank*) : *sub*-judge, *sub*-committee, *sub*-division.
Subter- (*under, secretly*) : *subter*-fuge.
Super-, sur- (*above*) : *super*-fluous, *sur*-face, *sur*-vive.
Trans-, tra- (*across*) : *trans*-mit, *trans*-gress, *tra*-duce, *tra*-ffic.
Tri-, tre- (*three, thrice*) : *tri*-angle, *tri*-nity, *tri*-vial, *tre*-ble.
Ultra- (*beyond, excess*) : *ultra*-marine, *ultra*-radical.
Vice-, vis- (*instead of*) : *vice*-roy, *vis*-count.

152. Greek Prefixes :—

Amphi- (*on both sides*) : *amphi*-bious, *amphi*-theatre.
An-, a- (*not*) : *an*-archy, *an*-ecdote, *a*-pathy, *a*-theism.
Ana- (*again, back*) : *ana*-logy, *ana*-lyse, *ana*-tomy.
Anti-, ant- (*against*) : *anti*-podes, *anti*-pathy, *ant*-agonist.
Apo-, aph- (*from*) : *apo*-logy, *apo*-state, *apo*-stle, *aph*-orism.
Archi-, arch- (*chief*) : *archi*-tect, *arch*-bishop.
Auto- (*self*) : *auto*-car, *auto*-graph, *auth*-entic.
Cata-, cath- (*down*) : *cata*-ract, *cath*-edral, *cat*-echism.
Dia- (*through*) : *dia*-logue, *dia*-meter, *dia*-gnosis.
Dis-, di- (*in two*) : *dis*-syllable, *di*-phthong, *di*-lemma.
Dys- (*ill, badly*) : *dys*-entry, *dys*-pepsia.
Ek-, ex- (*out*) : *ec*-stasy, *ex*-odus.
En- (*in*) : *en*-thusiasm, *em*-phasis, *el*-lipsis.
Eu-, ev- (*well*) : *eu*-phony, *eu*-logy, *ev*-angelist.

Epi-, **eph-** (*on*) : *epi*-taph, *ep*-och, *eph*-emeral, *ep*-isode.
Hemi- (*half*) : *hemi*-sphere.
Hyper- (*above, beyond*) : *hyper*-critical, *hyper*-bole.
Hypo-, **hyph-** (*under*) : *hypo*-crite, *hypo*-thesis, *hyph*-en.
Meta-, **meth-**, **met-** (*after*) : *meta*-phor, *meth*-od, *met*-eor.
Mono-, **mon-** (*single*) : *mono*-poly, *mon*-arch, *mon*-k.
Pan-, **panto-** (*all*) : *pan*-orama, *panto*-mime.
Para-, **par-** (*beside*) : *para*-ble, *para*-graph, *par*-allel.
Peri- (*around*) : *peri*-od, *peri*-phrasis, *peri*-meter.
Pro- (*before*) : *pro*-gramme, *pro*-phet, *pro*-blem.
Syn- (*with*) : *syn*-od, *syl*-lable, *sym*-bol, *sym*-pathy, *sy*-stem.
Tri- (*thrice*) : *tri*-pod, *tri*-syllable.

153. General results, regarding the uses of Prefixes :—

(*a*) Prefixes denoting the **undoing** of something done :—

Teutonic :—
un- : *un*-bolt, *un*-tie, *un*-lock, *un*-fold.

Romanic :—
dis- : *dis*-mount, *dis*-arm, *dis*-appear, *dis*-close.
de- : *de*-odorise, *de*-plete, *de*-camp, *de*-throne.

(*b*) Prefixes denoting a **Negative**, with one Suffix :—

Teutonic :—
un- : *un*-happy, *un*-safe, *un*-ready, *un*-certain.
-less : hap-*less*, law-*less*, hope-*less*, spot-*less*.
n- : *n*-one, *n*-ever, *n*-or, *n*-either.

Romanic :—
ne-, **neg-**, **non-** : *ne*-uter, *neg*-lect, *non*-sense.
dis-, **di-** : *dis*-contented, *dif*-ficult, *dif*-fident.
in- : *in*-human, *ir*-rational, *im*-moral, *ig*-noble, *il*-legible.
ab- : *ab*-normal.

Greek :—
a-, **an-** : *a*-pathy, *an*-archy.

(*c*) Prefixes indicating something **good** :—

Teutonic :—
well- : *wel*-fare, *wel*-come, *well*-bred.

Romanic :—
bene- : *bene*-volent, *bene*-fit, *ben*-ignant, *ben*-ison.

Greek :—
eu-, **ev-** : *eu*-phony, *ev*-angelist.

(*d*) Prefixes indicating something **bad** :—

Teutonic :—
mis- (from *miss*) : *mis*-deed, *mis*-take, *mis*-hap.

Romanic :—
mis- (from *minus*) : *mis*-carry, *mis*-use, *mis*-fortune.
male-, **mal-** : *male*-factor, *mal*-ignant, *mal*-treat.

Greek :—
dys- : *dys*-entery, *dys*-pepsia.

Exercise 40.—*On Word-building.*

(*a*) 1. Supply the feminine forms of *sultan*, *hero*, *testator*, *shepherd*, *spinner*, *fox*. 2. Break up *mistrustfully*, *unwholesomeness* into syllables, and show how each syllable contributes to the meaning of the words. 3. What are the suffixes in the following words :—*farthing*, *foremost*, *kingdom*, *fatten*, *English*, *thirsty*. 4. Reverse the meaning of each of the following words by adding a prefix :—*happy*, *possible*, *rational*, *contented*, *valid*, *noble*, *sense*. 5. Give four examples of diminutive forms in English nouns. 6. Form adjectives from *disaster*, *two*, *wheat*, and adverbs from *gay*, *holy*, *other*, *south*, *week*. 7. How are verbs formed (*a*) from nouns ; (*b*) from adjectives ; (*c*) from other verbs. Give two examples of each, and show the exact force of the change of the word. 8. By the use of a suffix, change each of the following nouns into an adjective, and give the force of each suffix : —*sister*, *fame*, *quarrel*, *slave*, *silver*. 9. What is meant by saying that the word *bicycle* is a hybrid ? 10. Write words (one in each case) containing the following prefixes and suffixes :—*ante-*, *anti-*, *auto-*, *vice-*, *-ess*, *-ness*, *-ry*, *-kin*. (*Oxford and Cambridge*, *Junior and Senior.*)

(*b*) 1. How are Compound verbs formed ? Write down ten Compound verbs with different prefixes, giving the meaning of these. 2. Give the diminutive forms of *stream*, *hill*, *duck*, *lass ;* and the meaning of the prefix in each of the following words : *mischance*, *importunate*, *retrospect*, *subterfuge*, *constant*. 3. Why is co-temporary an incorrect form ? What different forms do *cum*, *in*, *ad*, *inter*, *per* assume in composition ? 4. Write down suffixes employed to denote (1) the agent, (2) diminution, (3) gender. 5. Give with examples three affixes (suffixes) of Latin origin, by which Abstract nouns in English are formed. 6. Give the exact force of the following prefixes and affixes (suffixes) :—man*hood*, spin*ster*, tire*some*, spark*le ; mis*give, *for*get, *be*troth, *in*nocent. 7. What is the force of the prefixes in the words *impossible*, *except*. From what languages are they respectively taken ? Write down three other examples of the use of each of these prefixes. 8. Explain the meaning of the following prefixes, and write words formed by means of them :—*un-*, *ante-*, *bi-*, *circum-*, *inter-*. 9. Give (i.) three prefixes of Latin origin, and (ii.) three noun suffixes ; and by examples show what effect they have upon words in which they are introduced. (*Preceptors'*, *Second and Third Classes.*)

(*c*) 1. Give the different ways of forming adverbs in English. 2. Explain the force of the syllables in *Italics* in the following words : spin*ster*, head*long*, twen*ty*, *im*proper, hill*ock*, eld*est*, king*dom*, *be*sprinkle. 3. In the following words what is the force of the parts printed in *Italics ?* —*a*round, numer*ous*, *a*loud, govern*esses*, *re*cite, Eng*lish*, Italia*n*. 4. Mention *two* ways in which *abstract* nouns can be formed from *common* nouns, and give *two* examples of each. 5. What is meant by *diminutives* and *augmentatives*. Illustrate by examples the suffixes used in the formation of such words. 6. What are *compound* adjectives ? Give *three* examples. 7. Give the meanings of the following Latin Prefixes, and illustrate each by *two* English words :—*ab-*, *bis-*, *con-*, *non-*, *pro-*, *se-*. 8. Give the meanings of the following *prefixes*, and *two* instances of the use of each :—*in-*, *per-*, *dis-*, *re-*. (*Preceptors'*, *Second and Third Classes.*)

(*d*) 1. Say what you know about the Feminine endings in *vixen*, *spinster*, *duchess*, *baxter*, *margravine*, *infanta*, and *testatrix*. 2. Mention six English Inseparable prefixes ; and give two examples of words formed with each of them.. 3. What is the force of the prefix *un*dismayed, *mis*lay, *be*hind, *for*give, *with*stand, *pre*fix, *extra*vagant, *post*pone, *super*scription, *an*archy, *epi*taph, *peri*meter ? 4. Give the meaning and function of the following prefixes (with *two* examples in each case), and state whether they are English or Latin :—*be-*, *con-*, *for-*, *gain-*, *in-*, *pro-*, *re-*, *with-*. 5. Give the derivation and meaning of each of the following suffixes, with two examples of each :—*-ard* or *-art*, *-fy*, *-kin*, *-ock*, *-ous*, *-some*, *-ster*, *-tude*. 6. Give the meaning and function of the following suffixes ; and state whether they are added to nouns, or verbs, or adjectives :—*-ing*, *-lock*, *-m*, *-red*, *-ther*, *-s*, *-ward*. 7. Give examples of the following suffixes, and state their derivation and their meaning :—*-ster*, *-kin*, *-ly*, *-tude*, *-let*, *-ous*, *-fy*, *-ise*. 8. Explain with examples the force of the following prefixes and suffixes :—*be-*, *for-*, *with-*, *cata-*, *intro-*, *-der*, *-nd*, *-ship*, *-eer*, *-le*, *-ment*. 9. Give the origin and meaning of the prefix in each of the following words :—*ad*vent, *contra*dict, *for*lorn, *hyper*critical, *inter*pose, *mis*take, *re*open, *trans*marine, *un*kind, *with*stand. 10. Give the meaning and derivation of the suffixes (distinctly specifying these) of the following words :—*wisdom*, *bounty*, *slavish*, *clayey*, *worship*, *blackness*, *longitude*, *sepulchre*, *strengthen*, *gamble*. 11. Explain the force of the terminations in any five of the following :—*oxen*, *vixen*, *maiden*, *holden*, *wooden*, *open*, *often*. 12. With what different suffixes, and derived from what sources, do we form Abstract nouns ? Give one or two examples of each. 13. Point out the force of the prefix in each of the following, explaining the words themselves :—*hypercritical*, *antechamber*, *cisalpine*, *synchronous*, *percolate*, *cataract*. (*Preceptors'*, *First Class.*)

CHAPTER XXXII.—SOUNDS, SYMBOLS, AND SPELLINGS.

SECTION 1.—LETTERS, ACCENT, SYLLABLES.

154. A letter (Latin *litera*, Fr. *lettre*) is a mark or symbol that stands for a certain sound. Without letters men can talk as fast as they like, but they cannot either read or write. A word, until it is written, is merely a sound, perceptible to the ear, but not to the eye.

Letters are subdivided into two great classes, vowels and consonants.

155. Vowel is from Lat. *vocalis*, Fr. *voyelle*,—L. *vox*, *vocis*, the voice. A vowel, as its etymology implies, stands for a *voice-sound*, *i.e.* a sound or tone produced by the unimpeded passage of the breath, without the help of a consonant. Thus it is quite as easy to say *e* as *be*.

156. **Consonant** (Lat. *con*, together with, *sonantem*, sounding).—This, as its name implies, stands for a sound that cannot be easily, if at all, produced except in company with a vowel. Thus it is not easy to pronounce the letter *b*, until we connect it with some vowel, as *be*. In fact, we find it so difficult to sound *b* by itself, that we have called the consonant *be*, not *b*.

157. **The English Alphabet**.—Our alphabet consists of 26 letters, of which 5 are vowels, 19 are consonants, and 2 are semivowels, *i.e* dubious letters.

Vowels.—A, a; E, e; I, i; O, o; U, u.

Consonants.—B, b; C, c; D, d; F, f; G, g; H, h; J, j; K, k; L, l; M, m; N, n; P, p; Q, q; R, r; S, s; T, t; V, v; X, x; Z, z.

Semivowels.—Y, y; W, w.

The letter *y* is superfluous as a vowel; for it expresses precisely the same sound as *i*. Thus there is no difference of sound between the first syllables of *sin*-ner and *syn*-tax. As a consonant, however, the *y* is indispensable; for we could not express such words as *yoke*, *yet* without it.

The letter *w* as a vowel is even less useful (if this were possible) than *y*; for it cannot stand alone as *y* can, but is seen only in such combinations as *aw*, *ew*, *ow*, all of which can be quite as easily spelt *au*, *eu*, *ou*. As a consonant, however, the letter *w* is indispensable; for it enables us to express such words as *will*, *wax*, *wet*.

Note.—The vowels *i* and *u* (care being taken that *u* here stands for the *u* in *full*, and *not* for the *u* in *tune*) acquire the consonantal sounds of *y* and *w* respectively, when they are followed by other vowels. Thus *opinion* is sounded as if it were spelt *o-pin-yon* (three syllables). Similarly if we attempt to sound *uilliam* we get *William*. The letter *w* is merely a double *v*, though it is called a "double *u*." The symbol *v* is merely another form of *u*, and in Latin during the classical period *u* was the only symbol used.

158. **Digraph, diphthong**.—It is necessary to understand clearly what is meant by these two words.

A *digraph* is a compound **letter**; a *diphthong* is a compound **sound**. "Digraph" is from Greek *di*, two or twice, and *graph*, to write: it therefore means "a double letter." "Diphthong" is from Greek *di*, two or twice, and *phthong*-os, a sound; it therefore means "a double sound."

Owing to the fewness of our vowel-*symbols* and the multiplicity of our vowel-*sounds* we are sometimes forced to use a digraph for expressing a vowel-sound that is simple or uncompounded, as *au.* On the other hand, it sometimes happens (such is the perversity of our spelling) that we use a single letter to express a vowel-sound that is compound; as *u* in *tu-bu-lar.*

Similarly we sometimes use a digraph to express a single consonantal sound, as *ph* in *Philip;* and a single consonant to express a double sound, as *x* in *tax.*

159. Voiceless and Voiced Consonants.[1]—Consonants are subdivided into two great classes, the Voiceless and the Voiced. Voiced is the name given to those consonants which can be sounded to a slight extent *without the help of a vowel;* the Voiceless are those to which no sound whatever can be given without this help. The Voiced therefore have something of a vocalic character, and are a connecting link between Voiceless consonants and Vowels.

Consonants as thus distinguished go for the most part in pairs. All consonants not included amongst these pairs are Voiced, with the exception of *h,* which is Voiceless.

Voiceless.	*Voiced.*	*Voiceless.*	*Voiced.*	*Voiceless.*	*Voiced.*
k	g	s	z	p	b
ch	j	t	d	f	v
sh	zh	th(in)	th(is)	wh	w

The distinction between Voiceless and Voiced can be easily verified by any one who will make the experiment on his own organs. We can sound *ka,* for instance, so long as the *k* is followed by a vowel. But if we cut off the *a* and try to sound the *k* alone, we cannot produce any sound whatever, though we are conscious of a feeling of muscular tension in the tongue. There is no *voice* in it; and hence the consonant *k* is classed as Voiceless.

On the other hand, if we take the combination *ga,* and cut off the *a,* we find that without the assistance of this or any other vowel it is possible to make an audible guggle. This consonant is therefore classed among the Voiced.

[1] *Voiceless* and *Voiced* are the names adopted by Professor Skeat. **Surd** (silent) and **Sonant** (sounding) are equally suitable. The names Hard and Soft, Sharp and Flat, are also used; but they are not suitable. An apple may be hard or soft, but not a consonant.

The following facts are of very wide application :—

I.—When two consonants come together, voiceless consonants are assimilated in sound to voiced ones, or voiced to voiceless.

(*a*) In monosyllables the first letter usually holds its ground, and the second has to give way to it. Compare the *s* in *cats* with that in *lads*. In the first the *s* remains voiceless, because it is preceded by the voiceless *t*. In the second the *s* becomes a voiced letter, *i.e.* receives the sound of *z*, because it is preceded by a voiced *d*. Similarly compare the *d* in *looked* with that in *loved*, the *s* in *caps* with that in *cabs*.

(*b*) In dissyllables and compound words the first letter usually gives way to the second one; as in *five*-teen, sounded and spelt as *fif*-teen; *cup-board*, sounded, though not spelt, as *cub-board*; *black-guard*, sounded, though not spelt, as *blag-guard*.

This process is very commonly at work in prefixes. Thus we have a*c*cent for a*d*cent, a*ff*lict for a*df*lict, a*pp*ear for a*dp*ear, a*ss*ent for a*ds*ent, a*tt*ain for a*dt*ain, a*gg*rieve for a*dg*rieve, a*ll*ot for a*dl*ot, a*nn*ul for a*dn*ul, a*rr*ive for a*dr*ive, inte*ll*ect for inte*rl*ect, o*cc*ur for o*bc*ur, o*ff*er for o*bf*er, o*pp*ose for o*bp*ose, pe*ll*ucid for pe*rl*ucid, po*ll*ute for po*rl*ute, su*cc*eed for su*bc*eed, su*pp*ort for su*bp*ort, etc.

II.—A voiceless consonant often receives the sound of a voiced one, when it is placed between two vowels. Thus in *breath* the *th* is voiceless; but in *breathe*, where it stands between two vowels, it is voiced. Again *rise* is sounded as *rize*, not as *rice*. *Lathe* is sounded, not as *lath*, but with the sound *th* as in *th*(is).

III.—When one consonant is substituted for another, as sometimes happens, a voiceless consonant is displaced by a voiceless one, and a voiced by a voiced. This is especially seen in doublets,—that is, pairs of words derived from the same original elements, but differently spelt :—

Croo*k*, cro*ss* (*k* substituted for *s*, both voiceless). A*p*titude, a*t*titude (*p* and *t*, both voiceless). Aprico*ck* (older spelling) and aprico*t* (*k* and *t*, both voiceless). Bar*b*, bear*d* (*b* and *d*, both voiced). W*r*ap, *l*ap (*r* and *l*, both voiced). P*r*u*n*e, p*l*u*m* (*r* and *l*, *n* and *m*, both pairs voiced). *W*ard, *g*uard (*w* and *g*, both voiced).

In *sh*oe (A.S. *sc*ó) we find *sh* substituted for *sk* (both voiceless). So too in *sh*e (Midland *sc*é). In "see*th*e," "so*dd*en," voiced *th* is interchanged with voiced *d*; so too in mur*th*er (older spelling), mur*d*er. In the 3rd Sing. "cast-*s*" (older form, cast-*es*, cast-*eth*) we find the voiceless *s* substituted for the voiceless *th*.

In A.S. final or medial *h* was sounded almost like *k*, as in "Lo*ch* Lomond." A survival of this occurs in the word *next* (= *nekst*), which in A.S. was spelt *nehst*. In modern English this *h* has been usually respelt as *gh*. In the words "lou*gh*" and "hou*gh*" (sounded as *lok*, *hok*), the original sound of the *k* has been retained. But in certain other words, as *enough*, *laugh*, *rough*, *trough*, *tough*, *cough*, the sound of *f* has been substituted for the sound of *k*, both letters being voiceless.

160. Accent, Emphasis, Quantity.—Roughly speaking, both accent and emphasis are the effect of *loudness* (which helps to produce distinctness), while quantity depends on the *time* that it takes to pronounce a syllable.

When we lay stress upon a *single syllable*, *i.e.* pronounce it more loudly and distinctly than the other syllable or syllables of the same word, this is called **Accent** (Latin *ad*, to, *cantus*, a song).

Sup-ply′, sim′-ply. Re-bel′ (verb), reb′-el (noun).

When we lay stress upon *an entire word*, *i.e.* pronounce it more loudly and distinctly than any other word of the same sentence or phrase, this is called **Emphasis** (Greek *en*, in or on, *phasis*, speech).

I appeal from Philip *drunk* to Philip *sober*.

Quantity means "the amount of *time* occupied in uttering a vowel or syllable." If the time so occupied is short, the vowel or syllable is said to be short; otherwise, it is said to be long.

A vowel can be long either by nature or by position. (1) Vowels long by nature are exemplified in *fate*, *fraud*, *smote*, *bite*, etc.; vowels short by nature are seen in *fat*, *pod*, *hit*, *wet*, etc. (2) Vowels long by position, but short by nature, are seen in *west*, *land*, *flint*, *stump*, *bond*. The vowels themselves in such words or syllables are not long, but they are said to be made long by position, because they are followed by a strong combination of consonants, which prevents the syllable from being sounded rapidly.

161. Importance of Accent in English.—In English as now spoken quantity counts for very little: accent is all-important. Thus the word *guard* is certainly a long syllable when it stands alone; but in the combination "blackguard" (sounded as *blag′-guard*) the accent thrown upon the first syllable compels us to make the second syllable as short as we can pronounce it. Again, the diphthong *u* (i.e. *u* sounded as *yoo*) is long by nature, as in *tube*. But in the adjective *tu′-bu-lar* the second *u*, though long by nature like the first one, is, owing to the want of accent, made as short as we can pronounce it.

Such is the effect of accent in our language that an unaccented syllable sometimes disappears altogether. Thus *ap-pren′-tice* has been reduced to *pren′-tice; dam′-o-sel* (older spelling) to *dam′-sel; co-rone′* (Lat. "corona") to *crown; la-ven′-der-ess* to *laun′-dress; with-draw′-ing-room* to *draw′-ing-room; pun′-ish* to *punch; sa′-cris-tan* to *sex′-ton; pa-ral′-y-sie* (Gr. "paralysis") to *pal′-e-sy, pal′-sy; en-sam′-ple* to *sam′-ple; dis-port′* to *sport; hy-drop′-sy* to *drop′-sy; af-fray′* to *fray; es-quire′* to *squire; a-mend′* to *mend; ap-peal′* to *peal; de-spite′* to *spite.*

The part of speech to which a word belongs often depends upon the accent. If the choice lies between a verb and a noun, both spelt alike, the verb has the accent on the last syllable, the noun on the first. Of this we have at least sixty examples.

Com-pound′ (verb), com′-pound (noun). Con-duct′ (verb), con′-duct (noun). Con-fine′ (verb), con′-fine (noun). Con-vert′ (verb), con′-vert (noun). Con-vict′ (verb), con′-vict (noun), etc.

If the choice lies between a verb and an adjective, the verb has the accent on the last syllable, as before:—

Ab-sent′ (verb), ab′-sent (adj.). Fre-quent′ (verb), fre′-quent (adj.).

If the choice lies between a noun and an adjective, the noun has the accent on the first syllable, as before, and the adjective on the second:—

Com′-pact (noun), com-pact′ (adj.). Min′-ute (noun), mi-nute′ (adj.). In′-va-lid (noun), in-val′-id (adj.).

Note.—Sometimes, however, there is no difference of accent; as *con-tent′* (adj. and verb), *con-tents′* (noun); *con-sent′, re-spect′, her′-ald, sup-port′* (all nouns and verbs); *con′-crete, pa′-tient* (both nouns and adjectives). Such examples are not common.

162. Syllabic division.—In dividing a word into syllables we must be guided by the pronunciation (which of course is very much affected by the accent), not by the etymology. "Word-division," says Professor Skeat, "has nothing to do with etymology. From a practical point of view *im′-pu-dence* is right, being based on the spoken language. It is only when we take the word to pieces, that we discover that it is formed from *im-* (for *in-*), the base *pud*, and the suffix *-ence.* Yet we divide the word as *im′-pu-dence*, not as *im-pud′-ence.* The spoken language has *pe-ruse′* at one moment, and *pe-ru′-sal* at another. It rightly regards ease of utterance, and nothing else."

We divide "banquet" into *ban′-quet;* we are compelled to

do so by the accent. But if we followed the etymology we should have to divide it into *banqu-et*, and ignore the accent altogether; for the stem of the word is *banque*, Fr.

SECTION 2.—VOWELS: SOUNDS, SYMBOLS, AND SPELLINGS.

163. Twenty vowel-sounds.[1]—If our alphabet were more perfect than it is, we should have one separate symbol to express each separate sound. Unfortunately it is very imperfect; for we have only five vowel-signs (*y* having been excluded as superfluous) to express four times as many sounds. Of these twenty vowel-sounds, sixteen are simple, and four are diphthongs. (The phrase "phonetic symbol" used below means the symbol used to express or denote the *one particular sound* assigned to it. The reason why some are bracketed as pairs is explained in § 164.)

A. Four sounds[2] frequently denoted by the symbol *a*; one short, and three long; all simple, none diphthongal.

{ 1. Short: the sound of *a* in *marry*. Phonetic symbol **ă**.
{ 2. Long: the sound of *a* in *Mary*. Phonetic symbol **â**.

3. Long: the sound of *a* in *mason*. Phonetic symbol **ā**.

Note. Observe that (3) is quite a distinct sound from (2). In sounding (2) you have to open the mouth a great deal wider than in sounding (3). In (2) the *a* is always followed by an *r*; in (3) it never is.

4. Long: the sound of *a* in *path*. Phonetic symbol **å**.

E. Two sounds commonly denoted by the symbol *e*; one short, and one long; both simple, neither diphthongal.

---

[1] The list of twenty sounds here given, though not the same as that given in current school-books, will, I trust, be accepted as correct; for it is the one on which all the best authorities are agreed, -Professor Skeat, Mr. Sweet, Miss Laura Soames, and Dr. Murray (in the introduction to the Oxford Dictionary). Dr. Murray's system is much more elaborate, but the basis is the same. As to the phonetic symbol most suitable for each sound, authorities are not equally unanimous. I have myself adopted those symbols which seemed likely to cause the least difficulty to a beginner, and which come nearest to those used in the current Dictionaries.

[2] To the four *a* sounds given above, some writers add two more, viz. the *a* in *fall* and the *a* in *want*. The latter is evidently a mistake. It creates a redundancy and leads to confusion; for the *a* in *want* is identical in sound with the *o* in *not*, and it never has the sound of *o* except when it is preceded by *w*. In fact, it is an *o* sound, and its connection with *a* is both accidental and exceptional. The former is not an *a* sound either, and is not expressed by *a* except when the *a* is followed by *l*. Professor Skeat associates only four sounds with the symbol *a* (see his Note printed in page 459 of my *English Grammar Past and Present*).

5. **Short**: the sound of *e* in *fed*. Phonetic symbol **ĕ**.
6. **Long**: the sound of *ee* in *feed*. Phonetic symbol **ē**.

I. Two sounds commonly denoted by the symbol *i*; one short, and one long: the short is simple, the long diphthongal.

7. **Short**: the sound of *i* in *bit*. Phonetic symbol **ĭ**.
8. **Long**: the sound of *i* in *bite*. Phonetic symbol **ī**.

O. Three sounds commonly denoted, and a fourth occasionally denoted, by the symbol *o*; two short and two long; all simple, none diphthongal.

9. **Short**: the sound of *o* in *not*. Phonetic symbol **ŏ**.
10. **Long**: the sound of *o* in *frost*. Phonetic symbol **au**.

Note.—Since the usual spelling is *au*, as in "fraud," this has been made the phonetic symbol in preference to *o*. But the use of the digraph *au* does not make the sound less simple than it is. In fact (10) is nothing more than (9) drawled or lengthened. If *dog* is drawled, it has the sound of *daug*. If the first syllable of *laurel* is shortened (as in practice it always is), it has the sound of *lŏrel*, rhyming with "moral." *Not* is merely the short of *naught*.

11. **Short**: the sound of *o* in *o*-mit. Phonetic symbol **o'**.
12. **Long**: the sound of *o* in *tone*. Phonetic symbol **ō**.

Note.—There is a great difference between (11) and (9). In sounding (9) you have to open your mouth rather wide, whereas in sounding (11) you almost close it. No. (12) is merely No. (11) drawled or lengthened.

OO. Two sounds commonly denoted by the digraph *oo*; one short, the other long; both simple, neither diphthongal.

13. **Short**: the sound of *oo* in *stood*. Phonetic symbol, **o͝o**.
14. **Long**: the sound of *oo* in *stool*. Phonetic symbol, **o͞o**.

U. Two sounds commonly denoted by the symbol *u*; one short, the other long; the short simple, the long diphthongal.

15. **Short**: the sound of *u* in *duck*. Phonetic symbol **ŭ**.
16. **Long**: the sound of *u* in *duke*. Phonetic symbol **ū**.

Oi. One sound commonly denoted by the digraph *oi*; diphthongal.

17. **Long**: the sound of *oi* in *toil*. Phonetic symbol **oi**.

Ou. One sound commonly denoted by the digraph *ou*; diphthongal.

18. **Long**: the sound of *ou* in *mouse*. Phonetic symbol **ou**.

Lastly, we come to two sounds, one short, the other long, and both simple or non-diphthongal. These have been called the Obscure, Neutral, or Indefinite sounds. For the expression of these sounds we have no vowel in our alphabet. So the expedient which the best authorities have agreed upon is to use ə (inverted *e*) for the phonetic symbol.

{ 19. Short: the sound of *er* [1] in gath′-*er*. Phonetic symbol **ə**.
{ 20. Long: the sound of *er* [1] in con-*fer*′. Phonetic symbol **əə**.

164. General results.—We have thus twenty vowel-sounds, of which sixteen are pure or simple, and four are mixed or diphthongal. The sixteen simple sounds are subdivided into (*a*) eight short, viz. **ă, ĕ, ĭ, ŏ, o′, ŏŏ, ŭ,** and **ə**; and (*b*) eight long, viz. **â, ā, ȧ, ē, au, ō, ōō,** and **əə**. The four diphthongs are **ī, ū, oi,** and **ou.**

Sounds which in the above description are bracketed together as short and long are real pairs. Thus, the *a* of *Mary* is the drawled or lengthened sound of the *a* in *marry;* the *o* of *frost* is the lengthened sound of the *o* in *not;* the *o* of *tone* is the lengthened sound of the *o* in *o*-mit; the *oo* of *stool* is the lengthened sound of the *oo* in *stood;* the *er* in con-*fer*′ is the lengthened and accented sound of the *er* in gath′-*er*.

On the other hand, the sounds which are not bracketed together as short and long are not pairs. Thus the *ee* in *feed* is not the long sound of *e* in *fed;* the *i* of *bite* is not the long sound of *i* in *bit;* the *u* of *duke* is not the long sound of *u* in *duck*. Though the same vowel is used in each case, the sounds are entirely distinct. For instance, the sound of *ee* in *feed* pairs not with *ĕ*, but with *ĭ*. The sound of *ĭ* is actually expressed by *ee* in the word "breeches" (sounded short as if it were spelt *brĭches*). Again, the sound of *ā* pairs not with *ă*, but with *ĕ;* thus *waist*′-coat is sounded short as if it were spelt *wĕst*′-coat.

165. How the four diphthongs are produced.—Let us take each diphthong in turn.[2]

---

[1] In Scotland, however, and in some of the northern counties of England, the *r* is trilled, that is, distinctly sounded as *r*. Owing to this peculiarity of the Northern dialect, I have been reluctantly compelled to adopt from Mr. Skeat, Mr. Sweet, Miss Soames, and Dr. Murray the awkward-looking symbol **ə**. This sound is so natural to human speech that hesitating speakers use it to fill up the pauses in their sentences. In books such pauses are printed thus:—"I —*er*—am aware —*er*—that," etc.

[2] It has been pointed out by phoneticians (Skeat, Sweet, Soames, Dr. Murray) that the long vowels which I have written as **ā** and **ō** are usually

ī. The first vowel-sound that helps to make this diphthong is obsolete in modern English, though still heard in the north-country dialects, where the *a* of *man* has retained a sound intermediate between **ă** and **à** (Nos. 1 and 4). This intermediate sound rapidly followed by the *i* of *bit* produces a third sound distinct from either. The spelling, *ai*, is seen in the word *aisle* (sounded as *īl*).

Note.—The sound of *à*, when added to *i*, would produce a diphthong, like the sound of *ai* in *Isaiah*, *naive*, *Kaiser*.

ū. Made up of *ĭ* + *ōō*. These, when sounded rapidly in succession, give *yōō*, like the *u* in *duke* (sounded as "dyōōk."

oi. Made up of *au* (see No. 10 in § 163) + *ĭ*. The utterance of these two simple sounds in rapid succession produces a mixed sound distinct from both.

ou. Made up of *à* (see No. 4 in § 163) + *ŏŏ*. The utterance of these two simple sounds in rapid succession produces a mixed sound distinct from both.

Note.—We now see very clearly what was stated above in § 158, that the use of a digraph or two letters to express a sound by no means indicates that the sound is diphthongal or mixed. Thus **ī** and **ū**, though expressed by single vowels, are both diphthongs; while **au, ŏŏ, ōō, ee**, though expressed by digraphs, are all simple sounds.

166. Spellings of the twenty vowel-sounds.—We shall follow the order of vowels, simple and diphthongal, given in § 163.

1. **ă** : m*a*d, pl*ai*d, h*a*v*e*, s*al*mon, thr*e*sh.
2. **â** : M*a*ry, *ai*ry, b*ea*rer, h*ei*ress, m*ayo*ralty, th*e*rein.
3. **ā** : f*a*tal, f*a*t*e*, t*ai*l, pl*ay*, camp*aign*, str*aigh*t, v*ei*n, th*ey*, r*eig*n, w*eigh*, st*ea*k, g*ao*l, g*au*ge, *eh*, d*ah*lia, h*alf*penny. French words: f*ê*te, conj*é*, ball*et*, champ*a*gne, dem*e*sne.
4. **à** : p*a*th, *a*rt, h*ea*rt, cl*e*rk, *au*nt, baz*aa*r, p*al*m, hurr*ah*, pl*ai*ster. Fr. words: v*a*se, écl*at*.
5. **ĕ** : b*e*d, h*ea*d, *a*ny, s*ai*d, s*ay*s, l*eo*pard, l*ei*sure, r*ey*nard, *a*t*e*, fr*ie*nd, Th*a*mes, b*u*ry.
6. **ē** : m*e*, th*e*m*e*, s*ee*n, *ea*ch, f*ie*ld, s*ei*ze,[1] k*ey*, C*æ*sar, pol*i*c*e*, inval*i*d, qu*ay*, p*eo*ple, B*eau*champ.

---

sounded with the glides *i* and *u* respectively, as a^i, o^u, and that hence these vowels are in a certain sense diphthongal. They are not diphthongal, however, to the same extent that **ī, ū, oi**, and **ou** are. For the sake of simplicity I have followed Miss Laura Soames in treating them as simple vowels, not as diphthongs.

[1] The following is a list of all the words in which *ei* has the sound of *ē*:—conceive, deceive (and their derivatives), ceiling, seize, either, neither, plebeian, weir, weird, seignory, inveigle, counterfeit.

7. **ĭ** : bit, nymph, pretty, give, surfeit, married, happy, guinea, donkey, women, busy, breeches, sieve.

8. **ī** : idol, try, mine, lyre, sign, high, height, die, rye, island, aisle, choir, indict, eye.

9. **ŏ** : from, want, shone, laurel, knowledge, yacht, hough.

10. **au** : haul, law, lost, tall, talk, pour, ought, broad, sore, lord, war, water, aught, Vaughan, gone.

11. **o'** : hero, follow, heroes, followed, furlough. Fr. depôt.

12. **ō** : no, note, both, toad, toe, dough, mow, brooch, oh, yeoman, sew, Cockburn. Fr. mauve, beau.

13. **ŏŏ** : stood, full, could, wolf.

14. **ōō** : fool, tomb, shoe, move, soup, through, truth, blue, juice, sleuth-hound, slew, rude, manœuvre.

15. **ŭ** : shut, blood, son, come, touch.

16. **ū** (=yōō) : du-ty, tune, due, suit, few, feud, lieu, view, impugn.

17. **oi** : coil, boy.

18. **ou** : loud, down.

19. **ə** : Chi'-na, Sa'-rah, suf'-fer, squir'-rel, but'-ton, Eu'-rope, thor'-ough, tor'-toise, fa'-mous, meer'-schaum, waist-coat, cup'-board, pleas'-ure, col'-lar, mar'-tyr, bun'-kum, an'-chor, ran'-cour, mur'-mur (all in unaccented syllables. This sound is never accented).

20. **əə** : herd, erred, heard, bird, stirred, turn, blurred, word, colo-nel (sounded as ker'-nel). (All in accented syllables.)

One hundred and ninety spellings (not counting the French words) for twenty vowel-sounds.

167. Same spelling with different sounds.—We may now invert the process, and show how the same symbol (*i.e.* the same spelling) may be used to denote different sounds :—

a : cat, tall, path, many, made, care, want, steward.
a—e : rave, have, are.
ai : maid, said, plaid, aisle.
au : aunt, haunt, gauge, mauve, meer-schaum.
e : he, her, clerk, bed, pretty.
e—e : there, here.
ea : heat, steak, heart, head.
ei : vein, leisure, seize, sur-feit, height.
ey : they, key, eye.
ew : new, sew.
i—e : bite, niche, police.
ie : field, die, sieve.
o : hot, cold, wolf, women, whom, son, button, lost, hero.
o—e : cove, prove, love, move, shove.
oa : load, broad, cup-board.
oe : shoe, toe.
oo : hook, fool, brooch, flood, door.
ou : pour, young, thou, soup, soul.
ough : rough, hiccough, cough, hough, trough, bough, though, through.

al : *fall*, *palm*, *shall*, *hospital*.
ol : *cold*, *wolf*, *golf*, *sym'-bol*.
ar : *ar'*-row, *art*, col-*lar*.

SECTION 3.—CONSONANTS : SOUNDS, SYMBOLS, AND SPELLINGS.

168. Twenty-five Consonantal sounds.—In English as now spoken there are altogether *twenty-five* consonantal sounds. The symbols used to denote these sounds, if we place them as nearly as we can in the order of the alphabet, run as follows :—

1. b	4. g	7. k	10. n	13. s	16. w	19. ch	22. th(in)
2. d	5. h	8. l	11. p	14. t	17. y	20. ng	23. sh
3. f	6. j	9. m	12. r	15. v	18. z	21. th(is)	24. zh
							25. wh

169. Simple and Compound.—Out of the twenty-five sounds enumerated above all are simple or uncompounded except two, viz. *j* and *ch*. These are called by Dr. Murray (in the Oxford Dictionary) "consonantal diphthongs," because he, with other phoneticians, has analysed *ch* into *t* + *sh*, and *j* into *d* + *zh*.

Though we have to accept this analysis on the word of the best authorities, it would be very inconvenient to write *tsh* for *ch*, and *dzh* for *j*. Moreover, the two sounds in question are of such frequent occurrence in our language, that *j* and *ch*, even if the sounds are diphthongal, deserve a place in the list of our consonantal symbols.

170. Redundant consonants.—It has been said that "our alphabet contains four redundant consonants—*c*, *j*, *q*, *x*." Assuming that the analysis of the sounds expressed by *j* and *ch* respectively is correct, the statement may be admitted for the following reasons :—

C is superfluous, because (1) when it precedes *a*, *o*, or *u*, it expresses the sound of *k* ; (2) when it precedes *e* or *i*, it expresses the sound of *s* ; (3) when it is combined with *h*, as in *church*, the digraph *ch* has been analysed into *tsh*.

J is superfluous, because it has been analysed into *dzh*.

Q is superfluous, because it is never used except in combination with *u*, and the combination can be expressed equally well by *kw*, as in *awkward*.

X is superfluous, because in such words as *extra* it is equivalent to *ks*, and in *example* to *gz*.

171. Main divisions of consonants.—The consonantal sounds can be classified according to the organ chiefly used in uttering them. Any part of our bodily structure that helps us to utter articulate sounds may be called an organ of speech. The chief organs are the tongue, the throat, the palate, the teeth, and the lips. By means of these organs the breath is modified as it passes through the larynx.

The most important of all these organs is the tongue; for the loss of this organ involves the loss of articulate speech. Since the tongue is the necessary helpmate to the other four organs, there is no separate class of Lingual (Lat. *lingua*, tongue).

The main divisions of consonants are as follows:—

I. **Gutturals** (Lat. *guttur*, throat): *k, g, ng.*
II. **Palatals** (Lat. *palatum*, palate): *ch, j* | *sh, zh* | *y, r.*
III. **Dentals** (Lat. *dent-em*, tooth): *t, d* | *s, z* | *n, l* | *th*(in), *th*(is).
IV. **Labials** (Lat. *labium*, lip): *p, b, m* | *f, v* | *wh, w.*

I. **Gutturals**: these three sounds are produced by raising the *back* of the tongue against the *soft* palate, viz. that part of the palate that lies farther back in the throat (Lat. *guttur*):—*k*, as in *k*een; *g*, as in *g*ood; *ng*, as in thi*ng* or fi*n*-ger. The last, though expressed by a digraph, is as simple a sound as the other two. It occurs only when it is followed by another guttural, *k* or *g*, as in bla*n*-ket, fi*n*-ger, or when it comes at the end of a word, as in thi*ng*, ridi*ng*. There is a great difference of sound between the *n* of fi*n*-(ger) and the *n* of fi*n*. The former is a guttural, which you cannot utter without opening your jaws; the latter a dental, which you utter with closed teeth.

II. **Palatals**: all these sounds are produced by raising the *front* of the tongue towards the *hard* palate, or palate proper (viz. that part of the palate that lies further forward than the soft palate):—*ch*, as in *ch*air; *j*, as in *j*oke; *sh*, as in *sh*ip; *zh*, as in sei*z*ure; *y*, as in *y*ield; *r*, as in *r*ob. All of these are simple sounds with the exception of the first two (§ 169).

III. **Dentals**: all these sounds are produced by bringing the point of the tongue towards the teeth or upper gums:—*t*, as in *t*ail; *d*, as in *d*og; | *s*, as in *s*eal; *z*, as in *z*eal; | *n*, as in *n*ame; *l*, as in *l*ine; | *th*(in), as in brea*th*; *th*(is), as in brea*the*. In sounding the first pair, *t* and *d*, the point of the tongue touches the upper teeth. In sounding the second pair, *s* and *z*, it comes very near the roots of the upper teeth, but does not quite touch them. In sounding the third pair, *n* and *l*, it touches the upper gums. In sounding the fourth pair, *th*(in) and *th*(is), it is placed between the upper and the lower teeth.

IV. **Labials**: all these sounds are produced by closing the lips:—*p*, as in *p*oor; *b*, as in *b*oon; *m*, as in *m*oon; | *f*, as in *f*ox; *v*, as in *v*ixen; | *wh*, as in *wh*ine; *w*, as in *w*ine. In sounding *p*, *b*, and *m* the lips are closed against each other, while the tongue is left to rest on the lower jaw. In sounding *f* and *v* the edges of the upper teeth are pressed against the lower lip, while the tongue rests on the lower jaw. In sounding *wh* and *w* the lips are rounded with the corners drawn together, while the tongue is almost in the same position as in sounding *g*. Hence *w* and *g* are liable to be interchanged, as in *w*ard (A.S. *w*eard), *g*uard (French spelling).

172. The Glottal "h" (Greek, *glottis*, mouth of the wind-pipe). "Glottal" is the name given to the open throat-sound expressed by the letter *h*. In sounding *h* we make no use of the palate, tongue, teeth, or lips. It is a mere breath-sound or aspirate, and stands alone in our alphabet.

The uncertainty about sounding or not sounding this unfortunate letter appears to have arisen in some way from the collision between English and French, which resulted from the Norman Conquest. In Anglo-Saxon the *h* was very distinctly sounded; in French very indistinctly. Hence the confusion.

173. Minor subdivisions of Consonants.—There are a few subdivisions of consonants, which cross with the four main divisions described above, and sometimes with one another.

Sibilants (Lat. *sibilantes*, hissing). On account of the hissing sound which they express, the name "sibilant" has been given to the letters *s*, *z*, *sh*, and *zh*.

Liquids (Lat. *liquidus*, flowing). This is the name given to the letters *l*, *m*, *n*, *r*, *ng*.

Nasals (Lat. *nasus*, nose); the name given to the three letters *n*, *m*, *ng*. These are called nasals, because in forming the sounds which they express the breath passes up the nose-passage and escapes through the nostril. If the nose-passage is blocked by a cold, *ng* (a guttural) is sounded almost as *g* (another guttural), *n* (a dental) almost as *d* (another dental), and *m* (a labial) almost as *b* (another labial).

Note.—When an *intrusive* consonant, *i.e.* one not belonging to the root, is inserted into a word, the intruder is usually of the same class as the consonant going before:—

Num-*b*-er (Lat. *num-er-us*); hum-*b*-le (Lat. *hum-il-is*); ten-*d*-er (Lat. *ten-er*); gen-*d*-er (Lat. *gen-er-is*). Observe the *m* and *b* are both labials, while the *n* and *d* are both dentals.

174. Spellings of the Consonantal sounds.—We shall take each of the twenty-five sounds in the order in which their respective symbols are given in § 168:—

1. **b**: *b*ond (initial); e*bb* (final), *bu*oy, cu*p*-board.
2. **d**: bon*d*, la*dd*er, call*ed*, hor*de*; wou*ld*.
3. **f**: *f*elt, whi*ff*, *ph*legm, lau*gh*, ha*lf*, o*f*ten, sa*pph*ire, li*eu*-tenant (where *ieu*=*ef*).
4. **g**: *g*ame, e*gg*, *gh*ost, *gu*ard.
5. **h**: *h*ot, *wh*o.
6. **j**: *j*ob, *g*ist, *G*eor*ge*, ju*dge*, ju*dg*ment, sol*di*er, Greenwi*ch*, *g*aol.
7. **k**: *k*ill, *c*all, a*cc*ount, ba*ck*, bis*cu*it, *q*uell, li*qu*or, grote*sque*, a*che*, lou*gh*.
8. **l**: *l*ake, ki*ll*, is*l*and, ais*le*, gaze*lle*, sera*gl*io, Woo*lw*ich.
9. **m**: *m*end, ha*mm*er, hy*mn*, la*mb*, progra*mme*, phleg*m*, Ha*mp*den, dra*chm*.
10. **n**: pi*n*, i*nn*, deig*n*, *kn*ee, *gn*aw, Jo*hn*, Linco*ln*, We*dn*esday, rib*and*, bor*ne*, An*ne*, coig*ne*.
11. **p**: *p*lace, ha*pp*y, ste*ppe*, Cla*ph*am, hiccou*gh*.
12. **r**: *r*ain, bo*rr*ow, *rh*ythm, *wr*ite, Nor*w*ich.
13. **s**: *s*elf, ki*ss*, den*se*, *c*ell, dan*ce*, *sc*ene, coale*sce*, *sch*ism, quar*tz*, *sw*ord, has*t*en, i*sth*mus, *ps*alm, creva*sse*.
14. **t**: we*t*, ke*tt*le, ga*z*e*tte*, *Th*ames, look*ed*, *tw*o, de*bt*, indi*ct*, recei*pt*, ya*cht*; cas*te*.
15. **v**: *v*est, ha*ve*, na*vv*y, o*f*, ne*ph*ew; hal*ve*.
16. **w**: *w*ine, *wh*en, s*u*ave, ch*o*ir.
17. **y**: *y*ield, un*i*on, hallelu*j*ah. French vi*gn*ette (*gn*=ny) cou-ti*ll*on.
18. **z**: *z*eal, fi*zz*, hi*s*, clean*se*, sci*ss*ors, *X*erxes, fur*ze*, Wedn*es*day, Chi*sw*ick, Win*ds*or, ven*is*on, *cz*ar, bu*si*ness.
19. **ch**: *ch*ur*ch*, ni*che*, la*tch*, na*tu*re, ques*ti*on, righ*te*ous, violo*nc*ello.
20. **ng**: thi*ng*, fi*n*ger, to*ngue*, ha*nd*kerchief, Birmi*ngh*am.
21. **th**(is): *th*en, soo*the*.
22. **th**(in): brea*th*, Ma*tth*ew.
23. **sh**: *sh*all, A*s*ia, ti*ss*ue, pen*si*on, mousta*che*, fu*ch*sia, mi*ssi*on, fa*shi*on, offi*ci*ate, so*ci*al, o*ce*an, con*sci*ence, *sch*edule, vi*ti*ate, por*ti*on, lun*che*on, *ch*aise.
24. **zh**: sei*z*ure, lei*s*ure, occa*si*on, transi*ti*on. Fr. rou*ge*, ré*g*ime, ju*j*ube (sometimes sounded as *jujube*).
25. **wh**: *wh*ile (often sounded merely as *w*, except in North Britain).

One hundred and sixty-six spellings (not counting the French words) for twenty-five different sounds.

175. Same spelling with different sounds:—

c: violoncello, cat, city.
ch: a*che*, *ch*aise, su*ch*, dra*ch*m (silent).

j : *J*ew, *ju*jube, hallelu*j*ah.
ge : rou*ge*, villa*ge*, *ge*t.
gi : *gi*ve, *gi*nger.
ti : no*ti*on, ques*ti*on, transi*ti*on.
s : ha*s*, ga*s*.
sc : *sc*ene, *sc*arce.
sch : *sch*eme, *sch*edule.
si : occa*si*on, disper*si*on.
th : *th*in, *th*is, *Th*ames.
x : e*x*tra, e*x*ample, *X*erxes. Fr. beau*x*.
ph : nym*ph*, ne*ph*ew.
gh : *gh*ost, lau*gh*, hou*gh*.
qu : li*qu*or, *qu*een.

176. Causes of discrepancies in spelling.—In the earliest form of English every simple sound was expressed by its own particular symbol, and no sound (with very few exceptions) had more than one symbol. The spelling therefore was in the main "phonetic." But the phonetic system was marred and eventually ruined (*a*) by the mixture of French words with English consequent on the Norman Conquest; (*b*) the disuse of marks to denote the lengthening of vowels; (*c*) the loss of the Old English symbols *æ* and *ǽ*, which left the vowel *a* much more work to do than it had before; (*d*) changes in the pronunciation both of vowels and consonants,—changes that were seldom accompanied by a change of spelling; (*e*) the respelling of many of our words during the Revival of Learning (A.D. 1500-1600), so as to bring them more in accordance with the classical originals: thus *vitailles* was respelt as "victuals" (Lat. *victus*, food); *dett* as "debt" (Lat. *debit*-um); *dout* as "doubt" (Lat. *dubit*-are); *sutil* as "subtle" (Lat. *subtil*-is).

Exercise 41.

(*a*) 1. Distinguish between *emphasis, accent, quantity.* 2. Give two instances in which words, identical in spelling, are distinguished one from another by accent. 3. "A perfect alphabet would contain a separate letter to represent every simple or elementary sound." Show that the letter *a* in English represents several simple or elementary sounds. 4. What single letters in our alphabet represent compound sounds? 5. "Our alphabet contains four redundant letters—*c, j, q, x*." Discuss this statement. 6. Write two words of one syllable, in the first of which the letter *i* represents a pure vowel sound, and in the second a diphthongal sound. 7. How do you account for the fact that the spelling of English words is often at variance with their pronunciation? 8. Give one example under each of the following to show that in some words—

(i.) The letter *i* represents a diphthongal sound.
(ii.) The letter *s* is written where *z* is sounded.
(iii.) A letter is not sounded at all.

9. State and illustrate the different sounds of the letter *s*. (*Oxford and Cambridge Locals.*)

(*b*) 1. What consonants are redundant in the English alphabet, and in what respects is our alphabet defective in consonants? 2. The sound of *a* in *hate* is expressed in several different ways in written English (as in *bait, may, whey, weight, gaol, gauge,* etc.). Show that there are also several ways in which the sound of *e* in *me* is represented in writing. 3. Give four true Diphthongs, four Liquids, four Sibilants, and four Labials. 4. Explain the terms *letter, diphthong, Labial, Palatal.* How many sounds has the combination *ough?* 5. Quote examples of English words containing *ei* or *ie* (four of each), and of verbs ending in *ceed* or *cede* (two of each). 6. What is a *diphthong?* Give six examples, all different, of so-called diphthongs which are not really diphthongs. 7. How many *true* diphthongs have we in the English language? Quote three words as examples of each of them. (*College of Preceptors.*)

CHAPTER XXXIII.—PECULIAR PLURALS: ORIGIN AND USES.

177. Man, men, etc., see § 7 (i.).—The eight Plurals there shown are called **Mutation**-plurals, because they are formed by a change or mutation of the inside vowel of the singular. Once there were many more such plurals than there are now. The original plural of *man* was "*mann-is.*" The *i* in the ending *-is* had the effect of changing the *a* of *mann* or *man* into a sound more like itself; thus *mann-is* became *menn-is.* The effect of *i* in thus changing the preceding vowel is called Vowel-mutation in English and *Umlaut* in German. When the *-is* was dropped, nothing but the vowel-change was left to distinguish the Plural from the Singular. This Mutation-method became obsolete when the Anglo-Saxon system of grammar decayed.

178. Ox, oxen, etc., see § 7 (ii.).—The four Plurals there shown are formed by a process that is now as obsolete as that of vowel-mutation (§ 177). In Old English *-an* (now written *-en*) was not less common as a Plural ending than *-as* (now written *-es* or *-s*). But *-as* or *-es* became much more common when the decay of Anglo-Saxon was setting in. Afterwards, when French influence had begun to work (about 200 years after the Norman Conquest), the French Plural in *-s* drove the nail home, so that *-s* or *-es* became eventually the sign of the Plural for almost all our nouns.

179. Foreign Plurals.—We have some Plurals which have been borrowed direct from foreign nouns :—

Latin Plurals.—From *-um* (Sing.) to *-a* (Plur.): addend-*a*, agend-*a*, dat-*a*, errat-*a*, strat-*a* (stratum-*s* is sometimes used).

From *-us* (Sing.) to *-i* (Plur.): alumn-*i*, fung-*i*, radi-*i*, geni-*i* (or genius-*es*).

Other Latin Plurals are: genera (genus), stamina (stamen), indices (index), series (series), species (species), apparatus (apparatus).

Greek Plurals.—From *-is* (Sing.) to *-es* (Plur.): analyses, bases, hypotheses, parentheses, oases, bases.

From *-on* (Sing.) to *-a* (Plur.): phenomen-*a*, criteri-*a*.

Italian Plurals: banditti (or bandits), dilettanti.

French Plurals: beaux, bureaux, chateaux, messieurs, mesdames.

Hebrew Plurals: cherubim (or cherubs), seraphim (or seraphs).

180. Nouns of Multitude.—These are a kind of Collective noun (§ 17) which have a plural sense, though they remain singular in form. See § 100, Rule IV.

The *poultry* (=fowls) are doing well. These *cattle* (=cows) are mine. These *vermin* (=insects, etc.) do much harm. These *people* (=persons) have returned home.

181. Some nouns, which take a Plural at ordinary times, use the Singular instead of the Plural to express some specific quantity or number :—

A twelve-*month*. A three-*foot* rule. An eight-*day* clock. A six-*year*-old horse. A fort-*night* (contraction of "fourteen nights"). Forty *head* of cattle. Twelve *pound* weight. Ten *sail* of the line. A six-*penny* piece.

Note.—*Six-pence* has a Collective sense denoting a single coin, which makes the noun appear to be Singular, so that we say *a sixpence* (Singular), *sixpences* (Plural). The latter is really a double Plural.

182. Two forms of Plural, each with a separate meaning :—

Brother	Brothers,	*sons of the same mother.*
	Brethren,	*members of the same society.*
Cherub	Cherubim,	*angels of a certain rank.*
	Cherubs,	*images or models of a cherub.*
Cloth	Cloths,	*kinds or pieces of cloth* (Distributive).
	Clothes,	*articles of dress* (Collective).
Cow	Cows,	*individual cows* (Distributive).
	Kine,	*cattle* (Collective).
Die	Dies,	*stamps for coining* (Distributive).
	Dice,	*small cubes used in games* (Collective).
Genius	Geniuses,	*men of genius or talent.*
	Genii,	*fabulous spirits of the air.*

Index	Indexes,	*tables of contents.*
	Indices,	*signs used in algebra.*
Pea	Peas,	(Distributive).
	Pease,	(Collective).
Penny	Pennies,	=*penny-pieces* (Distributive).
	Pence,	(sometimes Collective).
Staff	Staves,	*sticks or poles.*
	Staffs,	*departments in the army.*
Stamen	Stamens,	*male organs of flowers* (Distributive).
	Stamina,	*endurance, vigour*, lit. *threads* (Collective).
Shot	Shot,	*little balls discharged from a gun.*
	Shots,	*discharges; as, "He had two shots."*

183. Different senses of Singular and Plural :—

Singular.	*Plural.*
Advice, counsel.	*Advices*, information.
Air, atmosphere.	*Airs*, demeanour.
Ban, a curse (under a *ban*).	*Banns*, announcement (*banns* of marriage).
Beef, flesh of ox.	*Beeves*, cattle, bulls and cows.
Compass, range or extent.	*Compasses*, an instrument.
Copper, a metal.	*Coppers*, pennies.
Domino, a king of mask.	*Dominoes*, the game so-called.
Force, strength or energy.	*Forces*, army.
Good, benefit.	*Goods*, movable property.
Iron, a metal.	*Irons*, fetters made of iron.
Minute, of time.	*Minutes*, of a meeting.
Physic, medicine.	*Physics*, natural science.
Return, coming back.	*Returns*, statistics.
Salt, seasoning substance.	*Salts*, smelling salts.
Sand, a kind of matter.	*Sands*, a tract of sandy land.
Vapour, invisible steam.	*Vapours*, dejection.
Vesper, evening.	*Vespers*, evening prayers.
Water, the element.	*Waters*, springs.

184. Two meanings in the Plural against one in the Singular :—

	Singular.		*Plural.*
Colour,	colour.	*Colours*	1. Kinds of colour. 2. *Flag of regiment.*
Custom,	habit.	*Customs*	1. Habits. 2. *Toll* or *tax.*
Element,	simple substance.	*Elements*	1. Simple substances. 2. *Conditions of the air.*
Effect,	result.	*Effects*	1. Results. 2. *Goods and chattels.*
Letter,	1. Of Alphabet. 2. Epistle.	*Letters*	1. Of alphabet. 2. *Epistles.* 3. *Learning.*
Manner,	mode or way.	*Manners*	1. Modes, ways. 2. *Behaviour.*

Singular.		Plural.	
Number,	as in counting.	*Numbers*	1. As in counting. 2. *Poetry.*
Pain,	suffering.	*Pains*	1. Sufferings. 2. *Trouble, care.*
Part,	portion.	*Parts*	1. Portions. 2. *Abilities.*
Premise,	a statement or proposition.	*Premises*	1. Propositions. 2. *Buildings.*
Quarter,	a fourth part.	*Quarters*	1. Fourth parts. 2. *Lodgings.*
Spectacle,	anything seen.	*Spectacles*	1. Things seen. 2. *Eye-glasses.*

185. Two meanings in the Singular against one in the Plural:—

Singular.		Plural.	
Abuse	1. Wrong use. 2. Reproaches.	*Abuses,*	wrong uses.
Foot	1. Part of body. 2. Infantry.	*Feet,*	parts of body.
Horse	1. A quadruped. 2. Cavalry.	*Horses,*	quadrupeds.
Issue	1. Result. 2. Offspring.	*Issues,*	results.
Light	1. A lamp. 2. Radiance.	*Lights,*	lamps.
People	1. A nation. 2. Persons.	*Peoples,*	nations.
Powder	1. A medicinal mixture. 2. Gunpowder.	*Powders,*	medicinal mixtures.
Practice	1. Habitual act. 2. Professional connection.	*Practices,*	habitual acts.
Stone	1. A piece of rock. 2. Fourteen pounds.	*Stones,*	pieces of rock.
Wood	1. A forest. 2. Timber.	*Woods,*	forests.

186. True Singulars used as Plurals.—By a "True Singular" we mean that the final *s* is part of the original Singular noun, and not a sign of the Plural.

Such nouns, though Singular by etymology, are liable to be considered Plural on account of the final *s;* and all except the first of these named below are now always used as if they were Plural.

Summons (Fr. *semonce*).—This noun is still correctly used as a Singular; as "I received *a* summons to attend"; "*This* summons reached me to-day." The plural form is *summonses.*

Alms (A.S. *ælmesse*).—"He asked *an alms*" (New Testament). But now the word is generally used as if it were Plural; as, "I gave alms to the beggar, and for *these* he thanked me."

Eaves (A.S. *efese*).—The edge or lower borders of the roof of a house. The word is now always used as a Plural; as, "The eaves *are* not yet finished."

Riches (Fr. *richesse*).—This too is really a Singular; as, "In one hour *is* so great riches come to naught" (*New Testament*); but now, on account of the final *s*, this noun is always used as a Plural; as, "Riches *do* not last for ever."

Cherries (Mid. Eng. *cheris*): cf. Latin, *ceras*-us.—The *s* looked so like a Plural ending, that a Singular *cherry* was coined.

Peas (A.S. *pis-a*, Singular).—When the *a* was lost, the final *s* looked like a Plural, so a Singular *pea* was coined.

The vaunting poets found nought worth a *pease*.—SPENCER.

187. True Plurals used as Singulars.—In such nouns the final *s* is really a sign of the Plural:—

Amends.—This is sometimes used as a Singular and sometimes as a Plural; as, "*An* honourable amends" (ADDISON).

Means.—This is now almost always used as a Singular; as, "By *this* means."

News.—This is now almost always used as a Singular; as, "Ill news *runs* apace." Mid. Eng. *new-es*(plural); French, *nouvelles*.

Innings.—This is a word used in cricket to denote the turn for going in and using the bat. It is *always* used as a Singular; as, "We have not yet had *an* innings"; "Our eleven beat the other by *an* innings and ten runs."

Gallows.—The frame-work from which criminals are hanged. This noun is used as a Singular; as, "They fixed up *a* gallows."

Odds.—A word used in betting to denote the difference of one wager against another. "We gave him *a* heavy odds against ourselves."

Sledge.—A respelling of *sleds*, plural of *sled*, which is still used in Canada for "sledge." This is always used as Singular.

CHAPTER XXXIV.—GENDER OF NOUNS: ORIGIN AND HISTORY.

188. Different Words for Masculine and Feminine: see § 9.—The origin of the words belonging to this list is given below:—

Bachelor, maid, spinster.—Late Lat. *baccalarius*, origin unknown. A.S. *mægd-en*, little maid (the *-en* being Diminutive). A.S. *spinn-estre*, a woman who spins (the *-estre* denoting a female).

Boar, sow.—A.S. *bár* (male pig). A.S. *sugu*, sow. No connection with "swine," A.S. *swín*.

Boy, girl.—Dutch *boef*, Frisian *boi*, boy. Old Low German *gör*, child, with diminutive suffix *-l* added to it: hence *girl*.

Brother, sister.—A.S. *bróthor* (cf. Lat. *frater*). A.S. *seostor*, Norse *systir*; cf. Latin *soror* for *sosor*.

Buck, doe.—A.S. *bucc-a*, male fallow deer. A.S. *dá*, doe.

Bull, cow.—A.S. *bull-uc*, a bull-calf. A.S. *cú*, cow.

Bullock or **steer, heifer.**—A.S. *bull-uc* as above. A.S. *steór*, steer; A.S. *heáh-fore* (lit. a high, *i.e.* full grown cow-calf).

Cock, hen.—A.S. *cocc*, of imitative origin. A.S. *henn-e*, hen.

Colt or **foal, filly.**—A.S. *colt*, the young of any animal. A.S. *fol-a*, male young; Norse, *fyl-ja*, a female foal.

Duck, drake.—Middle Eng. *duk-e*, a bird that bobs the head (Feminine). A.S. *ened-rake*, *end-rake*. Perhaps the *en* of *endrake* became confounded with the Indefinite article *an*, leaving only *drake*. In A.S. *ened* means "duck." But Dr. Murray declares himself unable to ascertain the meaning of *rake*, though he has decided that it did not signify "lord" or "master," as is usually asserted. *Rake* is not a suffix, as has been stated.

Drone, bee.—A.S. *drán*, the hummer. A.S. *beó*, *bí*, bee.

Earl, countess.—A.S. *eorl*, a man. Old Fr. *cont-esse*, Fem. of "count."

Father, mother.—A.S. *fæder*, father. A.S. *móder*, mother.

Friar or **monk, nun.**—Old Fr. *freire*, brother (cf. Lat. *frater*). A.S. *munec* (Late Lat. *monachus*, one who lives alone). A.S. *nunne*, a nun or spiritual mother.

Gaffer, gammer.—The first is the short of Eng. *grandfather*; the second of Fr. *grand-mère* (grandmother).

Gander, goose.—A.S. *gós*, from the root *gan-s*, in which the *s* is only a suffix. A.S. *gan-d-ra*, in which the *ra* is a suffix, and the *d* is an intruder, as in *ten-d-er*, Lat. *ten-er*.

Gentleman, lady.—Fr. *gentil-homme*, a well-born man. For *lady*, see below under **Lord.**

Hart, roe.—A.S. *heort*, hart. A.S. *ráh*, roe.

Horse, mare.—A.S. *hors*, a runner, courser. A.S. *mere*, mare.

Husband, wife.—Norse, *hús-bóndi* house-occupier. A.S. *wíf*, woman or female.

King, queen.—A.S. *cyn-ing*, one of noble kin. A.S. *cwén*, woman.

Lord, lady.—A.S. *hláford*=*hláf-weard*, loaf-keeper. A.S. *hláf-dige*, loaf-kneader.

Man, woman.—A.S. *mann*, person of either sex. A.S. *wíf-man*, a female person.

Milter, spawner.—"Milter" means a fish with *milt* or *milk*. "Spawner" means a fish that scatters eggs. Old Fr. *espandre*, to scatter.

Nephew, niece.—Old Fr. *neveu*, Lat. *nepot-em*, a grandson. Old Fr. *niece*, Lat. *neptis*, grand-daughter or niece.

Ram or **wether, ewe.**—A.S. *ram*, a male sheep. A.S. *wether*, a yearling. A.S. *eowu*, a female sheep; cf. Lat. *ov-is*.

Sir, madam, or **madame.**—Fr. *sire*, Lat. *senior*, older. Fr. *madame*, Lat. *mea domina*, my lady.

Sire, dam.—Origin as above.

Son, daughter.—A.S. *sunu*, son. A.S. *dóhtor*, daughter.

Stag, hind.—Origin of "stag" unknown. Its derivation from A.S. *stig*-an, to mount, is disputed. A.S. *hind*, female deer.

Uncle, aunt.—Fr. *oncle*, Lat. *avunculus*, a little grandfather. Old Fr. *ante*, Lat. *amita*, a father's sister.

189. Peculiar forms in "-ess" or "-ss":—

Abb-ess: Old Fr. *ab-esse*, Late Latin *abbat-issa*, the Fem. form of *abbas*, *abbat-em*, father.

Duch-ess: Old Fr. *duc-esse*, *duch-esse*; Lat. *duc*-em, leader.

Mistr-ess: Old Fr. *maister-esse*, Fem. form of *maistre*, master. "Miss" is a contraction of *mistress*.

Marchion-ess: Late Lat. *marchion-issa*, the stem of which is *marchion*-(em), prefect of the marches or border.

Murder-er, murder-ess.—The stem of both is *murder*: the former has A.S. suffix *-ere*, which denotes a male agent; the latter the French suffix *-esse*, which denotes a female agent.

Sorcer-er, sorcer-ess.—Parallel to the above. The stem of both is *sorcer*, from Old Fr. *sorc-ier*, Lat. *sort-iarius*.

Songster, songstress.—Originally the *-ster* of "song-*ster*" denoted a Feminine. When the Fem. force of *-ster* had been forgotten, the final *er* appeared to signify a male, as in "murder-*er*," "sorcer-*er*." So the *er* was changed to *-ess*, to form a Feminine.

Empr-ess, govern-ess, nur-se.—In these three words the suffix is from Lat. *-icem*, not *-issa* or *-esse*: imperatr-*icem*, gubernatr-*icem*, nutr-*icem*.

Lad, lass.—It used to be said that *lad* and *lass* were from the Welsh *llawd* and *llodes*. But this is now abandoned. No one knows the etymology of either word. It has been suggested that *lad* may mean "one led," Middle English *lad*, pp. of *led-en*, to lead.

190. Other peculiar endings:—

Widow-er, widow.—The older forms were "widuw-*a*" (Masc.) and "widuw-*e*" (Fem.). To make the difference more distinct, the *-a* of the Masc. was displaced by the suffix *-ere* or *-er*, denoting a male agent as in "murder-*er*," "sorcer-*er*."

Wizard, witch.—"Witch" was not long ago of the Common gender: "Your honour is a *witch*."—SCOTT. "Wizard" *witt-ish-ard*, Old Fr. *wisch-ard* or *guisc-art*, sagacious.

Sultan, sultan-a.—The final *a* is an Italian feminine.

Bride-groom, bride: A.S. *brýd*, a bride. To give this stem a masculine sense A.S. *guma* (male) was added; in Eng. the *r* of "groom" is an intruder.

Fox, vixen: A.S. *fox*, a fox. A.S. *fyx-en*, Middle English *fix-en*, *vixen*, a female fox; the final *-en* being a Fem. suffix. The *o* of *fox* was changed to *y* or *i* by the law of Mutation or Umlaut described in § 177.

CHAPTER XXXV.—ORIGIN AND USE OF CERTAIN ENDINGS.

191.—The following is an alphabetical list or glossary of certain endings, the origin and use of which are considered more especially worthy of attention:—

-ar (1): A.S. *-ere* (person, agent). Li-*ar* (for li-*er*).
-ar (2): Lat. *-aris*, *-arium*, *-arius*: schol-*ar*, vic-*ar*, cell-*ar*.
-ble: Lat. *plex* (fold), dou-*ble*. Also Lat. *-bilis*, fee-*ble*, dura-*ble*.
-d (1).—Sign of the Past Participle of Weak verbs. In A.S. this was *-t* or *-d*. Cf. Latin "ama-*t*-us," Gr. "Chris-*t*-os," Christ, anointed.

-d (2).—Sign of the Past tense of Weak verbs. A.S. *-de*, *-te*, or *-the*. No connection at all with the preceding. But when the final *e* was lost, nothing was left to keep them distinct.
-'em, as in "kill *'em*." From A.S. *hem*, "them," with the *h* omitted.

-en (1), Teutonic: A.S. *-en*. Seven uses have been served by this suffix:—(*a*) diminutive, maid-*en*; (*b*) feminine, vix-*en*; (*c*) agent, hav-*en*, that which holds or has; (*d*) plural, ox-*en*; (*e*) passive Part. beat-*en*; (*f*) quality, wood-*en*; (*g*) Trans. verb, dark-*en*, to make dark.
-en (2), Teutonic. Obsolete Infinitive ending, of which we see examples in—

> In peace may pass-*en* Lethe lake.—SPENSER.
> Thinks all is writ he speak-*en* can.—SHAKSPEARE.
> The soil that erst so seemly was to see-*n*.—SACKVILLE.

The Simple or Noun-Infinitive in A.S. had no "to" before it, and ended in *-an*, which in Mid. Eng. became *-en*; the *-en* being eventually dropped. What we now call the Gerundial or Qualifying Infinitive always had "to" before it in A.S., and ended in *-anne* or *-enne*; as *tó bind-enne*, "to bind," "for binding." Here *tó* is simply the preposition "to." The ending *-enne* was gradually reduced to *-en* and eventually disappeared like the *-en* of the Simple Infinitive.
Meanwhile the Simple Infinitive, in compensation for the loss of its ending *-en*, took to itself the preposition "to" borrowed from the Gerundial Infinitive. Thenceforth the two Infinitives became undistinguishable in form.

Note.—It is a very great mistake to suppose that the old ending *-enne* or *-en* has reappeared in modern Eng. in the form of *-ing*; and that hence "bind-ing" is a form of Infinitive. A correct explanation of *ing* is given under **-ing**. See also footnote to p. 77.

-en (3): Latin *-enus*, ali-*enus*, ali-*en*.
-er (1), Teutonic.—Three uses are served by this suffix:—(*a*) A.S. *-ere*, agent, rid-*er*, robb-*er*; (*b*) A.S. *-ira*, *-ra*, Comparative suffix, hott-*er*; (*c*) A.S. *-er*, Frequentative suffix, chatt-*er*.
-er (2), Romanic.—Two uses are served by this suffix:—(1) Lat. *-arius* or *-ator*, agent, arch-*er* (arc-*arius*), lev-*er* (lev-*ator*); (2) French Infinitive *-re*, rend-*er* (Fr. rend-*re*).
-eth: sign of 3rd Sing. Pres. (older form). See below, **s** (*c*).
-ies: Plural ending of Singulars in *y*. An older form of the Singular ending was *-ie*; as *citie*, *cities*.
-ing (1).—The Suffix used for forming abstract nouns from verb-stems. A.S. *-ing*, or more usually *-ung*. Thus "wrít-*ing*" or "wrít-*ung*" (writing) was a pure noun; as "the writing of letters." (Very erroneously this *-ing* has been supposed to be an Infinitive ending for **-en** (2). It has even been called the "Flexional Infinitive." This is purely fictitious, devoid of all historical warrant.)

-ing (2).—The Suffix *now* used for forming the Present Participle of verbs: a corruption of A.S. *inde*, and therefore entirely distinct from **-ing** (1). At the end of a word *-ing* is more easily sounded than *-ind*, and so the latter was ousted (A.D. 1350). See § 107.

Note.—What we now call a Gerund is merely a confusion between **-ing** (1) and **-ing** (2). When we leave out the "of" which ought to follow the verbal noun **-ing** (1), and give it all the participial forms, Past and Present, Active and Passive, of **-ing** (2), we call this thing a Gerund. The Gerund began to appear about 1500 A.D.

-ish (1), Teutonic: A.S. *-isc*: pal-*ish*, woman-*ish*, peev-*ish*.

-ish (2), Romanic: Verb-suffix from Lat. *-esc*, Fr. *-iss*: pun-*ish*.

-le (1), Teutonic: two chief uses—(*a*) Diminutive nouns, as freck-*le*; (*b*) Frequentative verbs, as crumb-*le*.

-le or **-el** (2), Romanic: Diminutive nouns: mod-*el*, circ-*le*.

-ling (1): A.S. *-el*, *-ing*, double Dim., as dar-*ling*; (2) A.S. *-linga* or *-lunga*, adverbial suffix, as dark-*ling*.

-ly, Teutonic.—Two purposes served by this suffix:—(*a*) A.S. *lic* (like); for forming *adjectives*; chiefly added to nouns; as god-*ly* (god-like), man-*ly* (man-like): sometimes added to adjectives; as clean-*ly*, good-*ly*; (*b*) A.S. *lic-e* (adverbial form of *lic*); for forming *adverbs*; as tru-*ly*, rough-*ly*. This adverbial suffix is sometimes added to Participles, as knowing-*ly*, learned-*ly*.

-on (1), Teutonic; as wag-*on*, wai-*n*.

-on (2), Romanic: two uses—(*a*) agent, patr-*on*; (*b*) augmentative, milli-*on*.

-on (3), Greek: phenomen-*on*, criteri-*on*.

-or (1), Teutonic.—A.S. *-ere* (male agent): sail-*or*.

-or (2), Romanic: appears in three different characters:—(*a*) Agent, as mot-*or* (Lat. *-or*), emper-*or* (Lat. *-ator*); (*b*) Abstract: err-*or* (Lat. *-or*); (*c*) Lat. compar.: super-i-*or*, exter-i-*or*.

-s: There are three uses served by the inflection *s*. (*a*) Sign of the Plural. In A.S. the form was *-as*, which in Middle English became *-es* (see § 178). Now the *e* is omitted, except after nouns ending in *ch*, *s*, *x*, or *sh*; as march-*es*, glass-*es*, box-*es*, bush-*es*. (*b*) Sign of the Possessive. In A.S. this was *es*; but now the *e* is elided and an apostrophe put in its place. In the Tudor period the *es* is occasionally seen:—

> Larger than the mounës sphere.—*Mid. Night's Dream*, ii. 1.

In A.S. certain Feminines did not take this inflection; hence the contrast between *Lord's day* and *Lady day*, *Wednesday* (Woden's day) and *Friday* (Freia's day). (*c*) Sign of the 3rd pers. Sing. Present tense. In A.S. this was *-eth* or *-th*. The form *-eth* is now used only in poetry. The *th* has become *s*, on the principle that one dental (voiceless) has been substituted for another dental that is also voiceless. See § 159 III., and § 171 III.

-ther: A.S. *-ther*. Three uses served by this suffix:—(*a*) Comparative, as in fur-*ther*; (*b*) Agent, as in mo-*ther*; (*c*) Adverbial, as in hi-*ther*.

-ves.—Plural ending of nouns, whose Singular ends in *f* or *-fe*. The letter *f*, when placed between two vowels, as in "wives," is more easily sounded as *v*, and was so sounded in A.S. Those nouns which form the Plural in *fs* or *fes* are of French origin, not Teutonic.

-y (1), **Teutonic.**—Serves three purposes :—(*a*) Dimin., as dadd-*y*; (*b*) Adjective, as might-*y*; (*c*) Verb, as ferr-*y*, the Causal form of "fare"; see § 62, p. 40.

-y (2), **Romanic.**—Serves two purposes :—(*a*) for *-atus*, as deput-*y*, one who is deputed; jur-*y*, one who is sworn; (*b*) for *-ia, -ium, -ies*; as famil-*y*, stud-*y*, progen-*y*.

-y (3), **Greek**: for *-ia*, as energ-*y*.

CHAPTER XXXVI.—ORIGIN AND HISTORY OF CERTAIN WORDS.

192. This chapter consists of an alphabetical list or glossary of certain words in common grammatical use, whose origin and history are more especially worthy of attention.

A (1), **an, any, one, only, once.**—All based upon A.S. *án*, "one." "Any" is A.S. *ǽn-ig*. "One" was so spelt in A.D. 1500 to make it look more like Lat. *un-us*, with which, however, it has no connection in origin. "Only" is A.S. *án-lic* (one-like). "Once" is A.S. *án-es* (of one), Adv. Possessive (§ 149). "A" is merely a contraction of *an*.

A (2).—Disguised preposition (§ 55*a*); as "four *a* (on) day."

Ago: A.S. *á-gán* (agone, agon, ago), Past Part. of "go"; looking back from time present to time gone or past.

Am, is, are.—The verb "to be" is a patch-work of three separate roots, (1) *-es*, (2) *-wes*, (3) *beó*. "Am," "is," "are" are all from the first. "Am" is A.S. *eam* for *es-m*: cf. Latin *su-m*, Gr. *es-mi*. "Is" is A.S. *is* for *es*, *es-t*: cf. Latin *est*, Gr. *es-ti*, German, *ist*. "Are" is from *ar-on*, northern dialect, the *s* being changed to *r*.

As, a contraction of *also* (all so), A.S. *eal-swá*.

Aught: A.S. *á-wiht*, one whit.

Aye (1), yes. Apparently a corruption of *yea*, A.S. *geá*.

Aye (2), **ever**: A.S. *áwa*; cf. Latin *æv-um*, an age.

Bad, worse, worst.—A patch-work of two roots. "Bad" is from A.S. *bæd-el*, an effeminate man. "Wor-se" is A.S. *wyr-sa*, in which *-sa*, the original Comparative suffix, has not been changed to *-ra*, as it has been in almost all other adjectives. "Wor-st" is from A.S *wyrr-est*, Superlative of *wyr*.

Be, been, being.—All these are based on the third root named under **am**. "We *be* twelve brethren."—*Old Testament*. The *n* of "been" is the regular participial ending of Strong verbs.

Breeks, breeches.—These are two forms or spellings of the same plural. This plural is a double one, made up (1) of A.S. *brec*, plural of *bróc*, as "feet," "foot," by vowel-mutation, see § 177; (2) the superadded plural ending *-s* or *-es*.

Can, could.—"Could" (in which the *l* is an intruder, in imitation of *should, would*) is from A.S. *cú-the*, past tense of the Weak conjugation. Hence "un-couth," literally "unknown," "strange." There is no such word as *can-s* in the Present tense, because *can* was originally the Past tense of a verb, which had lost its Present form even in A.S.

Dare, durst.—The root is *dars*, hence Past tense *dors-te*, "durst." The Pres. has the form of *dare*, A.S. *dearr*, because the final *s* of *dars* was changed to *r*.

Deer: A.S. *deór*. In A.S. it was of the Neuter gender, and Neuters of a certain class had no Plural inflection. Hence in Eng. too the form of the Plural is the same as that of the Singular.

Do, did: A.S. *dó* (Pres.), *dy-de* (Past). The latter is believed by some to be a *reduplicated* Past, like Latin *pell-o, pe-pul-i*. But this is doubtful. The *-de* of *dy-de* might be merely the regular ending of Past tense in Weak verbs; see above **-d** (2).

Dozen: Old Fr. *dos-aine*, Latin *duo-decim*, two + ten.

During.—Properly the Pres. Part of the verb *dure* or *endure*, to continue. "During this week" was originally "this week during or enduring," absolute construction. By an inversion of the order of the words, "during" has assumed the status of a preposition.

Each: A.S. *ǽlc*, contraction of *á-ge-lic*, ever like, all alike.

Eight: A.S. *eah-ta*, Lat. *oc-to*. Medial *h* in A.S. was sounded almost as *c* or *k*. In Eng. this letter passed into *gh* which in many words became silent.

Either: A.S. *ǽg-ther*, contraction of *á-gi-hwæther*, "ever which of two." The negative form is *neither*.

Eleven: A.S. *end-lufon*, Gothic, *ain-lif*, where *ain* means "one," and *lif* means "over," "left." So "eleven" literally means "ten and one over."

Enough: A.S. *ge-nóh* or *ge-nóg*, Mid. Eng. *i-nóh* or *e-nógh*.

Ere: A.S. *ǽr*; hence *ear*ly from *ǽr*-lic.

Every: A.S. *ǽfre*, ever, and *ǽlc*, each. In Mid. English it was *ever-ich*. The *ch* became eventually silent, and was dropped.

Evil: A.S. *yfel*. No connection with *ill*. See **Ill** below.

Except: Lat. *except*-us, excepted. "God and his son except."—MILTON. Here *except* is a participle, formed direct from *except*-us; and the construction is absolute. By an inversion of the order of the words *except* has become a preposition; cf. **During**.

Far, farther, farthest.—In A.S. the forms were *feor, fyr-ra, fyrr-est*. But the analogy of *fore, fur-ther, fur-thest* was too strong, and so the original forms have been superseded.

First.—This is the regular and oldest Superlative of *fore*. A.S. *fore* (Posit.), *fyrst* (Superlative for *for-ist, for-est*). The *o* became *y* by Mutation or Umlaut, through the effect of the vowel *i* in the suffix *-ist*. See § 177. Cf. *fox, fyxen* in § 190.

Fore, former, foremost: A.S. *fore*, standing in front. The Comp. "former" was not seen before the sixteenth century. It comes from an old Superlative *for-ma*, to which the Comparative suffix *-er* has been added, making *for-m-er*. "Foremost" is also modern, and comes from *for-ma + est*; it has therefore two Superlat. suffixes *-ma* and *-est*.

Forth, further, furthest.—These are duplicates or doublets of the preceding. But the real Positive is "fore," not "forth." The latter is merely an extension of A.S. *fore*. The real Compar. and Superl. are *fur-ther, fur-thest*, not *furth-er, furth-est*.

Good, better, best.—A patch-work. "Good" is merely a re-spelling of A.S. *gód*, good. "Better," "best" are from a root *bat*, the base of the verb *batt-en*, to feed or make fat; allied to *boot*, profit.

Have, had: A.S. *habb-an*. In the Past tense *had-de* the radical *b* was dropped.

Her: A.S. *hire*, in which *hi* was the base, and *-re* was a sign of the Genitive and the Dative cases. The A.S. Dative we now call the Objective. Thus in Mod. Eng. (as *hire* in A.S.) *her* stands for two cases, Possessive and Objective.

Hers.—A double Possessive: *he-r-s*. For the Possessive *r* see **Her.** Compare "ours," "yours," "theirs."

Hight: A.S. *hēht*, Reduplicated Past tense of *hāt-an*, to call. The only *certain* instance of a Reduplicated Past in English. This is clearly reduplicated, since the *h* is repeated. See remarks under **Do.**

Him: A.S. *him*. The *m* (attached to the base *hi*) was in A.S. the regular form of the Dative case; cf. *who-m*. The old Accusative was *hine*, *hi-ne*, which has survived only in the colloquial form *'un*: "I saw *'un*"=I saw *hine*, the *h* being silent.

His (1): A.S. *his*. The *s* (attached to the base *hi*) is the regular sign of the Genitive or Possessive.

His (2): as in "Jesus Christ *his* sake." In such phrases (on account of the uncertainty of the letter *h*) *his* has been written for *is*. The particle *is* or *his* was written as a separate word *after foreign proper names* merely as a sign of the Possessive case, because such names could not be regularly declined.

Hisn.—A form used only by peasants. The *n* in A.S. was a regular sign of the Possessive; cf. *mine, thine*. Hence *hisn* is a double Poss. Cf. *ourn, yourn*, used by rustics in southern counties.

I: A.S. *ic*, which in Mid. Eng. became *ich*. A Somersetshire peasant in Shakspeare is made to say, "*Ch'ill* (=*ich* will, *I* will) pick your teeth."—*King Lear*, iv. 6.

Ill: Northern dialect *illr*. No connection with "evil."

Is: 3rd pers. Sing. of "am." See **Am.**

It, its.—"It" is from A.S. *hit*, the *h* being omitted: Neuter gender of "he"; cf. Latin "i-*d*." In A.S. *his* was the Possessive form for the Neuter as well as the Masculine. "Its" occurs only once in the Translation of the Bible printed in 1611 (*Lev.* xxv. 5), and only three times in Milton's poetry. In Dryden's time it is thoroughly established. "Its" is written without the apostrophe, because no such form as "it-*es*" ever existed.

Let (1): A.S. *lǣt-an*, to permit. } The two verbs are quite distinct,
Let (2): A.S. *lett-an*, to hinder. } though now spelt alike.

Little, less, least.—A patch-work from two distinct roots. "Little" is from A.S. *lyt, lyt-el*; the *-el* is Diminutive. The Comp. and Superl. are from the root *læs*, adverb, as shown in the next line.

Less: A.S. *læs-sa* (Comparative of *læs*), in which the *-sa* is the original form of Comp. suffix, that preceded *-ra* (*-er*). So *læs-sa* became simply *less*. "Lesser" is a double Comparative, and modern.

Least: A.S. *læs-st*, Superlative of *læs*.

Many.—Either (*a*) adjective, A.S. *manig*; or (*b*) noun, A.S. *manigu* or *menigu*, multitude. The "of" is usually omitted after (*b*) the noun; as "a great many (of) men," a large number of men.

May, might.—"May" is from A.S. *mæg*, as "day" is from "*dæg*," the *g* being changed to *y*. "Might" is A.S. *meah-te*, Weak Past tense. There is no such form as "may-*s*" in 3rd Sing. Pres. for the reason given under **Can.**

Methinks. See **Think** below.

Million : Lat. *mille.* The *-on* is augmentative : a big thousand.

Mine : A.S. *mín.* The *n* was a sign of the Genitive or Possessive case. Hence in the south of England we hear the working classes say *hisn, ourn, yourn.*

More, most.—These have no connection either with "many" or "much," though they have been tacked on to them to furnish Comparative and Superlative forms. "More" is from A.S. *má-ra.* "Most" is from A.S. *mǽ-st.* The base of both is *má.*

Much or **mickle** : A.S. *myc, myc-el.* The *-el* is Diminutive.

Must : A.S. *mós-te,* for *mót-te.* Weak Past tense of the verb *mót-an.* This verb has survived in the almost obsolete phrase, "So *mote* it be," so may it be.

My.—Merely a contraction of A.S. *mín,* mine. Compare Indef. article *a,* which is merely a contraction of A.S. *án,* one.

Near, nearer.—"Near," though now considered a Positive adjective, and used sometimes as a Preposition, was originally a Comparative, A.S. *neáh-ra,* of which "nigh-er" is merely a modern spelling. "Near" has a Comparative force in—

> The *near* in blood, the nearer bloody.—*Macbeth,* ii. 3.

Next.—Merely another spelling of *nigh-est ;* A.S. *néh-st.* In A.S. the medial *h* was sounded almost as *c* or *k.* Hence *néh-st* is now spelt as "next." See § 159, III.

Nigh : A.S. *neáh,* or *néh,* as shown already. For A.S. *neáh* or *néh, neáh-ra, néhst,* we have now substituted *near, nearer, nearest.*

Not, naught.—"Not" is merely a more rapid pronunciation of "naught" ; since *ŏ* is the short sound of *au ;* see § 163, under **O.** "Naught" is a modern spelling of A.S. *náwiht :* see **Aught.**

Notwithstanding.—Properly, two words "not withstanding," not preventing, not standing in the way. "Nothwithstanding these facts" was originally "these facts not withstanding" ; absolute construction. By a change of order "notwithstanding" has now assumed the status of a preposition. Cf. **During, Except.**

One, only. See **A** (1).

Or.—Contraction of Middle Eng. *outher* or *auther,* A.S. *áhwæther.* "Or" is not a contraction of "other," nor a doublet of "either." In A.S. *áhwæther, á* means "one," and *hwæther* "which of two."

Often : A.S. *oft ;* Middle English, *ofte.* Final *n* is an intruder.

Other : A.S. *ó-ther,* which at first meant "second." It is a Comparative adjective, and *-ther* is a Comparative suffix. Cf. Latin *al-ter ;* and see **Far, Forth.**

Ought : A.S. *áh-te,* he owed. "You *ought* him a thousand pounds."—SHAKSPEARE.

Our, ours : A.S. *úre, úres.* The *r* is one sign of the Possessive, and the *s* is another. So *ours* is a double Possessive.

Out, utter, uttermost : A.S. *úte* or *útan, útor, útema* or *útemest.* "Uttermost" is merely a respelling or rather misspelling of *utemest.*

Own : A.S. *ágen,* possessed or owned. Strong form of Past Part.

Past.—A participle, originally absolute, which by change of position became a preposition. "Half *past* four" = half, four (having) passed. Compare **Except, During, Notwithstanding**.

Pending.—Similar to the above. Pending notice = notice pending.

Prithee: for "I *pray thee*."

Quoth: A.S. *cwæth*, Strong Past of A.S. *cweth-an*, to say.

Rather.—Comparative of *rathe*, "early." A.S. *hræth*, quick.

Save.—An adjective (Lat. *salvus*, Fr. *sauf*) which through change of position has become a preposition: "all *save* one" = all, one being safe or reserved. See above, **Pending, During**, etc.

Score.—Used in English for either Sing. or Plur. In A.S. *scor-a* was Plural only. Original meaning "notch" cut in a stick called *tally*.

> Our forefathers had no other books but the *score* and the *tally*.—
> *Henry VI.* Part II.

Second: Lat. *secund-us*. It superseded A.S. *óther*, which at first meant "second," but eventually acquired a different sense.

Self: A.S. *self* or *silf*, signifying "same," identical"; as in *self-same*. Observe then that in A.S. *self* was an *adjective*, not a noun. As an adjective it was put after the pronoun in the same number and case. Hence we find such forms as *ic selfa* (Nom.), *mín selfes* (Poss.), *mé selfum* (Dative), *mec selfne* (Acc.). In the Mod. period *self* acquired the status of a noun, with a plural *selves*, like "shelf, shelves." So we get the forms *myself*, *thyself*, *herself*, *ourselves*, *yourselves*, where the noun "self," or "selves" is qualified by a Possessive pronoun. In *himself* the word "self" is still an adjective. In *themselves* there is a confusion between "self" as noun and "self" as adjective. In strict grammar it should be either *themself* or *theirselves*. The latter is common among peasants in the southern counties of England.

Shall, should: A.S. *sceal* or *scal* (Pres.), *scol-de* (Past). There is no such form as *shall-s*, because *shall* belongs to the same class of irregular verb as **can, may**. On *sc* changed to *sh*, see p. 135.

She.—Not from the A.S. *seó*, as has been asserted, but from the Midland *scǽ*, which in modern English has been regularly respelt as "she." (*Scǽ* occurs in the last two chapters of the *Old English Chronicle*, that were written in the Mercian or Midland dialect.)

Sheep: A.S. *sceáp* or *scép*. Plural the same as Singular, for the same reason as that stated under **Deer**.

Since.—So spelt for *sins;* contraction of Mid. Eng. *sithens* (now almost obsolete), in which the final *s* is the Genitive adverbial suffix: cf. *alway-s*. See § 149. "Sithen" is from A.S. *síth thám*, after that.

Some: A.S. *sum*.

Such: A.S. *swylc*, from *swá* (so) and *líc* (like). Hence the modern phrase "such-like" is pleonastic.

Swine: A.S. *swín*, pig. Plural the same as Singular for the reason stated under **Deer**.

Than, then: A.S. *thænne* or *thonne*. No distinction was made between *than* and *then* before the modern period. In Shakspeare we have *than* in the sense of "then" rhyming with "began"—

> And their ranks began
> To break upon the galled shore and *than*
> Retire again.—*Rape of Lucrece*.

That: A.S. *thæt, thæ-t.* The *t* is a mark of the Neuter: cf. i-*t*, Lat. i-*d*, illu-*d*, quo-*d*.

The (1), Def. Article: A.S. *the;* used in A.S. not for the Def. Article, but for an indeclinable Relative. In A.S. the Def. Article in the Nom. Case was *sé* (Masc.), *seó* (Fem.), and *thæt* (Neuter).

The (2), Adverb used with Comparatives: A.S. *thý*, Instrumental Case of the Demonstrative pronoun. See § 40 (*b*).

Their, theirs: Northern dialect *their-ra.* The *s* is a sign of the Possessive, and *-ra* was another such sign. So "theirs" is a double Possessive.

Them: A.S. *thám, thá-m*, Dative case: cf. hi-*m*, who-*m*.

These, those: A.S. *thǽs, thás.* No difference between them in A.S. Both were plurals of the same Singular. The distinction is modern.

They: Northern dialect, *their, thei.*

Thine, thy: A.S. *thín*, in which *n* is a sign of the Possessive. "Thy" is merely a contraction of "thine."

Think (1): A.S. *thenc-an*, to think or reflect.

Think (2), in "me-thinks": A.S. *thync-an*, to seem. See § 85.

This: A.S. *thes* (Masc.), *theós* (Fem.), *this* (Neuter).

To wit: A.S. *tó wit-enne*, "for knowing"; Gerundial or Qualifying Infinitive. On the loss of *-enne*, see **-en** (2).

Twelve: A.S. *twá-lif, i.e.* ten and *two* (twá) *left* (lif), or "two over." Compare the etymology of **Eleven**.

Unless.—Formerly written "*on lesse* that," *i.e.* on a less supposition than, if not. Here *un* stands for the prep. *on*. For the origin of "less" see **Less**.

Was, wast, were.—All these are based on the root *wes*, one of the three roots out of which the verb "to be" is conjugated (see **Am**). "Was" is A.S. *wæs*. "Were" is A.S. *wǽr-on*, in which an *r* has been substituted for *s*, as in *ar-t* for *as-t*.

What: A.S. *hwæt*, Neuter of *hwá*. *Hwæ-t;* cf. Lat. quo-*d*.

Which: A.S. *hwilc*, short for *hwí-lic*, why like.

Who, whose, whom: A.S. *hwá*, *hwæ-s* (Gen.), *hwǽ-m* (Dative).

Whole.—An ill-spelt doublet of *hale*, A.S. *hál*, sound.

Why: A.S. *hwí*, Instrumental case of *hwá*.

Will, would.—"Would" is A.S. *wol-de*, where *-de* is the correct regular ending of the Past tense in the Weak conjugation. In *won't* we have *wol not*, *wol* being another form of the root: cf. Latin *vol*-o, *vol*-untary.

Wont (accustomed): A.S. *wun-od*, pp. of A.S. *wun-ian*, to remain. *Wont-ed*=*won-d-ed*, with two participial endings.

Worse. See **Bad.**

Worth, as in "Woe *worth* the day" *i.e.* Woe befall the day. "Worth" is all that remains of A.S. *weorth-an*, to become, once very widely used.

Wot, wist: A.S. *wát* (Pres. tense), *wis-te* (Past tense). The root of the verb is *wit*, which in the Past is changed to *wis*. The only form of this verb that is now much used is the phrase "to wit."

Yclept: A.S. *ge-clipod*, called. The *ge* prefix has become *y*.

You, your, yours: A.S. *eów, eów-er, eów-r-es.* The last is a double Possessive; cf. *ou-r-s, thei-r-s.*

Exercise 42.

(*a*) 1. Write short notes on the forms—*kine, riches, children.* 2. Why is the parsing of words in the English of to-day more difficult than in the older forms of the language? 3. What is case? What case-forms are found in English? Give two examples of each. 4. State what you know about the history of the changes that have taken place in the inflection of (*a*) the Present Participle, (*b*) the Past Participle, (*c*) the Infinitive mood in English. Parse and account for the form *do* in "I can *do* it." 5. Give instances of obsolete ways of forming the plural of nouns in English. How was it that they became obsolete? 6. Mention three nouns, of which the plural form has a different meaning from that of the singular. 7. Write short notes on the words—*vixen, drake, nearer.* 8. Show that our language possesses inflections which mark (1) gender, (2) number. 9. Give examples of English Past Participles which are formed by obsolete processes. Comment on the forms of the Past Participles—*done, drunk, beaten, made, wrought, bereft.* 10. Write notes on the history of *myself, his, hers, every, which;* and state the conditions under which the last two are now used. 11. Mention four Common nouns which have been derived from names of persons or places. 12. Give the usual adverbial suffix by which adjectives are turned into adverbs (*a*) in Old English, (*b*) at the present time. Explain by notes on the words -*seldom, hither, once, asleep, to-morrow* in what other ways adverbs are made. 13. Enumerate with examples the several grammatical uses served by the inflection -*s*. Write notes on the history of any two of them. 14. Name the chief Indefinite and Distributive adjectives; and in the case of any three of them point out what changes they have undergone in meaning and form. 15. Write down examples of all the suffixes that give a negative or contrary meaning to a word. 16. What is a diphthong? From the following words make a list of those which contain true diphthongs:—*aunt, build, buoy, eye, few, fought, gaol, powder, seat, soul, suit.* 17. Explain how the function of a Relative pronoun in a sentence differs from that of a Personal pronoun. State what you know about the history of the Relative pronouns *what* and *which*, and parse *what* in the sentences "I am what I am," and "I did not repeat what you said." 18. State and illustrate the uses of the verb *to be*. Comment on the history of the forms *am, is, are, was.* 19. Give examples of the employment of the suffix -*en* in the formation of Nouns, Adjectives, and Verbs, and state the force of the suffix in each case. (*Cambridge, Junior and Senior:*)

(*b*) 1. Note anything remarkable in the formation of the following words: —*any, could, first, every, naught, next, least, might, prithee, methinks.* 2. Account for the selection of the suffix which is in common use for forming the plural of English nouns. 3. Describe the several ways of indicating gender in English nouns. Explain the origin of the following forms:—*executrix, duchess, sir, woman, drake, widower, daughter.* 4. Classify conjunctions according to (*a*) their use, (*b*) their origin. Give an example of each class. 5. Explain with examples the terms—Root, Stem, Primary Derivative,

Secondary Derivative. 6. Give the derivation of *eleven* and *twelve*. 7. Give the rules for the division of words into syllables. Divide, stating the reason in each case—*tablet*, *table*, *counter* (noun), *counteract*. 8. "Pronouns have more traces of old forms than other parts of speech." Briefly justify this statement, and give examples. 9. What was the origin of the verbals in *-ing?* In what ways are they used? (*Oxford, Junior and Senior.*)

(*c*) 1. Account for the contradictory forms—*Lord's day* and *Lady-day; Wednesday* and *Friday*. 2. Write the plurals of *alkali*, *shelf*, *attorney*, *Percy*, *alms*, *gallows*, *man-servant*, *logic*, *trout*, *cloth;* and the plurals of any six foreign words in common use. 3. State the different ways of forming adverbs in English. 4. State what you know about the forms—*worse*, *further*, *better*, *next*, and *uttermost*. 5. Annotate the following words:—*drake*, *bridegroom*, *gander*, *bachelor*, *spider*. 6. What is meant by the plural of a noun? Write the plurals of *memorandum*, *journey*, *folio*, *sow*, *cow*, *axis*, *salmon*, *cloth*, *James*, *Miss Williams*. 7. Write down four nouns which have double plurals, and point out the difference of meaning in the two forms. 8. State what you know about the following words:—*filly*, *goose*, *lady*, *wizard*, *sir*. 9. Comment on any peculiarities that exist in the following words:—*vixen*, *Thursday*, *Friday*, *other*, *worst*, *next*, *rather*, *nethermost*. 10. Give the derivation and meaning of each of the following words:—*whilom*, *methinks*, *egotism*, *pea*, *perchance*, *forgive*, *untoward*. 11. Comment upon any peculiarities that exist in the following words:—*pease*, *riches*, *Lady-day*, *least*, *farthing*, *needs*, *darkling*. 12. Write the plurals of *ox*, *potato*, *chimney*, *Henry*, *penny*, *die*, *dye*, *lord-lieutenant*, *aide-de-camp*, *beau*, *portmanteau*, *brother*. (*Preceptors', Second and First Class.*)

(*d*) 1. Give the derivations of *whilom*, *why*, *than*, *neutralise*, *whole*. 2. State what you know about the words—*worse*, *less*, *rather*, *midmost*, *children*. 3. Give the rule for the formation of the plural of nouns ending in *y*. Write the plurals of *joy*, *journey*, *difficulty*, *colloquy*. Also of *chief*, *staff*, *quarto*, *die*, *cloth*. 4. Quote four nouns which in appearance are plural, but are in reality singular, and give the derivation of each. 5. Account for the omission of *w* in the pronunciation of *whole*. 6. Account for the doubled consonant in —ac*m*modate, assessor, co*r*roborate, i*n*nate, i*n*nocuous, inte*l*ligent, pe*l*lucid, ho*t*ter, wi*t*ty. 7. What is notable in the spelling or formation of *could*, *imbecility*, *opaque*, *connection*, *secrecy*, *colonelcy?* 8. Point out the force of the prefix in *un*dismayed, *mis*lay, *be*hind, *for*give, *with*stand, *pre*fix, *extra*vagant, *post*pone, *super*scription, *an*archy, *epi*gram, *peri*meter. (*Preceptors', Second and First Class.*)

INDEX OF SUBJECTS AND SELECTED WORDS.

The references are to pages.

Note.—For alphabetical list showing the origin and use of important endings and important words, see Chapters XXXV. and XXXVI.

THE END

WORKS BY J. C. NESFIELD, M.A.

Now Ready. Globe 8vo. Price 1s. 6d.

OUTLINE OF ENGLISH GRAMMAR. In Five Parts. By J. C. NESFIELD, M.A.

I.—NOUNS, ADJECTIVES, PRONOUNS, ADVERBS, PREPOSITIONS, AND CONJUNCTIONS. II.—VERBS AND THEIR INFLECTIONS. III.—PARSING AND ANALYSIS. IV.—ANALYSIS AND CONVERSION OF SENTENCES: SEQUENCE OF TENSES. V.—ANALYSIS AND DERIVATION OF WORDS: SOUNDS AND SPELLINGS.

THE USES OF THE PARTS OF SPEECH AS SHOWN BY EXAMPLES. By J. C. NESFIELD, M.A. Oxon. Globe 8vo, sewed, 6d.

ENGLISH GRAMMAR FOR ELEMENTARY SCHOOLS. By J. C. NESFIELD, M.A.

Book I.—Uses of the Parts of Speech as shown by Examples. Globe 8vo, sewed, 3d.

Book II.—Modifications of Subject, Predicate, and Object, by Words, Phrases, and Easy Sentences. Globe 8vo, sewed, 4d.

Book III.—Parsing and Easy Analysis. Globe 8vo, sewed, 5d.

Book IV.—Analysis and Word-forming by Prefixes and Suffixes. Globe 8vo, sewed, 6d.

Now Ready. Globe 8vo. Price 3s. 6d.

HISTORICAL ENGLISH AND DERIVATION. By J. C. NESFIELD, M.A., Author of "English Grammar Past and Present."

EDUCATIONAL TIMES.—"In Mr. Nesfield's carefully written volume of 284 pages we have a practical introduction to historical etymology and syntax, based on good authorities (Skeat, Murray, and others), but affording ample evidence of direct deduction and comparison. It is well calculated for an advanced study of English, and is, on the whole, very clearly and systematically arranged."

SCHOOLMASTER.—"Mr. Nesfield's book shows considerable knowledge of a wide and important subject, a clear view of its several parts, and great industry and skill in the treatment of each."

MACMILLAN AND CO., LTD., LONDON.